Survivor

One Man's Battle with HIV, Hemophilia, and Hepatitis C

VAUGHN RIPLEY

iUniverse, Inc.
New York   Bloomington

Survivor
One Man's Battle with HIV, Hemophilia, and Hepatitis C

iUniverse books may be ordered through booksellers or by contacting:

iUniverse
1663 Liberty Drive
Bloomington, IN 47403
www.iuniverse.com
1-800-Authors (1-800-288-4677)

ISBN: 978-1-4502-6030-5 (pbk)
ISBN: 978-1-4502-6031-2 (cloth)
ISBN: 978-1-4502-6032-9 (ebk)

Library of Congress Control Number: 2010913917

Printed in the United States of America

iUniverse rev. date: 9/29/10

This book is dedicated to my soul mate.

Help Support AIDS Research
Ten percent of author royalties are donated to AIDS research through
the AIDS Research Alliance www.aidsresearch.org

"Dyin' ain't much of a livin' boy."
–JOSEY WALES

chiv-al-rous (shiv'al rus), *adj.* 1. having the qualities of chivalry, as courage, courtesy, and loyalty. 2. considerate and courteous to women; gallant. 3. gracious and honorable toward an enemy, esp. a defeated one, and toward the weak or poor. – *syn.* 1. fearless, dauntless, valiant; courtly; faithful, true, devoted. – *ant.* 1. cowardly, rude, disloyal.
Random House Dictionary, 2nd Edition Unabridged

Acknowledgments

There are so many people who have been there for me through support, inspiration, and downright tenacity. I would like to express my deepest gratitude to all of you. I can't possibly thank everyone with a blurb, but here is a try:

Butterfly kisses and thanks to Trinity for the inspirational push to complete this legacy. There were many an evening where just a smile from you charged my emotions and helped me continue this story. I am amazed on a daily basis how you grow into a woman. You have endured some pretty tough things in your life, and you've always ended up on top. I look forward to walking you down the aisle my darling daughter.

Great big rhino kisses and thanks to Xander for magically appearing in my life and helping me to renew my love of life. I look forward to living vicariously through you. You are one tough kid and I figure you'll be an even tougher man; which is to be expected of Ripley men. Even at this young age, I am proud of how you carry yourself. It is with great pride that I say, "I'm his father."

Thanks to Scean for punching me in the mouth when I needed it. Your chivalry has always been a motivator for me. We have been to Hell and back together … Somehow, we survived. You are my best friend and always will be. I expect nothing less of a brother than what you have given me. Hopefully, I have done the same for you.

Hugs, kisses, and thanks to Mom for all of those extended stays with me at the Hospital Motel, keeping me under your wing, and guiding me along my path to manhood.

Thanks to Dad for helping me to mature and passing on your love of music. You've always been there for me, and I am eternally grateful.

Great big bear hug to George. I can't believe that I spent the first 24 years of my life without really knowing my father. I appreciate that you have entered my life and been there for me as a role model and mentor.

Big thanks to Greg for being there for me as a friend and cousin. You have inspired me in ways that cannot be conveyed in written word. Rock on, Rush-boy!

Super-duper thanks to John Thompson and James Nicoll for helping me with ideas and the final design of my book's cover.

Thanks to Monica, Kelly, Laine, Raeghn, Mel, Robin, Dick, Diana, Dawn, James, Patty, Jacob, Quincy, Becky, Judy, Dano, Billy, Marcie, Greg, Kimmy, Michael, Katie, Ski, Ben, Danny Boy, Maggot, Eric, Shawn, Kirk, Chill, Toe, John, Nick, Robert (Mike), Emily, Pete and John, Mikey, Keith, Mildred, Barb, Beverly, Tan, Daphna, Alan, Kang, Scot, Joey, Lar… MVSlider, Liam, John, Adam, Marc, David, Megan, Denise, Grog, Doug, Ink, Joe, Kazmij, Sadiki (WTJHAND), Kohler, Scott, Shogun of Harlem, Andrew, Ben, Sang, Fred, Josh, Sean, Sue, Terry (Dokiel), Katty, Ally, Red, Patti, Zee, Indy, and Vig to name but a few of my closest friends and family who made this book happen by experiencing life with me!

A "thank you very much" must be go out to Rick Rock for being there as a big brother and mentor. You are my hero, man!

Thanks to Cat for proofreading my crappy rough draft—and, for helping me understand my target audience.

I am deeply grateful to my publisher, iUniverse, who not only gave me a platform to stand on, but they also gave me an extremely talented group of support personnel who helped me through the tough process of publishing my first book.

No one deserves more thanks, and credit, than my evaluator, Mark Mandell, who sifted through my rough and helped me to create a diamond. All authors should be so lucky to work with someone this patient, hardworking, and thorough.

This book would not have been possible without the endless efforts of several other fantastic folks at iUniverse, including Jade Council, project dominator *wink*, Angela Shryock, publishing consultant, Ashleigh Wiens, check-in coordinator, Eric Hanselmann, check-in coordinator, and of course, George Nedeff, my editorial consultant. My journey from fledgling writer to full-blown author was made easier and more enjoyable by them all.

Without the love and caring of my many doctors and nurses I would not be here today, so in no special order I extend scores of thanks to Dr.

Cooke, Dr. Posorske, Mary Ellen, Dr. Rick, Dr. Sauri, Dr. Choa, Dr. Kessler, and Charlotte. Obviously, doctors do an amazing job of keeping us all intact. Unfortunately, it is often a thankless job. I know that I speak for billions of people when I say, "thank you very much for all you do!"

I have a bunch of friends on my personal forum: http://vaughnripley. com/forum, and all of you have done so much to help boost my confidence during this publishing process. I'm not going to pinpoint each and every one of you, but you know who you are!! Thank you one and all, for your support and morale infusion. Also, thank you for making my discussion forum such a success. Pat yourselves on the back and take the rest of the day off!

And above all else, thanks from the bottom of my throbbing heart go out to my lovely wife, Kristine—without you and your belief in me, this book would never have been written. I have truly been blessed by being lucky enough to share life with someone as precious as you!

If I forgot to include you in my thanks, I am sure you will let me know; then I can thank you in person.

Preface

Survivor was written to share the story of my fight to live, despite the ailments that afflict me. Throughout the years I have found many parallels between my particular battles and those of my friends, family members, co-workers, and people in general. For this reason, I decided to put down in written word; what I have endured and what I did to live.

My hope is that every person who reads this book will not only be touched, but also glean something memorable and perhaps even magical in their pursuit of a fulfilled life. Many of my unorthodox approaches to survival may seem strange or even bizarre to some, but it is my intention to share my story in an honest and straightforward fashion.

Deciding to go further than simply writing a memoir, I included detailed information on how I approach life and deal with things that each of us runs into. It is my hope that you will walk away from *Survivor* with a renewed look at life and new ideas on how to deal with and control certain aspects of your own life.

Enough chitchat, let's get right to the meat!

* * *

More than 25,000,000 people have died from AIDS since 1981.

According to the National Institute of Health (NIH) web site an estimated 40,000,000 people were living with HIV/AIDS as of the end of 2003. And, approximately 1 of every 100 adults aged 15 to 49 are HIV-infected. An estimated 5,000,000 new HIV infections occurred worldwide during 2003 (that is approximately 14,000 new infections every day).

In 2003 alone, HIV/AIDS-associated illnesses caused the deaths of approximately 3,000,000 people.

The Centers for Disease Control and Prevention (CDC) estimates that as of 2003 nearly 950,000 United States residents are living with the HIV infection.

According to the National Hemophilia Foundation, the estimate for the number of people in the United States with hemophilia is approximately 20,000. *They approximate that 50 percent of the hemophilia population in the United States contracted HIV in the 1980's!* They also estimate a total number of HIV+ hemophiliacs at somewhere around 10,000. It is estimated that over 4,200 members of the HIV/hemophilia community have died since the onset of the crisis; this leaves approximately 5,800 of us still "alive and kicking" and hoping to stay that way until a cure comes along.

"What does all of this have to do with me?" you ask. To answer that we have to travel back in time a little ways—*insert eerie dream music here*.

The year 1967 was a mesmerizing year of success, misery, and magic. Lyndon B. Johnson was President and Hubert H. Humphrey was the Vice President. Vince Lombardi's Green Bay Packers beat the Kansas City Chiefs 35 to 10 in the first Super Bowl. Rocky Marciano retired as the undefeated boxing champ. Three Apollo astronauts were killed in a fire during a simulated space launch. Thurgood Marshall was sworn in as the first black United States Supreme Court Justice. Robert "Evel" Knievel jumped 16 automobiles on his motorcycle. China detonated its first hydrogen bomb. All over America, racial violence was becoming a national problem. Israeli forces fought to occupy the east bank of the Suez Canal. The world's first successful human heart transplant took place. The unmanned probes Surveyor 3 and Surveyor 5 landed on the moon and retrieved lunar soil for testing. One of the worst fires in department store history left 322 people dead in Brussels. Finally, at 3:03 a.m. on April 12, 1967, Vaughn Foster Ripley was born.

I was born Vaughn Foster Borden to Yahna Kristina Christensen in room 3139 at George Washington University Hospital. At birth, I was 21 inches in length and weighed a mere 6 pounds 13 ounces. I was born jaundiced and had ear trouble.

I received my middle name from my mother's friend Joanne who drove her to the hospital the night she gave birth to me.

I would like to take this time to thank those people who gave me my first gifts in this world. Marilyn Olson gave me a blue knit suit. Jan Loiselle gave me a precious toy dog. Sue Harris gave me a stretch suit. Mr. Kavich gave me my first rattle. Also, thanks to Jan Christmore, who gave me a stretch suit. Thank you all.

When I was 13 months old, I had one of my first medical problems. I had my adenoids removed and for three days I had a severe bleeding problem. As a last resort, my doctor used silver nitrate to stop the bleeding. I was given a factor VIII (pronounced factor eight) assay (sometimes called plasma factor VIII antigen), which is a blood test to measure the activity of factor VIII. Factor VIII is one of the proteins important for blood coagulation. After testing, I was diagnosed with hemophilia type A.

Hemophilia is a hereditary bleeding disorder characterized by excessive bleeding. Cutting through the obfuscation, it means that once I start bleeding, it is hard, *sometimes impossible,* to staunch. Because my blood is missing the coagulation factor VIII, doctors inject me with a serum (called factor VIII or cryoprecipitate) created from donated blood to help stop any bleeding problems.

My mother calls factor VIII my "bags of gold." The factor VIII is so minuscule in a bag of blood that it literally takes thousands of people donating blood to make one bag of serum for me. It costs a fortune to create these small bags because of the immense amount of plasma and intricate procedures.

Cost is only one of the downsides to factor VIII transfusions. Since so many people's donations are needed per dosage, diseases and viruses are also a huge factor. More than 90 percent of treated hemophiliacs develop hepatitis. In recent years, the more dangerous and deadly blood disorder Acquired Immune Deficiency Syndrome (AIDS) has stricken the hemophilia population with dire consequences.

In the early eighties, AIDS was found among the homosexual and intravenous drug user communities, but it is believed to have been around since at least 1976 (some studies have placed it back to the early 1920's or earlier). AIDS was unrecognized as a significant threat to the general populace until 1985 when Rock Hudson admitted being stricken. By the time Rock Hudson died in 1985 and the threat was recognized, hundreds of thousands of Americans were already infected and tens of thousands had already died. What most people were unaware of, or refused to admit, was that we were all eligible to be afflicted by this sickness and that this was not a disease reserved for homosexuals. In July 1982, three heterosexual hemophilia type A patients had developed Pneumocystis Carinii Pneumonia and other opportunistic infections. These were later to be classified as the first hemophiliacs to contract AIDS.

My first experience with AIDS came, not from Rock Hudson, but from one of my teachers in high school. He was an urbane man who loved teaching. When Dr. Davis died of AIDS, it suddenly became a reality to me.

Initially I felt secure believing that the blood transfusions that I was receiving were tested and out of harm's way. I have a letter from my doctor, which arrived days after Rock Hudson's death, dated October 9, 1985, stating that I tested HTLV-III negative. My life continued as normal and I was unworried about becoming HIV+.

* * *

In 1983 French scientists isolated the virus and named it Lymphadenopathy-Associated Virus (LAV).

In 1984, Dr. Robert Gallow claimed to have discovered the virus and named it Human T-cell Lymphotropic Virus (HTLV). Later, doctors around the world decided to name the virus, Human Immunodeficiency Virus (HIV). At this same time, the Health and Human Services Secretary predicted a brief epidemic and a cure by 1990 at the latest.

In doctor's lingo, if you are considered HIV+, you contracted the virus. If you are found positive, your level is determined by T-cell counts and viral load. In the early medical stages of AIDS history, any T-cell count below 200 was called the ARC stage. Once you reached zero, you were officially labeled as having AIDS. Over the last decade or two, that has changed to eliminate the ARC stage. Now, if your T-cell count drops below 200, you have AIDS.

In the eighties the American Red Cross announced that it was screening blood using the FDA approved Elisa Test, and only allowing *safe* blood into the transfusion community. Unfortunately for thousands of people, they were wrong. The HIV-tainted blood was being shipped without the knowledge of anyone.

* * *

On January 3, 1987 I was diagnosed as being HIV+. Somewhere between mid 1985 and late 1987, I was transfused with a bad batch of blood. To quote Huey Lewis, "Sometimes, bad is bad."

Chapter One

Before I was born, my parents were divorced. My parents, Yahna Christensen and George Borden, were married on March 21, 1963. By the time I was born, they had been divorced for some time.

On February 21, 1968, my mother remarried. My new father, Kim Ripley, adopted me and I received his last name. I grew up knowing Kim as "dad" and my parents didn't even tell me I was adopted until I was twelve years old.

For my first birthday, Dad gave me a ride on his motorcycle. Too bad I am unable to remember it. Surely it was a blast. This event probably led to my future, often dangerous obsession with two-wheeled vehicles. Just before I turned three years old, my mother took the training wheels off of my bike and I started riding on two wheels. I must have been cute riding that tiny ten-inch bicycle around the neighborhood.

* * *

Shortly after learning to ride my bike, I remember playing with a neighborhood friend in our front yard when a nondescript van pulled up. The driver put down his window and called my friend and me over. My friend immediately ran over and started talking with the man. I slowly approached the van and realized that he was asking us if we wanted to go for a ride. I had always been leery of strangers and this guy seemed suspicious, even to my young mind.

The man continued to try to convince us to go for a ride with him. My friend was becoming agreeable and was actually making his way into the van when I started screaming. Instinctively, I knew this was not a good situation and I was becoming extremely frightened. My screams alerted my mother and a neighbor. They both came running out to see what was wrong and the van sped off just short of my friend climbing in.

My mother immediately knew what was going on and could not believe how close we had come to being kidnapped. To this day, she is proud of the way my "Spidey-sense" kicked in and potentially saved two small children from being abducted and possibly hurt or lost forever.

Perhaps this incident is the reason I am so protective of my family and friends.

* * *

Immediately after their marriage, my parents got to work on adding to the family. Before you could blink an eye, I had two younger brothers. We started out in Arlington, Virginia where my two brothers, Scean Ashton and Laine Heath, were born. *The world will never be the same!*

Around 1970 my dad was working for a land-surveying firm, Rodgers and Associates, as a Party Chief. Essentially a Party Chief is the leader of a surveyor field crew. The company owner hired a new Field Coordinator (the Field Coordinator assigns and coordinates the work that survey crews do out in the field), named Wayne. It quickly became apparent to my dad that he and Wayne (his new boss) were not going to have a good relationship, so he started exploring his options.

Dad shared his situation with a friend of the family, Lee, who had worked for the government. Lee did some inquiries and eventually came up with a job idea for my dad.

This was soon after the discovery of large oil deposits on the north slope of Alaska and plans were underway to drill for this oil and pipe it to the southern coast to the Port of Valdez. The pipeline (eventually known as the Trans-Alaska Pipeline System) was to be approximately 800 miles long, over mountainous terrain and frozen tundra. Lee had a contact with someone in the oil industry who said the design consortium needed surveyors to do route surveying. The work conditions were going to be challenging but the pay was going to be great.

My dad was excited about the adventure and decided to pursue this path. The downside was that his family would not be able to accompany him to Alaska. The oil company offered to fly him to the "mainland" several times a year for an extended family visit. After my parents discussed this, they decided that they could endure this for two or three years in order to build a nice nest egg.

The plan was to temporarily move our family to Phoenix, Arizona near my mom's sister while Dad went off into the wilderness of Alaska to survey the Trans-Alaska Pipeline. With plans set, my parents put our house up for sale and started packing things for our westward trek. At the time we owned two vehicles a 1968 Ford and a Suzuki motorcycle. My parents resolved to sell the Ford and replace it with a pickup that had a camper. Dad mounted a motorcycle rack on the front bumper and was ready to go in no time.

We quickly got a contract on our house and also had a buyer for the Ford. Everything was going according to the plan until my parents were rear ended by a young boy driving his uncle's car. The kid must have been driving pretty fast, because the impact was hard enough to pile my parent's car into two cars in front of them. Suffice it to say that it was a bad accident.

The force of the accident was so hard that it broke the backs of their seats. After the initial screeching, smashing, and tinkling of glass, the hiss of steam broke the eerie silence that surrounded the scene.

Dad quickly surmised that my mom was severely injured and she was carted off in an ambulance. Doctors deduced that she had suffered extreme whiplash from the collision and was going to need months of physical therapy and rehabilitation to repair her injured body.

The car was a total loss. Because my dad had a buyer for the car, in his young and inexperienced thinking, he had decided not to renew the insurance. It had just expired a day or two before the accident. Of course you're thinking, *no problem, it wasn't his fault.* Dad thought that as well. But this saga continues—the driver's uncle decided to say that the kid was not an "authorized" driver and therefore his insurance company denied my parents claim. Since our family still owed payments on the totaled car, they continued to pay for it even though it no longer existed!

Needless to say, these events put a little kink in our plans. Oh, by the way, Dad had already quit his job by then and now we couldn't head west because of Mom's injuries. We ended up moving in with some good friends of my parents, Marilyn and Randy. In the meantime Dad got a temporary job at a surveying company in Arlington.

The bad news did not stop there. Next we found out that there were so many environmental issues regarding the construction of the pipeline that the project was on hold for months (perhaps even years). Dad never did get to go on that great adventure in the wild tundra of Alaska.

After Mom recovered enough to travel we decided to head to Arizona anyway and make our own adventure. We were having a grand time driving across the country until we got to Houston where the pickup developed an engine problem.

The truck was fixed after a few days and many dollars. The fuel tank was rather small on the pickup and this started to create problems in the west. We could only run about 150 miles on a tank with the load we were carrying, so we had to plan very carefully where we might get the next gasoline break. On several occasions when we drove late we actually had to park in the gas station to wait for them to open in the morning.

Before we knew it, we had arrived in Phoenix and bought a low-income house just north of the city. We also picked up an adorable puppy that we affectionately named Creek. Creek was half German Shorthair and half Weimaraner.

Our friends, Randy and Marilyn (whom we lived with after the famous car accident), visited us and liked it so much, that they moved out there too. They bought a house a few blocks from us.

My sister, Raeghn Lorraine, was born in Phoenix in January of 1972.

In Arizona we were exposed to many natural dangers and we were fortunate to have survived scorpions, rattlesnakes, and even a tornado. Many of my early life memories come from living in Arizona.

* * *

After about two years in Phoenix, we moved to Casa Grande into a mobile home near a big surveying project that my dad was working on.

One of my most vivid memories of Arizona is a tornado that came so close to our home that it actually knocked our mobile home completely off its blocks. This tornado also destroyed another mobile home only a couple of blocks away from us. I can remember my parents driving us around our neighborhood to inspect the damage. I sat with my face pasted to the window in awe and fear as I took in the fury of Mother Nature.

Along with the damaged homes, the neighborhood swimming pool had its chain-link fence mangled and torn out of the ground. This single incident gave me a respect of natural disasters that remains to this day.

Another fleeting memory is of my brother Scean mistakenly reaching for a rattlesnake thinking it was a frog. Luckily, in Casa Grande our neighbor was a local sheriff, and was able to shoot the snake before it struck him.

Along with the other troubles associated with the desert in Arizona, sand storms were fairly frequent and unbelievable. These storms could be seen for more than 30 minutes prior to their attack and they would sometimes fill the entire surrounding area. I vaguely remember two of our neighbors coming over during a terrible sand storm. They both wore SCUBA gear outfits to protect them from the weather.

Fortunately my experience with tornados, desert heat, and sand storms has merely given me a level of respect for weather and not an unwarranted fear or phobia.

Without warning, my dad's surveying company was closed by the IRS for not paying their taxes. My mother wrote a friend, Fritz, at my dad's old surveying company in Maryland asking if he could come back to Rodger's. Fritz replied saying that Dad would always be welcome back. We decided to pack up yet again and drive the wagon train eastward.

We sold the mobile home in Casa Grande to a very nice couple with a cute little boy. It turned out the "nice" couple was wanted by the FBI and when the heat was on they stole an airplane from a nearby airstrip and left us high and dry on the mobile home payments.

At that point in my life, exposure to danger was something that seemed "normal." Due in part to this, I learned how to cope and certainly survive danger. These skills would serve me well later in life when danger became commonplace.

We moved back east to Virginia with my Grandma Barbara while Mom and Dad house hunted in Maryland. Before long, my parents had found a nice townhouse for rent in a Gaithersburg community called, Quince Orchard.

* * *

Twice a year our family would pack into the car and drive up to Carlisle, Pennsylvania to my dad's parents' house in the woods. The house, which was over 150 years old, was situated on a 60-acre wooded lot. There was a fair-sized pond in the backyard that my Grandfather had built. We would go visit in the summer and get some swimming in and then again in the winter to do a little ice-skating.

Along with my grandparents, my aunt, Jocelyn, and cousin, Cathy would meet us in Carlisle and because they were from New York, this was the only time we got to spend time with them. We had many glorious summer days swimming in the pond along with snapping turtles and stocked bass.

Having grandparents close by gave me a sense of normalcy. My little world of hemophilia had me feeling like an outcast of sorts and simple things like trips to visit Grandma and Grandpa helped me to forget my misgivings of being different. Also, Grandpa was extremely well read and I felt a kinship due to my early passion for reading.

My Grandfather, Dr. Julien Ashton Ripley Junior, died on June 27, 1974. It was my first run-in with death. Because I was only seven when he died, my memories of him are very vague and nebulous. I did not know much about my Grandpa at the time of his death, but throughout the years I gathered little pieces of interesting information. For instance, during the Vietnam War he was arrested for protesting and even spent some time in jail for this protest.

Grandpa worked for eight years at Stanford in the Physical Sciences Program, and became an Emeritus Professor in 1973. He published a book, *The Elements and Structure of the Physical Sciences.* I read in a eulogium that was written by his associates that Grandpa would greet each day with the statement, "Good morning, morning." I wonder if I inherited some of my extreme optimism from his kind spirit.

Through my Grandpa, I am related to Alexander Graham Bell, the Bells and Grosvenors of *National Geographic,* and his cousin, S. Dillon Ripley, who was the head of the Smithsonian Institution. I sometimes think twice about saying that I am related to these famous folks, but I always fall back on the fact that my dad adopted me and I am "officially" in the family. Besides, the Ripley family relation to Alexander Graham Bell is through a marriage, so that makes me just as closely related to him as any of my adopted relatives.

Grandpa received his bachelor's degree in Physics from Yale. From there, he got his master's degree from Harvard. Then he received his PhD in the Philosophy of Science at the University of Virginia. He then returned to Yale, having been granted a Sterling Graduate School Fellowship for post-doctoral studies. Along his glorious educational path, Grandpa twice held National Science Foundation Summer Fellowships, was Associate Professor of Physics at Dickinson College, Chairman of the Department of Physics and Mathematics at Abadan Institute of Technology in Iran and Associate Professor of Physics at Wilkes College.

At Stanford, he taught the elementary course in the Physical Sciences, courses in the history of Science, the Philosophy of Science, and a wide variety of Undergraduate courses.

I attribute my tremendous love for continuing education and constant need to build my knowledge to my Grandfather. He was a perspicacious man with whom I wish I had more time to sit and ponder life. I know that he would certainly have had wise insight into my future challenges.

* * *

In 1975 we packed up a friend's camper and drove south to visit my mother's father in Georgia. Gardell Christensen raised my mother in a gypsy fashion. They went from town to town as he accepted artistic jobs at museums around the nation. All told, Mom went to nine different schools while growing up. Grandpa Christensen was an artist and a taxidermist and this helped him with his museum connection since these two talents combined to make for a perfect museum diorama designer. And, Grandpa was one of the best during his time.

He went on an expedition to Africa in 1938 to film and paint the African Okapi. He also helped to create the lion diorama and large elephant display at the New York Museum of Natural History. His diorama creations included many life-sized exhibits. During 1952, he created an intense scene titled "Buffalo Jump" in a Montana museum for K. Ross Toole, which depicts Native Americans forcing bison to fall to their death off a cliff.

Besides the dioramas, my Grandpa was also an extremely gifted painter and sculptor. He painted many wildlife scenes and sculpted animals. His sculptures include a grizzly bear, of which I have the original bronze casting.

I suppose that Grandpa Christensen had a big impact and influence on me because he was my maternal grandparent and my only "real" Grandfather since my dad's side of the family came to me through adoption. In several artistic and creative ways he did rub off on me genetically. I believe that my talent with art and drawing stemmed from this marvelous man.

* * *

After living in our townhouse for a short stint, we settled into a single-family home in Rockville, Maryland. We had a cute community and lots of friendly neighbors.

As kids, we "Riplets" (my dad's nickname for his children) were fairly normal and somewhat rambunctious, which contributed to our fair share of adventures. Here are a few of my favorites.

My brother Scean and I used to play kick ball with all of the local boys. One day, my little brother Laine was begging to play. He explained that he was big enough to play, and pleaded with us. We decided to let him play *on probation.* If he could prove that he was good enough to play, we would let him play from then on.

Fortunately while he played, no one kicked a ball his way. Laine was able to make himself look remarkably busy in the outfield. Things were really looking up for him when he was able to actually make it to first base. He surprised us all by speedily making it to third when the next kid kicked. Scean and I were surprised that he was doing so well.

Suddenly, his luck ran out as the next kid kicked the ball. His lack of terminology stopped him from knowing that the fourth base was called home plate.

I screamed, "Go home Laine!"

Everyone picked up the chant, "Go home Laine! Go home Laine!"

Slowly, Laine turned sadly toward us. With a look of dejection, he dropped his crying face into his arm and ran home.

We suddenly realized the situation. He must have thought we meant home as in our house. The poor kid never fully recovered from that incident.

* * *

One of our neighbors Mr. Dodd, owned his own company, and would park his company vans on our court. Many of the neighbors were grumpy about this issue and one day they suggested a possible solution. They acted as though they were joking, but there was real meaning when they asked us four Ripley kids to let the air out of old man Dodd's tires. There we were, four kids, one on each tire in broad daylight releasing the air from his van tires. My sister was only four years old, and she was there kneeling with the rest of us. Needless to say, we were framed and busted. We Riplets never received any punishment for that crime, because adults had put us up to it, but poor Mr. Dodd probably never forgave us.

* * *

I started the third grade when I was eight years old and all of the boys around me hated girls. If you touched a girl, you had to spray imaginary cootie killing aerosol on the offending body part. I was confused, because I thought girls were neat.

I clearly remember having a crush on my third grade teacher. And, I was the first of my friends to have a girlfriend. Her name was Donna and she was a blue-eyed, blonde-haired cutie. From the day I saw her, I knew that girls were okay. We were madly in puppy love and we even kissed once.

Donna was my first experience with the opposite sex. We spent many fun afternoons playing house and other games. She innocently introduced me to a whole new world away from my masculine friends. We were more like friends than boyfriend and girlfriend and it was a unique experience for me as a kid.

At the time I also had two best friends named Joe Freddy and Mike. We did everything together. We were a goof ball team, but we really cared about each other. Later in life I often find myself pondering what became of all of my youngster friends (someone should invent a tool called *Facebook*, and help us to reunite).

Hemophilia was a heavy burden on my eight-year-old shoulders. Many of the kids in school would pick on me because of my illness. More than once a bully would punch me for no reason and exclaim, "I want to see you swell up." I endured many levels of torture including name-calling (which was surprisingly more painful than the punches. Some of the kids called me a "homo-feel-ya" and it pained me in a way that I tried not to show. My mental skin was thickening from an early age.

Inside I built a rage that was pointed toward myself for being so different. I merely wanted a normal life where I could participate in contact sports and be like the "ordinary" kids. I felt a separation from everyone including my friends and longed for a day when a real cure would help me to fit in.

* * *

I spent many hours standing in one of the four corners of our living room. Any time you did something against the household rules, you were sentenced to time in the corner. One time, Laine had done something wrong and Dad made him stand in the corner. Forgetting that he was punishing Laine, Dad went out to the store and left him standing there. Laine was too frightened to move, so he ended up standing out there for hours. When Dad finally arrived home, he felt terrible for leaving him there, but kids are merciless and we just laughed at the situation.

Another time, we were all at the local drug store, by now Dad was used to us acting up. He looked over and saw a blonde boy in the toy section messing up the aisle. Dad hurried over and grabbed him by the arm. Spinning him around, he screamed, "What are you doing?"

The little boy looked in horror at the stranger who was scolding him.

Apparently, he was someone else's kid that Dad had mistaken for one of us. The whole situation was quite embarrassing for Dad, but amusing for us kids.

* * *

We had a nice basketball hoop on our court and the entire neighborhood would come play ball. We would get some interesting games going. One day, it was just a couple of us and we were shooting hoops. After a particularly nice shot, the basketball stayed stuck in our new net. Because we were all too short to reach it, retrieval of the ball was seemingly impossible. Frustration mounted as we tried everything, including shaking the pole, with no result. We realized that climbing it was a bad idea because the backboard was unable to support our weight.

Finally, I figured out that if I threw a rock just right, it could potentially knock the ball out of the net. After about three tries, I was still unable to free the ball, however, I did manage to break the entire back window out of our neighbor's car. My parents were less than pleased when they found out.

* * *

Let's just say that I have always had a fascination with electricity. For some reason, it excites and impresses me.

One day I decided to indulge my curiosity and see what would happen if scissors were actually inserted into the wall outlet. Since I was too frightened to do this myself, I decided to enroll my baby sister Raeghn to perform the experiment.

I tried to assure her that she would not be hurt. However, despite my best attempts, she did not believe me, and was unwilling to go along with my plans. I moved from assuring to begging. She still refused. Unfortunately for me, she was smarter than I thought and my hopes were fading.

So, in an effort to prove her wrong, I decided to make it appear as though I had inserted the scissors when I had not. I explained to her that nothing would happen as I moved the pointed blade slowly toward the electrical socket and that her fears were unfounded.

Hovering about a millimeter from the opening, I turned and said, "See, I told you that it wouldn't do anything."

At that moment, the electricity found a way to arc from the outlet to the scissors to me! Initially, I didn't feel any pain, but, soon after, my whole body jolted fiercely and a loud bang was followed with an explosion of sparks.

After I jiggled, and screamed some, I was knocked off of my feet by the power and sent sliding across the kitchen floor.

Raeghn was elated with my mishap and continues to doubt me to this day.

* * *

As kids, we had many similar adventures before the neighborhood was finally able to sigh in relief as we packed up and moved once again.

* * *

After Rockville, we bought a nice-sized house on a four-acre wooded lot in Laytonsville, Maryland. Our house was brand new and we had a creek running through the back yard. For us Riplets, it was a dream come true with an endless array of adventures ahead of us.

Dad built us a tree house in the back yard next to the creek, and we would play in it for hours. Playing army with the rest of the neighborhood kids was our biggest thrill. At night, we would play hide and seek. We had a rope swing over the creek and tons of trees to climb.

In 1977, Dad bought Mom a new four-wheel drive GMC Jimmy. Since Mom had the Jimmy, Dad wanted to trade our Suburban in for something else and my parents ended up buying a soft-top, blue CJ-5 Jeep.

I was obsessed with vehicles because it was a passion that I could have as a hemophiliac. I would spend countless hours reading car and truck magazines and studying different models of automobiles. I also started getting into making models of my favorite cars as a "safe" pastime.

In addition to my fascination with cars, I found an allure to four-wheeling. My father introduced me to driving off-road and it cultured a hobby that remains to this day. In the time that we lived in Laytonsville, Dad created lots of trails through the back yard with that jeep and I loved every minute of it.

* * *

On August 16, 1977, Elvis died without warning. Up until this point, Grandpa Ripley was the only person I knew who had died and he died when I was only seven years old. So, Elvis was my first real exposure to death. I was only ten years old, but my dad's old records and reel-to-reel tapes of Elvis had me hooked on his bluesy gospel rock style. I loved "Jailhouse Rock" and "I Got Stung" by "the King." His death affected me deeply and introduced me to the pain and suffering of losing someone. Perhaps it brought home to me my own feelings of mortality which, as a kid, you don't often think about. As a kid with hemophilia though, I was faced with these feelings on a regular basis as I was driven to the hospital for factor VIII nearly every week.

* * *

My dad took me into work one day and I got to play with his computer. It was an old Prime mainframe. I played *Adventure* and *Star Trek*. These were both text-based (no graphics or sounds) computer games that would bore the kids of today to death. Instantly, I was amazed and in love with computers. I instinctively knew that computers would play a major role in my life; I was just unsure how at that point.

* * *

Around this time I really started to understand what hemophilia meant. More than ever I wanted to fit in with the jocks and be able to participate in contact sports. I felt separated from my peers and it hurt me to feel so different. The kids did not make this easier by taunting me and laughing at my weakness.

One area that I found was developing rapidly was my mind and creativity. I started to understand that by reading and studying I could build a potential area that people respected. Before long, I had tapped this power and found some of the kids actually turning to me for advice on a plethora of subjects. My reading picked up and I was devouring books at a massive rate. Without wasting time on sports and some of the other standard time-takers, I was able to absorb myself in a world of books. Without knowing it, I was creating my path and future. The nerd in me was starting to surface and I was enjoying it. Perhaps contact sports were not the only thing in the world after all.

I was able to focus my mind and turn my physical deficiency into something positive. This was my first real glimpse of the power that my mind had to make up for my shortcomings. I had found a way to utilize my natural talents and forget about the illness related problems. Life was helping me to find a course through all of the obstruction that would bring me success and happiness.

* * *

In 1979, I started seventh grade and life was weird. When I started junior high school, I was more of a nerd than ever before. The main reason for this was because of hemophilia. I was forbidden to play any contact sports, and I had a doctor's note excusing me from most activities in gym class. So all through junior high I was primarily a swimmer and a cross-country runner, the "tamer" sports. This didn't stop me from occasionally testing my boundaries on skateboards and bicycles, much to the chagrin of my parents and doctors when they found out.

I joined the Chess Club and hung out with the "brainiacs." I was finding fantasy games like *Dungeons and Dragons* loads of fun. I was officially becoming a bookworm and loving it. In some ways I questioned if I was truly enjoying reading. I wondered deep down inside if I was merely conforming to what society said that I must do. But usually I was happy with my mental prowess and left the physical games to those with bodies equipped to handle it better.

* * *

Although I had a mischievous side, I was also tremendously mature for my age. Being only twelve years old did not stop me from shocking my hematologist during one appointment with words and courage beyond that of many adults. My mother and doctor were talking quietly about the fact that, as a hemophiliac, it was likely that I would lead a considerably shorter life than average.

Unwilling to just sit there listening to the negative spin on my life, I interrupted their whispering to announce, "Excuse me. I understand that I'll die younger than most people. But, I plan to live life to its fullest anyway."

The doctor's open-mouthed expression and the tears welling in my mother's eyes told me that I had spoken true words beyond my years. To this day, I try to live with that same positive outlook and motto.

* * *

In another of my "wiser" moments, I decided to say a few nice things on Mother's Day at church. During one part of the service, the Bishop asked for folks to come up and say something to their mother's. My heart was beating so hard that I could hear it knocking in my ears, but I stood and started walking briskly toward the front.

The instant Mom saw me stand I could see her eyes well up as she straightened herself and smiled proudly at me. Just the fact that I was willing to do this was more than enough for her. The walk to the podium at the front of the church seemed to take forever, and it felt as though every eye in the chapel was upon me.

I waited my turn as child after child went up and told how much they loved their mothers.

My turn came quicker than I had hoped for and I grabbed the microphone to adjust it to my height. A feedback screech frightened the crowd and drew their attention firmly toward me. I was stumbling for words and found that my throat felt dry and stuffed with cotton.

Finally, I leaned in and started to tell how important my mother was to my siblings and me. I told a few short stories that relayed how great she was in my eyes. From the stage, I could see the tears flowing down my mom's cheeks. At that moment, I decided to tell the whole church just how awesome my mother really was.

Choking back my own tears, I finished my stories by saying, "And finally, my mother always makes sure that we kids have everything that we need. She does this at her own expense. For, even though each of us has nice clothes and new shoes, she is stuck wearing holey underwear."

As I finished the entire congregation went dead silent for a moment and I feared that I had broken some church-related rule. Suddenly, without warning, the entire church broke out into boisterous laughter. Mom had a look of pure shock and embarrassment on her face.

When the laughter died down, I added one last thing, "I love you Mom and happy mother's Day!"

Even though I had unknowingly humiliated my mom with the underwear comment, she was still proud of me. She gave me a long hug when I returned to our pew and kissed me on the cheek. Mom did not stop her tearful thanks for quite a while.

* * *

Less suddenly than Elvis, John Wayne died on June 11, 1979. "The Duke" was my idol and everything I wanted to be in a man. I had seen many of his movies and was infatuated with his laconic style of dealing with bad guys. John Wayne was an inspiration to me in many ways.

I still quote his piercing drawl, "Pilgrim, you could've gotten somebody killed today and somebody oughta belt you in the mouth. But I won't. I won't. The hell I won't!" Or, perhaps that was Walter Eugene "Radar" O'Reilly.

When we were younger, we had taken a trip out to one of his ranches in Arizona. I can still remember seeing his ranch and thinking how cool it was that we were actually at one of John Wayne's houses. The main lesson that John Wayne, as both a person and movie persona, taught me was that the world was filled with injustice and unfairness, but you didn't have to take it. He never took it onscreen and off, and I certainly wasn't going to take it either!

By this time, the death thing was really starting to get to me and I was beginning to understand how fragile life truly was. If Grandpa, Elvis, and even John Wayne could die, then any one of us could also do so at any time. I went through a short phase of worrying about death. This worry was both for my own mortality and the transient nature of friends and family that surrounded me. I went through a period of worrying that my mother would die. I cried myself to sleep and never told anyone of my fears and worries.

* * *

Because I was such a wimp, seventh grade was kind of tough for me. I had learned to keep my hemophilia a secret, so most of the kids were unaware of my disability. Due in part to this fact, sometimes bullies would push me around. Damned if I do, Damned if I don't considering that bullies liked to pick on me because of either hemophilia or just my wimpy, skinny stature.

One of the kids at school named Solomon was bigger than the rest of us. He listened to Pink Floyd and his crowd was too *cool* for me. He knew about my health issues and used to protect me from time-to-time. It was an ironic relationship having the hippie hipster stand up for the straight and narrow nerd. We were exact opposites and yet somehow connected by a code of honor that no one would have believed Solomon followed.

I never did get to thank him, so—"Thanks, Sol."

The only real fight that I got into in seventh grade was with one of my best friends, Doug. Doug was a really nice guy and undeserving of my wrath. By punching him in the nose, I was taking my frustrations and fears out on him. The very thing that I hated bullies for, I was doing to someone weaker than me. *Pathetic* to say the least, but I allowed my aggression to build until it finally released on someone who not only didn't deserve it, but was also a good friend of mine.

Unfortunately Doug's glasses went flying through the air and shattered into pieces on the floor. The fight only lasted long enough for me to punch him. From there, everyone's concern was focused on the broken glasses.

We both went to the principal's office and waited for our parents. I think we had to split the cost of the busted glasses. I felt terrible, but we never discussed it again.

* * *

At 13, I went to Ann Arbor in Michigan to attend hemophilia camp. The camp was called, "Camp Bald Eagle." I met many other hemophiliacs and kids with von Willebrand's disease (another bleeding disorder similar to hemophilia).

It was an eye opening experience to meet so many hemophiliacs. I realized, for the first time in my life, that I had it relatively easy. Many of the other hemophiliacs had the disease so severe that they rode in padded wheel chairs to avoid bruising their feet or joints. And, almost everyone except me had to give themselves injections on a regular basis.

I felt a bond attending a camp with so many boys who lived like me. I found out that I was not the *only* person in the world with this illness and that thousands of other kids dealt with my same problems on a daily basis.

During my stay at Camp Bald Eagle, I collided with a counselor while playing Frisbee. Because the counselor was also a hemophiliac and he had broken his clavicle, everyone's attention went to him. I sat alone for over an hour waiting while he was tended to.

Most people immediately ask me about cuts when I explain my hemophilia to them, but the real danger lurks in internal bleeding. External cuts and lacerations can almost always be simply controlled via firm pressure. On the other hand, internal bleeds can sometimes be impossible (without factor VIII) to restrain. For this very reason, hemophilia is so dangerous and even deadly.

My thigh was really hurting me during the waiting period and I could feel the blood coursing between my muscle fibers and swelling my thigh to well beyond its normal shape and size. It was ironic that I was at hemophilia camp and supposedly in the hands of "safe" people and yet sitting waiting for care while I bled to the point of a dangerous level.

Panic was starting to set in and I finally called out to someone that I was having some pretty bad pain in my thigh. When the first counselor came over to have a look, he instantly became alarmed and called for additional help.

My thigh had swelled to two times its normal size and I required loads of factor VIII. I spent four months in physical therapy. This would start the "accident" phase of my youth.

* * *

One afternoon, while waiting for my school bus, I decided to jump up onto one of the concrete platforms that most of the kids used to sit on. My jump calculation was off by centimeters and my foot slapped into the block rather than landing on top of it, doing a number on my vulnerable tibialis anterior (shin muscle).

I instantly fell down and forward, landing with a splintery crack on my right shin. Pain shot through my leg and into my spine. The shock of the impact initially hid the amount of damage I had done. On top of that, I was embarrassed at my obvious failed leap.

Chills ran down my neck and I felt momentarily weak as I tried to casually walk from the scene. Each step on my right foot sent sheer agony all of the way up my body and into my head. I still couldn't understand why my leg was giving me so much trouble.

Finally, when I had gotten far enough from the accident site, I chanced a glance down my leg and my stomach crawled into a ball as I noticed the blood flowing freely out of the base of my pant leg, onto my sneakers, and eventually pooling on the ground at my foot.

I felt the color drain from my face as sudden shock and fear gripped my heart. As "cool" as possible, I limped into the school and headed nonchalantly toward the main office for help.

Because none of the teachers (except the gym teacher) were aware of my condition and they were ill prepared for an incident such as this. Instantly the halls and principal's office were full of raving adults. Funnily enough I was the one who remained calm and collected and I cautiously instructed a couple of the composed ones. They called 911 and had an ambulance come to get me immediately.

After receiving 17 stitches (eight internal and nine external ones) I spent most of the night and many hours over the next couple of days getting factor VIII.

More than 30 years later, I still carry the jagged scar as a constant reminder of the pain and suffering that I endured at the time.

* * *

On December 8, 1980 I faced a new horror when John Lennon abruptly died of a gunshot wound. Up until now, everyone had died of natural causes (or so I thought). This latest death was of biblical Cain and Abel proportions. I couldn't understand why anyone would kill someone as peace-loving and innocent as John Lennon. This new form of death gripped me with a terror beyond anything I had felt before. This murder opened my eyes to the potential violence of mankind. Before this point in time, such benevolent brutality was beyond anything I had imagined.

I found that a darker side was opening inside me as I adapted to the hard world that existed outside the safe boundaries of my house. I realized with intense clarity that I would have to harden myself to survive in this world. My reading used to consist of comforting books and an occasional fantasy. I now started reading the dark writing of Stephen King and instantly became enthralled with his scary style. I remember reading *Salem's Lot* and being so frightened that I lay in fear every night for more than a month after finishing it.

If the world really was as hard and dangerous as I now believed, my plan was to work my way clear of the fear and pain by reading things that would harden me.

* * *

Sometime during the eighth grade, this bully named Ritchie tried to pick a fight with me. I tried to avoid him, but he was relentless in following me. I explained that I had hemophilia and was unable to fight him, but he refused to listen to any form of reason.

Finally, we were walking in the hall and he shoved me. Everything went into slow motion; I swung a right hook in the general direction of his face. Next thing I knew, I was missing him by a mile, and his right hook was clobbering me. He hit me so hard that I flew into the lockers and fell to the ground with a horrible thump.

My face immediately swelled and colored as the blood rolled freely under the skin of my left cheek.

A teacher took us both to the office and we waited for our parents.

Ritchie was unaware that he could have killed me with that punch. He was apologetic when he found out. I accepted his apology and spent three days at the hospital receiving factor VIII to stop the bleeding in my face.

Trying to look normal, I carried my disfigured cheek and eye with dignity. The damage that was caused physically amounted to nothing compared to my psychological pain. I wore that black eye for half of my eighth grade year and my fellow students never failed to let me know. It even lasted long enough to show up in my yearbook photo.

* * *

While still in eighth grade, my Grandmother bought us our first computer. It was an Apple II+. Instantly, I saw how powerful and creative this machine was.

I was amazed at the computer's potential. I asked my father to help me learn to program it. He helped me some and then threw the computer manual at me and explained, "If you really want to learn how to use it, you'll have to read this." So, I read it. Twice.

I started programming in AppleSoft, which was a form of BASIC (Beginner's All-purpose Symbolic Instruction Code). Soon after, I was writing games and playing with graphical pictures and animations. As I progressed, I made many creations. I designed a graphical picture that was a castle. It was animated and raised a waving flag up a flagpole. I wrote a game where you flew a bomber and dropped bombs on ships that were sailing below in the sea.

Intrigued by the power of programming, I started learning a new language called GraForth, which was oriented toward graphics and music. I dabbled in creating weird Pink Floyd-like renditions of computer graphic freak shows.

No matter what I was making, I felt free. Computers allowed me to express myself in a way I had never done before. I had found the key to the rest of my life.

* * *

In 1981, as my family was traveling out West for our second family reunion in Dubois, Wyoming, the Centers for Disease Control (CDC) declared a new disease, later to be known as AIDS, as an epidemic. AIDS was first called GRID, or "Gay-Related Immune Deficiency" for lack of a more intelligent title. This name clearly showed where the social stigma stemmed. Little did I know then how this disease would later come to impact my life.

Chapter Two

We had been in Laytonsville for about four years, and it was taking its toll on Dad. With his office in Rockville, his daily roundtrip commute was a good 60 miles. He was already at work more than he wanted, but the trip itself was a burden. It probably didn't help having to maintain a four-acre yard and huge house while money was tight, in addition to raising three growing boys and a girl on the side.

As a result, we packed up again and planned to move two blocks from where we originally had lived in Rockville. Our new house was in the Richard Montgomery High School district (it starts in the ninth grade). Since school was already starting and my parents didn't want me switching after only being there for a month, my mother drove me into Gaithersburg and I rode on the public transportation (fancy way of saying "bus") for the remaining eight miles into Rockville.

Each day she would give me four quarters that would carry me to and from school on the bus.

One day, I had eaten my packed lunch a little early and was starving by the time lunch rolled around. So, I broke into my remaining 50 cents to buy something at the school cafeteria. My pleasure from the food was short-lived as I realized that I would have no way of catching the bus home. Panic overwhelmed me as I tried to think how I could call Mom and ask her to come further down *the Pike* (the main road between Rockville and Gaithersburg) to Rockville to pick me up. I decided against this idea and as the day ended, I tried to come up with a plan.

Finally with no better plan in sight, I just started running to Gaithersburg. I had been in cross country and was in reasonable running shape, but the eight-mile run from city to city was about twice as far as I had ever run before.

It was a fairly hot and muggy day as I started out strong, running at about a seven-minute mile pace. I calculated that, at this pace, it would take me close to an hour to run the course. An hour was reasonable as I could explain that I had just missed the first bus and had to take the second one. My spirits were high as I chugged along.

My elation with my plan started going downhill about 30 minutes into my run as my fatigued body started faltering. I had not had any water all afternoon and the heat was starting to take its toll on me. I slowed my pace a hair, tucked my head in a little and kept on running.

Unfortunately, my new pace was slower and I feared that I would be even later. My mind wrestled to think of explanations for the delay. Nothing made sense and, to make matters worse, I was getting cramps in my hamstrings. My dehydration was advancing rapidly to a possible heat stroke.

Knowing that I would face certain punishment, I struggled to keep running. My breathing was erratic and I was starting to feel a bit cool even though it was sweltering outside.

As if my body had a mind of its own, it continued to slow my pace down and I was feeling delirious as I rocked from one foot to the other in a trance. I was only about a mile from my meeting place with my mother and I knew that I could do it.

My vision grayed as I approached the bus area more than 70 minutes late. In my confused state I again worried about how to explain the delay to my mom. I didn't realize, as I approached her truck, that my body and demeanor would speak for itself.

She sprang out of the truck and approached me with concern in her eyes. "What's wrong, honey?" she queried.

I decided that the truth would be best at this stage, so I tearfully explained everything to her. She worried about my possible heat stroke and took me to a nearby 7-11 where we sat as I re-hydrated and rested.

My mother was amazed that I would take on such a daunting task when I could have simply called her and explained the situation. In hindsight I guess she was right, but it was a challenge and I knew my body was capable.

Fortunately I didn't have to ride the bus for long, because we moved into our new house shortly after that experience.

It was kind of cool moving back into the same neighborhood, because we already knew the area and the people. I still remembered a lot of my childhood friends and made several new ones at school.

* * *

There was a large oblong grass-filled court in the center of our neighborhood. And, as you can imagine, the neighborhood children would gather there to play games of all sorts. One of my favorites (and my doctor's most dreaded) was affectionately called, "Kill the Man With the Ball." Kill the man was a simple game that required only a football. Essentially, the ball was released into the middle of our court and we would all sprint in to grab it. Whoever got the ball was the target of everyone else. The entire game consisted of breaking tackles and blows to keep the ball as long as possible.

We spent many afternoons bruising and bashing each other playing this crazy game that was even crazier for a hemophiliac. To my parent's credit, they never knew that we played it. My doctor, however, was a good bit suspicious of my never-ending supply of bruises and internal bleeding.

On a couple of fortunate occasions, Joel (the neighborhood football stud) would appear for a few fleeting minutes to grace us with his presence. He was going into his senior year and was an unbelievable football-playing machine. He would pick up our ball and keep it as long as he felt like. We all tried to no avail to tackle or even grab him. His younger brothers, Jason and Jared, were the best at making attempts to bring him down, but even as a group, we could not stop Joel from prancing around the field.

It may sound silly to most folks, but the inability to play contact sports really hurt me. Perhaps it was the simple act of not being allowed that pained me the most, but I always wanted to participate in football or soccer. For this reason, I would play in the most aggressive neighborhood games.

One afternoon I told Joel how much I loved football and wished I could play. In an offhand manner he said, "Why don't you come out and offer to be the waterboy?"

His comment sounded funny at first, but then I realized that he was serious. And, the more I thought about it, the more it started making sense. As waterboy, I would be lined up on the sideline of one of the best high school football teams in the state. And, I would mingle with all of the athletes that I idolized and secretly wished that I could be like. I decided to go for it.

I approached my Woodworking teacher, who was also the varsity team coach, and asked him what he thought. He loved the idea and told me I could start right away. Before I knew it, I was at every practice mixing up Gatorade and preparing coolers of water. Once the season started, I would get to run out on the field during timeouts and give the star players water and Gatorade while the coaches conferred with them. It was a humbling experience to see these finely tuned athletes playing. Plus I was contributing in some small way to their success and, more importantly they treated me as if I was one of their own.

None of the players made fun of me or picked on me even though I had the somewhat trivial task of bringing them fluid. If anything, they respected me and treated me with dignity. I don't know if they laughed at me behind my back, but that's really not important. What is crucial is that I felt like an integral part of the team.

During my season with the varsity football team, I mentored under the wings of Chuck, Kevin, Pat, and Vernon. All of the players helped instill values in me and inspired me to become a better man. At the top of this list was Joel. I think that he was proud of me for taking his advice and he was always there to counsel me. Joel helped encourage a work ethic in me that remains to this day. Through his example and guidance, I realized that nothing comes easily in life. You must fight hard to make gains and improvements. Also, rewards are bountiful to those of us who decide to press harder and beyond the limits of what is expected by others.

On top of all of the lessons learned, it was also nice being in tenth grade and having many of the Varsity football players as friends. Many of the so-called bullies of my grade would not even consider pushing me around for fear of the big football players that would surely smash them into a fine dust for looking at me wrong. For the first time in my life, I was not pushed around by peers, but looked upon with admiration.

* * *

While in the tenth grade, I met Paul. He was soft-spoken and extremely logical. He reminded me a lot of Spock from *Star Trek*. Every problem that he considered had to have a logical answer or outcome. Paul and I quickly became close friends.

Paul and I built a group of friends that hung out and goofed off. Many days we would gather up local kids and play "Capture the Flag" until the late hours.

Paul loved being active and adventurous like me. However, his sensible side kept my need for adrenaline in check. Paul was just what I needed to feel like one of the guys and yet stay reasonably safe.

* * *

Along with my newfound popularity, I was also among the first kids in our grade to be driving. Since my parents let me take the GMC Jimmy into school, I was of some use to the other kids.

I was a maniac with the truck. I would take it over curbs and through people's yards just to impress my friends. On and off the street, I was becoming a terror to be reckoned with.

On one occasion, I was playing Capture the Flag with several friends and I decided to use my truck to get the flag. I ran this idea by Paul, and he thought it was a good one. So, we piled into my truck and I commenced to drive over many curbs, sidewalks, and grass areas to finally reach the enemy's flag station.

Once there, Paul jumped out of the truck and grabbed the flag. He instantly popped back into my truck and we sped off, spitting grass and mud all over the place.

While we were backing away from the flag station, my brother Scean dove onto the truck's hood and was hanging on for dear life. I swerved back and forth, trying to throw him from the vehicle to no avail. He clung as if his life depended on it. *And, it may have.*

Finally Scean dropped off and we returned the flag to our side and won that match. Of course Scean started arguing that he had tagged us out by touching the truck. We argued for some time about this and I don't remember now who actually won the argument. However, I will never forget Scean diving onto the hood of my truck with a look of extreme perseverance and then hanging on for his life. Looking back, it seems more like a scene from an action flick than us kids playing Capture the Flag. This was merely the beginning of my off-road adventures, which took my "wild side" to a whole new level.

* * *

When eleventh grade started, I bought the CJ-5 from my dad. By now I was a completely merciless, brutal, off-road maniac. Nothing could stop my straight-six four by four and me.

The first night that I owned the jeep, I went out and got stuck in some serious mud. Before my dad could arrive to rescue my brother Laine and me, it became dark and the rain started coming down in sheets. This was my first, but nowhere near my last, four-wheeling excursion.

* * *

One night while my parents were out of town, my friends Johnny and Mike helped me sneak out to a party. During the party, I drank soda because I feared alcohol at this stage in my life.

We hung out for a couple of hours and then heard some shouting at the far side of the yard. Meandering over, Johnny, Mike, and I saw a teenager yelling at an adult. It sounded as though they were arguing about the man's daughter and what the teenager had done to her. Finally the father stormed into the house and people started getting back to the act of partying. Moments later the man emerged from the house brandishing a revolver and went right up to the kid and stuck it in his face. Everyone standing around went dead quiet for a second and then burst into screams and mayhem.

The area cleared faster than anything I had ever seen, but I stayed put and stared on in fascination as the man yelled at the now completely pale boy. Shaking the gun around and making the teenaged boy extremely nervous the man continued to berate and lecture the kid before finally pointing the gun at the ground and eventually walking back inside the house.

This was the first real party that I had been to, so the excitement was beyond belief. Between seeing someone pull a loaded weapon on another person and all of the alcohol shenanigans, I received my money's worth!

Johnny, Mike, and I decided to split after the first group of police officers came in, and started harassing the party.

Once we arrived home, I snuck back in and went to bed.

Just before sleep took over, I heard a light knocking noise. It was Mike and Johnny tapping on the front door. I rushed down to see what they wanted before they woke up my brothers. They insisted that, instead of going to sleep, we should sneak out again.

I was still scared my brothers would hear us leaving, so we tried to push my jeep out of the driveway. My dad's boat, a 24-foot cabin cruiser, was parked in the back of the driveway on a trailer and the rest of the driveway was a steep hill. We had a two-foot long wooden four-by-four behind my back right tire to stop me from rolling back into the boat trailer. All three of us were rocking the jeep trying to push it up and out of the driveway. Each time we rocked it further, the jeep would hit the block of wood harder.

Finally, in one huge push we got it almost all of the way up the hill, and the jeep rolled back over the block and onto the trailer receiver.

Now we had done it! The jeep was stuck on the boat trailer and it had made the loudest crashing sound you could imagine. I quickly jumped in and started the jeep up. Revving the motor, I threw it into first gear and punched the gas.

Nothing. The jeep just sat there screaming as I pushed the engine past red line. Panicking, I looked out at Johnny, who was pointing to the rear tires. They were spinning freely in the air.

I threw the transfer case into four-wheel drive and had Mike and Johnny lock the hubs. Punching it one more time, I popped the clutch and did a four-wheel burnout up my driveway. We ended up making ten times the noise by trying to be quiet.

After stopping just long enough to put it back into two-wheel drive and pick up Mike and Johnny, we sped off.

The next morning, I sprinkled pine needles over the black tire lines that went clean out of our driveway and into the street.

My brothers never woke up once, and if my dad ever noticed the dent on top off his trailer, he never told me.

* * *

One of my eleventh grade classes was Shop where we would repair and paint automobiles. The teacher complained one day about a band of hooligans driving by his house and screaming and doing big burnouts in the middle of the night. When he described the offensive vehicle, Mike and I both immediately knew that it belonged to a fellow classmate named Tim.

Tim hung out with a couple of guys named Kenny and Mike. They were motor heads (into hotrods and such) and therefore I thought they were pretty cool. However, I liked my Auto Shop teacher and felt bad for him in this situation. So, Mike and I decided to tell him who had done this devious act.

Apparently Tim got into some trouble over this escapade and it quickly went around school that Tim and his gang knew we had ratted him out. He was officially on the hunt to make my life miserable. My stomach turned as I thought about the consequences of a run-in with one of these guys. You can imagine the build up of heartburn when I ran into not one, but all three in an otherwise empty stairway.

I whimpered for forgiveness and mercy, as I knew that my punishment would land me in the hospital at best. Out of the three, I probably had the best relationship with Kenny. Even though we didn't get along as friends we sort of had this unwritten agreement of respect for each other. Kenny was a nice guy who would occasionally get into trouble because of his affiliation with his motor head gang. He knew about my hemophilia and how dangerous it could be for me to take a beating so he stepped forward not allowing Mike and Tim to get a piece.

He looked me in the eye and told me that what I had done was wrong and I was going to pay for that. He then proceeded to slug me in the stomach. It was not a hard punch, but it was enough to hurt and my emotions mixed in to make the pain greater. Afterward, he told me I was lucky that he didn't punch me in the face and create a bleed. I knew in my heart that he had done what he had to do and yet somehow managed to treat me fairly.

Mike and Tim snickered as they all left me bent over in the stairway. I cried some and gathered my thoughts and strength before lifting my chin and heading off to class.

I learned a valuable lesson that day. Mostly it consisted of not ratting out other kids for silly stuff. But it also taught me that even kids from the other side have feelings and don't always want to send you to the Emergency Room. I never told Kenny how much it meant to me that he was compassionate enough to do what he did, because I did not want to ruin his reputation as a tough guy. But inside I was thankful and still clearly remember that day.

After me, the group sought out my buddy Mike and gave him some pain and suffering for being a nark as well. Unfortunately for them, Mike was a close friend with Johnny's older brother, Jimmy. Jimmy was a year older and looked out for Mike because he was small and often picked on. On top of that, Jimmy had no patience for anyone beating up a hemophiliac.

It was Kenny's turn to be on the receiving end and Jimmy wasn't nearly as nice as Kenny had been to me. Jimmy gave him a rather painful beating for picking on Mike and me. Afterward I could not celebrate because I felt bad for Kenny who had tried to make my chastisement as safe and easy as possible.

* * *

On another occasion, at a different construction site, I was kicking mud sky high again. Alan, Frank, and I were cruising through thick pools of gummy mud. This construction site was a housing development and it was filled with large deep holes that were excavated basements for the future houses. We slalomed narrowly around different pre-dug basements.

Finally coming to an extremely steep wall of dirt, I stopped and then started to back down the path we had come up.

Frank uttered something along the lines of, "What's the matter, your jeep can't climb that hill?"

I turned from Frank to Alan to the dirt wall. The wall was only about eleven or twelve feet tall. I calculated that with a given speed, I would be up it before possibly tipping over.

A sinister grin cracked my face. Backing further for room to run, I stopped and looked at Frank.

Alan was in the front seat and frowning. He quizzed, "Your not really gonna try drivin' up that, are you?"

My twelve-and-a-half inch wide mud-treaded Power Cat tires growled as full throttle was applied to them. Cackling, I approached the solid wall of dirt in a frenzy. The powertrain lurched as I slammed it into second gear.

Glancing in the mirror, I noticed Frank beginning to doubt this maneuver. As we neared the wall of sure death, I thought to myself, *He'll never question my jeep's prowess again.*

The engine was wound up as far as second gear could go. I was afraid to switch gears so I let the jeep engine redline as we hit the wall. It was so steep that the bumper hit before the tires, and we were almost unable to get enough upward force to climb it. At that instant I thought she was incapable of making it, but the front tires finally grabbed dirt, and we shot straight up at an unbelievable angle.

It was incredible; we were running at about 30 miles per hour straight up into the sky. For a second I knew how astronauts must feel strapped into their seats and launching into outer space.

Then reality kicked in as we capped the wall. The jeep was completely off of the ground and we were peaking when I realized my mistake. You are never supposed to drive at high rates of speed into unknown territory.

From the air, I could see the freshly dug basement immediately in front of us.

Before the front tires even hit the ground, I had the jeep in neutral, the parking brake on, and the brake pedal pressed to the floor.

We were still moving when I noticed Alan jumping out of the passenger side. He must have been undoing his seat belt while I was slamming brakes on. The jeep stopped with the front tires inside the wall of the new basement. Dirt was spilling into the deep hole.

Frank and I had a moment of realization as the jeep teetered on the brink of complete disaster. We knew that any moment, it would lose traction and topple into the dirt grave.

Suddenly, Frank tried to escape from the back of the vehicle. Knowing that his weight was holding us on the edge, I grabbed him and pulled him back in.

It did not make him feel any easier when I explained the situation to him. Sweat poured down my brow as I told him to remain calm.

Alan was outside assessing the situation, screaming things like, "Oh shit," and "There's no way."

After collecting myself, I slowly put the transmission in reverse and applied some gas. When the clutch reached its pressure point I felt the jeep drop forward.

Alan screamed about the front tires spinning as more dirt was torn out from under us.

Quickly I took the jeep out of four-wheel drive and punched the gas while releasing the clutch. The jeep struggled for a second and then righted itself by backing away from this near fatal wreck.

The worst was over, but we still had to go back the way we came. I was incapable of turning around, so we had to back down the hill we came up.

It was more like dropping, but we were able to manage it. That was the closest I had ever come to totaling my jeep.

* * *

My jeep was starting to show signs of weakness. The brakes started failing and they needed to be "bled" once a week. If I did not bleed the air out of them, some days the pedal would go straight to the floor without doing anything. I would have to pump them like mad to build up pressure and get them to work properly.

After a particularly tough day at work, I decided to go out cruising with Marc. We were driving down Route 355 when the car in front of us came to a screeching halt. There was no one stopped in front of this car, yet they stopped anyway for no apparent reason. At this point however, whether there was a squirrel, cat, dog, or something else crossing the street to make the driver slam on their brakes, it was inconsequential. Reacting, I hit my brakes hard. Chills ran up my spine as the brake pedal slid easily to the floor. I cursed and started pumping the brakes. Looking toward Marc I remembered we were doorless. I shouted, "Hang on!"

After about three hard pumps, the brakes finally grabbed and the jeep started protesting with a tire squeal. I was able to slow the vehicle to about 35 miles per hour before Marc and I crashed into the automobile ahead of us.

Upon impact I jerked forward and the jeep came to an abrupt stop. As we stopped, I noticed the car we hit lurching forward. Its front end actually lifted off the ground as the car flew about 20 feet forward. When it landed I noticed the damage that was done.

It was terrible; the rear end was completely demolished. The trunk had collapsed and was crushed into the rear seat. The car appeared totaled.

I looked to see if Marc was okay. His eyes were round with amazement, but he nodded *yes* to my questioning look.

I proceeded to unfasten my safety belt and climb out. As I approached the vehicle, I saw it was a girl driver. She saw me walking up and suddenly let go of the brakes and punched the gas pedal. As she screeched away, I stood there baffled.

Snapping out of it, I went back and climbed into my jeep. Marc and I drove to the next parking lot and pulled in. Climbing out, I almost cried thinking of the damage I must have received.

Unbelievably, there was no damage. Not even a scratch. The only evidence of an accident was a slim white stripe of paint on the bumper that must have come from the other car. I pulled out a flat-head screwdriver and scraped the offensive paint off.

To this day I don't understand why the girl left the scene of the accident. I figure that she must have been out in Daddy's car without permission, or was uninsured. Either way, I wonder how she explained the damage to the car.

Chapter Three

During my senior year at Richard Montgomery, I was working part time for my dad's land surveying company. I did a bit of everything for them. I used to enter data for several of their clients on a keypunch machine. Also, I would run printouts of mylar and paper when they needed me to. Most of the time I was running deliveries or errands. On many of these deliveries I was driving a company van or the bosses' cars.

I was driving one of the company's field trucks, an old beat-up Chevrolet Suburban, on a delivery one day. My friend Wade was riding shotgun and we were acting like the goofy children that we were.

At one point a new Corvette was coming the other way and Wade held out an empty coke bottle stating, "I bet you won't throw this bottle at that 'Vette."

I snagged the bottle with a sneer and started rolling down my window. Unfortunately, I had built quite a reputation as a person that would do any dare and this was one of those occasions. I could see the driver as we approached and I was worried about following through with this obscene action. Deciding quickly, I swung my arm out the window feigning to toss the bottle. My plan was to pretend I had thrown the bottle and then toss it after the car, hoping that Wade would not notice the difference. In this way I could look like the crazy guy that everyone believed I was and yet avoid getting into real trouble.

Everything was working perfectly until my arm reached the full extension during my swing. Apparently I was not holding on to the bottle firmly enough and it popped out of my grasp. In slow motion the bottle tumbled through the air and smacked dead center on the Corvette's hood and then bounced off the windshield.

"Holy crap!" Wade yelled as he looked over the seat to watch the car fly by. "I didn't think you would really do that."

I was stunned. Peering in my rearview mirror I calmly stated, "Of course I would. You dared me." Inside my stomach was already starting to turn.

It happened. His rear brake lights kicked on and smoke seeped from the tires as the Corvette driver slammed on his brakes and then started to turn around to chase me down.

Panicking I punched the gas to the floor. That old Suburban had a big block motor and it could move when you wanted it to. Wade and I were both thrown back in our seat as I accelerated away from the scene.

Following the windy road, I saw a turn ahead that would be blind to the Corvette for a moment. Turning to Wade I ordered, "Hold on!"

Knowing that the Suburban could possibly roll, I was a bit apprehensive about my next move, but the fear of what would happen if I didn't try it allowed me to give it a go. I slammed the brakes just before the turn and all four tires screeched their protest. Easing up on the brake pedal a little bit, I turned the steering wheel to the right. The Suburban groaned as the chassis twisted and we took that turn at about 40 miles per hour. The right rear tire hopped some and the entire truck threatened to tumble. Barely staying on the road, I was able to make another turn. Once I was out of view of the main road, I slowed and pulled into a driveway.

Sitting in the driveway, I was sweating profusely and I could see my hands shaking from the adrenaline. Turning to Wade I breathed a sigh of relief. I refused to believe we were safe until we had sat there for a couple of minutes and then a smile broke my face. Wade returned my smile with one of his own and then he started talking a mile-a-minute about how crazy that was.

Finally, I slid the truck into reverse and eased out of the driveway and headed back to our road. My mind was racing and I was wondering if the Corvette driver had caught a glimpse of the company name on the side of the truck. If he did, I wondered if he would call my office and report me.

Turning back onto the main road I fell back into the routine of making my delivery. The worries of him reporting me were pretty slim and it would have been practically impossible for him to read the company name while flying by wondering what had just slammed into his shiny new Corvette.

Suddenly my worst nightmare came true. Directly in front of me was the same 'Vette heading back the way he was originally going. Before I could react, he cut across the road and blocked my way. Unless I wanted to take it to the next level, this game was over. I quickly decided to stop and take my medicine.

The man climbed out from behind the wheel and charged up to my truck. He was intense and obviously very angry. I stammered and stuttered and tried to come up with some semblance of an excuse. My efforts were ridiculous and it was apparent that I was extremely nervous. Finally he finished stating that he was going to call my boss. He said this final part while purposefully glaring at the enormous sticker on the door of my truck.

He warned me about trying anything that stupid again and then stormed off to climb back into his little muscle car.

If he did ever call my company, I never heard about it. But, I did spend many days worrying about my dad calling me into his office to scream at me about the embarrassment I had caused his company.

* * *

I applied for my first real computer job at a popular computer software store. The owner of a local computer store asked me to come in for a job interview. I dressed up with slacks and a tie and worked on what I would say when interviewed.

As I waited for my meeting I was nervous. Sweat was building on my brow and in my hands. I kept wiping my hand on my pant thigh to remove the sweat, so that I could be ready to shake hands with the owner. I was finally called to be questioned and interviewed. I found out that one of the programmers would be doing the interview. Relief shot through me when I discovered that I would not have to meet with the bigwig. I was still nervous nonetheless, but it was a hair easier knowing that someone as important as the president of the company would not be doing the grilling.

The introductions were short and then the programmer shot right to the punch line. He looked at me sternly and asked, "What languages do you know?"

I shot back with supreme confidence, "I took some German and French in high school."

Of course my interviewer was referring to computer languages like BASIC, C, and so on. I was *obviously* unqualified for that job and I did not receive the job. But I did vow to improve my computerese and started diving into programming languages like Turbo Pascal and Turbo C. Later I started tinkering with Assembly and even Machine language.

* * *

Because money was tight and I was not very good at saving, I decided to sell my jeep. It was hard being without a car, but most of my friends had them, so I was able to manage.

Without my jeep, I began to look to other areas for "thrills."

Paul had some friends that liked to rock climb at a nearby *crag* (rock climbing areas, usually consisting of many rock faces, are called crags). He asked if I would like to try it and I immediately said, "Yes." Being a hemophiliac has never stopped me from trying exhilarating things. It has helped bring me down to earth after several accidents, but never stopped me from trying. Paul, Marc, and I decided to climb at an area a friend had described on the Potomac River. It is called Carderock and is located on the Chesapeake and Ohio (C&O) canal, downriver from Great Falls on the Maryland side.

Since money was an issue, we only used regular sneakers and no protective gear such as ropes and harnesses. At the time I was unaware that climbing could be a much safer sport with the proper equipment.

We had a great afternoon free-solo climbing everything that we could. Finishing up, I decided to try a slab that seemed too tough for tennis shoes. Giving it a go, I almost *flashed* (flashing is a climbing term used to mean climbing something on your first try) it. Unfortunately, I lost traction and started sliding. I was unaware that I could get better traction by using only feet and hands, so I lay down to try to use all of my body for friction.

Adrenaline was pumping as the realization that I would die from the 30-foot drop to rocks below kicked in. Paul was also looking a little terrified, which was not helping matters.

I slowly slid down the slab and headed for the edge that spelled imminent death for me. As I neared the edge, Paul told me that there was a small branch over my head. I reached up and tried to make purchase on this supposed branch.

"A little to your right," he said. Then he followed with, "Now left—up an inch."

Finally I was able to grab it. He was not kidding when he said *little*. It was the tiniest branch I had ever grabbed. Miraculously the branch held and stopped my progress toward the precipice.

I somehow managed to get over to the side of the climb and worked my way to safety. Needless to say, after this death-defying event, Paul and I stopped climbing.

* * *

In November of 1984, my Grandma Harriett (Dad's step-mother) died. I have many fond memories of hanging out with her on her hammock during beautiful summer days. With Grandma Harriett gone, the legacy of the Carlisle pond was fading quickly. We no longer took our trips each year to go visit the old Carlisle house and swim or ice-skate. That old house and its inhabitants will always remain firmly in my heart. It was a loving place that always made me feel welcome. When Grandma Harriett died, a piece of me died along with her.

* * *

After high school I decided to continue my education by going to a local community college, Montgomery College Rockville campus. At the time, without a vehicle, I was skateboarding to class.

I was skateboarding down a hill in our neighborhood and it was just starting to get dark out. Enjoying myself, I raced down the steep street and headed toward a park at the bottom of the hill.

Apparently someone had moved some warning cones from around a construction hole in the middle of the street as a joke. I rode right into the freshly dug asphalt without knowing it. The hole was only about three feet long, but it was enough for my skateboard to drop in. The depth of the hole was about six inches, which proved to be more than enough to swallow my skateboard. Suddenly I was floating and then my feet snagged the other side of the hole and I tumbled.

Slamming my hip into the street, I tumbled and scraped my way to a stop. I had injured my hip and elbow but felt fortunate to have avoided cracking my skull. Gathering my board, I limped home to find my hip starting a nasty internal bleed.

Three days of factor VIII and weeks of staying off my feet kept me out of my college classes. I was falling so far behind that my hematologist wrote me an excuse to allow me to drop out without failing.

* * *

Another close friend of mine was Emily. She lived about three miles away from my house and I used to walk there to hang out and talk for hours. At the time, Emily was my best friend and we spent tons of time together. Emily would lecture me about how dangerous the things I did (like skateboarding) were for a hemophiliac. She had a way of making me feel juvenile and I loved it.

Emily was a couple of years younger than me, but my immature mind and attitude had us communicating at a similar level. We could sit talking and philosophizing forever.

I was attracted to Emily, but afraid that acting on those feelings would endanger our friendship. She was one of the only friends I had that would talk to me so openly and honestly. It felt good to spill the beans about personal issues and such.

I valued her opinion highly and loved the time that we spent talking about life. I also looked forward to every meeting with her because she was willing to talk about things that most folks considered trivial or silly. We would sit in her room for hours just talking about whatever caught our fancy at the time.

I think that Emily was attracted to me as much as I was to her, but we both sort of avoided the subject. To my dismay, eventually our friendship faded and neither of us really knows why. Today, Emily is a doctor in New Mexico and I miss our long evenings of debate and camaraderie.

* * *

After dropping out of college, I decided to go to a Computer Technical School. My mother and I did some researching together and came up with a technical school named Computer Learning Center located in Virginia. While there, I learned how to program advanced C, FORTRAN, and COBOL—*YUCK!*

In order to make the long trip to class, my mother helped me with the purchase of a new (used) vehicle. We searched a little through the want ads and finally decided to go with a nice golden-colored Dodge Dart.

One rainy day, when driving to class, I did a donut and wrecked into a jersey wall. I was cruising along the Capital Beltway at about 60 miles per hour in my Dart. It had completely bald tires and no traction whatsoever. As I was crossing the American Legion Bridge in the fast lane, I hit a tiny puddle. This sent my car into an unrecoverable hydroplaning spin.

I remember clearly thinking, *Uh, oh. This isn't good.* As I was spinning, I took turns swinging my head around to look over each shoulder. I caught eyes with a middle-aged man driving a Saab. He looked terrified as I missed his automobile by mere inches and continued spinning. I laughed.

The Dart was starting to slow down when I heard a loud blast of an air horn. Snapping my head around, my mouth dropped open in horror as I saw a fully loaded flatbed 18-wheeler bearing down on my passenger side door. *OH NO!* I thought as I tried turning into my spin. By some miracle, the car gained traction at the last second and I shot into the center jersey wall with my left fender. The truck driver barely missed crushing my vehicle and sent an obscene gesture my direction as he passed.

I was starting to make a habit of dropping out of school. Without a vehicle, I was unable to continue attending the school and dropped out—*again*.

* * *

My dealings with women were starting to depress me. That was when Terri came into my life. She was exactly what I needed to help pick me up. She constantly reminded me that she had always had a crush on me and secretly wished for me. In high school I had worked in the library and she used to ask for a pass just to visit me. It was fun knowing that someone of the opposite sex was as attracted to me as I was to them.

Terri's parents were old enough to be her grandparents, but I got along with them nicely. I would walk over to her house and then we would stroll around the neighborhood and make out some. All of our kissing and such would move along to a point where we thought it would take us to the next level, but she would always intervene and stop our action before it got to hot and heavy.

I was still a virgin and wanted to stretch my proverbial wings, but Terri was adamant that we abstain from sex. So, I calmly complied.

Terri and I lasted a couple of months and faded. I think our relationship canceled because she felt like I was too good for her. I know that sounds strange, but oddly enough it is what she told me. Was I just a victim of the "it's not you, it's me" break-up?

Chapter Four

In May of 1986, at 19 years old, I lost my virginity. Margo was an older woman who would occasionally hit on me and tease me. I found her attractive, but I wanted my first time to be special. She continued tagging me along with talk of foreplay and sex and I finally cracked and agreed to a nighttime foray.

The sex was very fast—*shocker!!!*—and afterward, I regretted it. I had spent my entire adolescence saving myself for someone special. Then, I blew it on the first person that would let me. At least I had finally gotten past the unbearable stepping-stone of having sex for my first time.

* * *

It seemed as though women were popping in and out of my life like Uncle Arthur on *Bewitched*. Then, someone who had been a friend for nearly two years surprised me. Liane was a fun spirited, wild woman. She sprung life into me. We began dating on the last day of December in 1986. I stopped the little bit of alcohol curiosity I had recently embarked on, and started delving into life with her.

* * *

Paul and I were out hot-rodding in his Honda Civic one afternoon and it started to rain a little. We were flying through neighborhood streets at high speeds. As we rounded a particularly sharp curve, we both noticed a car stopped in the middle of our lane. In front of the stopped car was a taxi pulling out of a driveway.

Paul immediately hit his brakes and we started to slide. The car went quickly into a spinning slide and time appeared to slow down. I turned my head in slow motion from side-to-side trying to follow our slide path. Paul was doing the same thing, looking in all different directions as we spun two or three donuts.

As the car started to slow, we realized that we were going to wreck into a very nice Jaguar that was parked on the side of the road. I prepared for impact and watched in horror as we closed on the fancy vehicle.

At the last moment, the Honda grabbed a little traction and we swung away from the Jaguar with inches to spare.

As soon as we came to a complete stop, I screamed, "That was awesome!"

Paul turned to me and his face was red with anger. I think it took all of his willpower to not punch me. We were both breathing heavily and he suddenly yelled, "That was *not* awesome!"

Later that day, Paul and I drove back by the "scene" to check it out. We stopped to admire our 70 plus feet of extremely dark skid marks in the shape of several donuts. Following the skid marks, we finally ended up down by the jaguar and noticed that the skid marks came within inches of the car. I do not even know how that is possible, since the body juts out further than the tires. All I know is, we must have missed that vehicle by millimeters.

* * *

In another one of our ludicrous car situations, Paul and I created the "creek situation;" which lives today in infamy. In order to fully appreciate this story, please understand that Paul and I were always looking for ways to not only put our lives on the line in vehicles, but also racing each other at the same time. For the most part, these races were for temporary bragging rights.

My girlfriend Liane lived in my neighborhood and I used to cut through a couple of yards to get there quickly. Paul decided that he would race me in his car. Realizing that the driving would probably be close to six times further than my short jog through yards, I quickly accepted his challenge.

Unbelievably, when I got to Liane's house, Paul was already there. He must have driven 60 miles per hour most of the way.

After visiting with Liane for a brief time, I asked Paul how he beat me to her house. He explained that he was cooking the whole way. I asked him to show me and we proceeded back to my house to start the short road rally.

The problem was that it had started to sprinkle rain on our way back to my house. Paul shot out of my court and down the street very quickly. He calmly stated, "This is about the speed that I traveled."

Then we came to the first big turn and he performed the maneuver perfectly going from the outside to the inside and back out as he said, "Then I took this turn like this—"

Just as we were finishing the turn, everything went into slow-motion mode. By this time in my life, I had gotten pretty used to slow-motion mode. It normally meant that something bad was about to happen. The car started sliding and we slid off of the road.

As we hopped the curb and continued our slide across the grass, Paul turned to me with a calm expression and said, "Except, I didn't do this last time."

I chuckled nervously and said, "Tree," as we skimmed the edge of a small tree and continued on our muddy slide toward a creek.

We missed a couple more trees and a bush, and then came to a rocking stop on the ledge to the creek. The car was literally teetering on the lip that dropped about six feet down into the creek below.

Paul and I tried to stay as motionless as possible since the car was literally balancing on the edge of serious damage. Paul finally peeked out his door and said that he would not be able to exit without dropping the car into the creek.

Thinking quickly, I opened my door slowly and kept my weight on the vehicle while shifting out. Once outside of the car with my feet and weight still on the doorjamb, I told Paul that I thought I could hold the car with my weight while he exited.

Agreeing, he waited for me to use my leverage by working out to the end of the passenger door. Finally, he was able to exit. However, I could feel that the car was going to drop off of the ledge if I let go of it.

We agreed that we needed some assistance in getting the car unstuck and I decided to run the two blocks back to my house and get my dad to help us with his pickup truck.

I left Paul standing in the grass supporting his car from demolition and ran home. As soon as I got home, I calmly asked my dad, "Dad, could you come help me and Paul with his car." I wanted to sound calm and not stir everyone up, especially my mother.

Unfortunately, my Uncle Dano was over and they were engrossed in a conversation. I tried once again to ask calmly and not raise any undo suspicion. Once again, my father did not even notice I was talking.

Finally, I threw my hands down and yelled, "Dad! Paul and I slid off of the road and he is holding his car from dropping off a ledge into the creek! Can you please come and help us." Of course the whole house stopped what they were doing and turned to me with horror on their faces. They probably did not know whether to believe me or not.

Dad jumped up and we raced down the street in the truck to help Paul. Sure enough, there he was, clinging to his automobile as it teetered on the edge.

Dad was able to hook up the tow-strap and pull the Honda off of the edge without incident. This story still brings a smile to everyone in my family when we bring it up.

* * *

Four days after Liane and I started dating, my parents called me into the den and told me that the family doctor had called. In the moments that followed, I spilled into a numb world that can only be found by facing death. On January 3, 1987, I had a mental collapse as my mother and father explained to me that I was dying. Our family doctor had called with the news that I was HIV+. To add insult to injury, my parents were in the middle of a painful separation. My happy life had suddenly become miserable.

Deep down inside I knew that my parents weren't getting a divorce because of me contracting HIV, but I couldn't help wondering if I was the cause. In addition, this was a time when I needed my parents more than ever before or ever again and they were consumed with their own problems. Rightfully so, they were busy trying to work out their marital differences and seeing if they could patch their marriage. They had been married for nineteen years and were watching the wonderful family that they had built crumble apart right in front of their eyes.

I stoically pressed on with life while my insides felt like they were wrenched and twisted into a pulpy mess. I bravely faced each day with a smile and feared going to bed where I would shake uncontrollably and cry myself to sleep.

My parents brought me in to see the family doctor and he proceeded to explain the simple fact that I was going to die. He did not give me a timeframe, but it was clear that he was talking about sometime in the very near future.

Turning from my nearly tearful family physician, I found my mom's tear streaked face sadly looking at me. Swallowing, I then turned to see my dad who also had tears welling up in his eyes. I had never seen my dad cry, and there he was crying freely. The entire room was lugubrious. Finally I turned back to my doctor and started laughing. I laughed sheepishly as if I had some hidden joke that they didn't know about. My mother came to me and hugged me and my laughs turned to cries. I cannot remember how long I wept, but we did leave the doctor's office lucidly understanding that my days were numbered.

We didn't talk on our ride home and I desperately grasped at strings to figure out what was going on in my life.

I was a teenaged boy facing my untimely death. Words cannot do justice to the waves of emotion that tore through my mind and body.

* * *

Liane was three years younger than me and her parents were already partially against us dating. I was scared to face them with this new fact.

I explained everything to Liane and we sat and shed tears for hours. Her mother questioned our behavior, but never got involved. I thought we should break up, but she, now more then ever, wanted to stay together. We decided that telling her parents was not a good idea. In case anyone is considering me a role model, I do not condone this behavior.

We dated for three more months solid. Then on and off we slowly separated. By the time my birthday came around in April, we were completely split apart.

I fell into an abyss of pain and agony. In an unexplainable rage, I started hating gay people. I blamed them for what was happening to me. I felt that their promiscuous conduct gave me this Godforsaken disease. Later in life I would realize that this type of thinking was unfair and untrue. But, at the time I needed something tangible to blame my pending death on.

* * *

Because of hemophilia I had become a fairly decent swimmer and loved going to the pool. My buddy Marc and I used to go down to our neighborhood pool to hang out and get in some occasional swimming. I had not been to the pool since finding out I was HIV+, so I was a bit nervous about showing up and seeing how people reacted, but Marc convinced me that no one would mind. From the moment we walked in, I could feel the eyes upon me. Perhaps most of it was sheer paranoia, but I felt as though the whole world had stopped to stare at this brazen lunatic that brought such a dangerous disease into their midst.

Because a pool is so chlorinated and my disease is tough to transmit, I knew that there was no danger to others, but I could not help thinking that they were all whispering about me. I started feeling extremely uncomfortable and explained this to Marc. He reassured and calmed me by elucidating the simple fact that I was being paranoid and no one was looking at me or talking about me.

I finally calmed enough to dive into the water and do a little swimming. Again I was feeling the eyes upon me and I uncomfortably got out of the water and made my way back to our seats. More than ever, I felt as though folks were peering at me as if I had some nerve coming and putting them all in danger. Whether the looks were really happening or not, I realized that my obsession with everyone's concern was going to drive me crazy. So, I started thinking about leaving.

As I was explaining my predicament to Marc, a lifeguard approached us and I felt dread sink deeply into my stomach. He casually walked right up to me and asked, "Do you have AIDS?"

I felt my cheeks turn cherry-red as a fear gripped me and surely showed on my face. I was shocked beyond belief at this blunt personal question and responded quickly with a nervous, "No."

I felt inside that I was clearly lying out of panic and was immediately ashamed of my perjury. The lifeguard was starting to say something about some of the people telling him that I had AIDS when I stood and rushed out of the pool with a glazed look on my face. By the time I was in the parking lot, my eyes were filled with tears, and I kept up my fast pace.

Finally I ran. I felt betrayed by my community. My friends. My support system. No one should have to go through something this horrendous. It scarred me for life.

Marc caught up to me and was very apologetic. He was surprised and clearly shaken by the whole situation. My stomach was already starting to feel better away from all of those prying eyes and whispering rumors.

This was the first of countless awkward and embarrassing situations that I would face in the coming years. Prior to this book, I rarely told this story, because it hurts so much and I am ashamed at the leper that society deemed me.

* * *

I started drinking again. This time it was more heavily. As often as I was doing it, my drinking could have been considered breathing. I picked up a few other bad habits like smoking cigarettes and constantly brooding over obstacles in life. Why was I being picked to die? I mean, I had a checkered past, but I was no more worse than the next guy. Why me?

It got to the point where I was constantly blasted or worse. Drinking was taking me into a shielded spot. Dying never crossed my mind (nor anything sane) while I was drunk. I had all new friends and we hung out for hours on end getting more-and-more drunk. The drinking was getting so heavy that sometimes I forgot who or where I was. I became so addicted, that I woke up in the morning and would pound some beers and end up drinking all day long.

The drinking had completely taken control of me. I was unmindful, because it made me forget about AIDS. My dad moved out to an apartment of his own. Alcohol also helped me in dealing with my parent's separation.

At this time, I had a motorcycle that I had illegally tagged. I used it to ride my friends around in a drunken stupor. We would fly up and down the neighborhood streets riding wheelies and screeching to halts nearly missing parked cars. We thought this was funny and entertaining. I was on the brink of suicide and could see no path home to safety.

In addition to the drinking, I started smoking pot. When I was younger I had sworn that I would never do anything as stupid as smoke pot and now I easily adapted it into my daily routine.

As is normally the story, the pot led to stronger drugs. Before I knew it, I was snorting cocaine and taking doses of acid. The LSD was even better at hiding my problems, because it lasted longer and took me completely away from reality. In addition to these mainstream drugs, I also started smoking PCP-laced pot, which was called "love boat." And, PCP-laced parsley, which was called "green."

I never actually injected needles into my system, but I did try heroin by snorting it mixed with cocaine. This was a bad combination, because it took all of the bad side effects of each drug and amalgamated them into a strengthened single drug.

I reached the nadir of my life when I started smoking crack cocaine. This extremely addictive drug was spiraling me into a terminal velocity with death.

Because I had convinced myself that I was already dead, the drugs were merely a soother that would help me on my way faster. I was on a suicidal rampage that could only end in a terrible fashion.

Chapter Five

In mid July of 1987, I was taking my friend James home. When we arrived at his house, there was an angel sitting on his stoop. Everything appeared to be moving in freeze frame motion, as if a gigantic strobe light was pulsing. It was probably a mixture of all of the drugs I had recently ingested and the situation, but I felt strength emanating from this being.

She was wearing gray cotton shorts, a light tee shirt, and sneakers. Her hair was light brown and absolutely gorgeous, and those brown eyes were full of compassion. To top it all off, she had a terrific body.

My heart leapt into my throat as I asked James, "Who is that?"

James replied coolly, "That's just my sister, Kristine."

I could feel his eyes upon me, as I breathed in and felt my body ache. She was absolute beauty and I was scum of the earth. What could I possibly expect her to think of me?

With a grunt, James climbed off of my motorcycle, slapped me five, and said, "Peace, bro."

At the time I had shoulder length bleached blonde hair, skull-covered shorts, a dangling earring, and blue eyes that had more red in them than blue.

I wound up the throttle, sent a vicious sneer in their direction, and bellowed, "Late."

Releasing the clutch lever, I sped out of there with a screech of rubber and fleeting thoughts of James' beautiful sister.

* * *

After partying for hours, I was driving James home again. Once again, his sister Kristine was sitting on their front stoop. I was in awe at how pretty she looked. All that I could think of was meeting her.

Now I know there is an unwritten rule about dating your friend's sister. But this stunning woman had me spellbound. I turned to James in a daze and quizzed, "Do you think, you could ask her to come over here?"

With a sigh, James clambered off of the motorcycle and waved in my direction. What he did next, took a lot of courage. I know he was afraid of me seeing his sister. I was HIV+ and a drunken, drug-addicted hoodlum to boot. Yet, he still went over and talked Kristine into saying hello to me.

She started walking my way and I was mesmerized. Her hair was bouncing with the motion of a musical conductor. Swaying from side to side, her hips moved in slow motion. As she approached me, I was hypnotized by her beautiful brown eyes.

"Hi," she said.

I stumbled for the right thing to say, and blurted out, "Wanna ride on my bike?"

She accepted my invitation hesitantly looking toward her brother. As soon as she hit the seat, I punched the throttle and we rocketed out of there. As we rode I realized that each time I accelerated she would grip me tighter. So, she was in for the ride of her life. By the time I stopped at a nearby park, I was filled with confidence and assumed that she wanted me. Spinning, I asked, "Wanna go over to that gazebo?"

She acted surprised and unhappy. I felt awkward and uncomfortable. Finally, she asked, "What are you doing?"

I replied, "Oh, well I thought—"

She frowned and asked if I could take her home. I complied and drove her home.

That was my first run in with my one and only *true love*.

* * *

Kristine was four years younger than me and I was "robbing the cradle." Her parents knew I was HIV+, and it bothered them (to say the least) that we were dating. Looking back at us, I would not want my daughter dating me either!

We continued to date and Kristine's parents finally sent her to New York to get her away from me. We fell apart for a while.

In the mean time I picked up where I had left off with my old friends and vices. I was still living at home with my mom and it was cramping my style. The only problem being that I was a bum and unable to afford moving out. So, I tried to straighten my act up and got a job working for IBM.

Because of my drinking habit, I was incapable of holding a job. Unfortunately, I would start a job, work some, and then quit, because it was, *too tough*. So I spent the next year or so going from one career to another. I was straying far from computers and was taking all available blue-collar jobs. I worked at many restaurants, on construction sites, and for a couple of local land surveying companies. None of the jobs were what I wanted and I had a hard time holding them.

* * *

One day while showing off to the high school girls, I wrecked my motorcycle while riding home from work. The rear tire was balding (this seems to be a recurring problem of mine) and a couple of radial threads were showing. The front tire was worse, if that was possible. I was riding by my old high school and decided to impress the women folk. I popped a wheelie and rode it like a champ for about 40 feet. My head was swelling with pride as I set the bike back down. Unfortunately as I dropped the front tire down it blew out with a loud explosion. From there, the bike immediately slid and started into an end–over-end tumble. After about three or four flips, it slid to a screeching halt.

At the time there was no helmet law in Maryland, and being the sensible hemophiliac that I am, I never wore one. Consequently, my Varnet shades were demolished as my face smacked against the pavement. I also tore up a nice pair of slacks. My tie and shirt were ruined with my blood. That temporarily ended my short motorcycle days and sent me to the hospital to receive my dosage of factor VIII.

* * *

Contrary to my doctor's wishes, my motorcycle days were far from over. My friend Frank had recently purchased a 600 Honda Hurricane. He came by and let me take it for a spin. I was riding through my neighborhood at breakneck speed. After a couple of wheelies, I decided to spook Frank. I knew that he could hear his engine whining as I zipped through the back streets, so I cranked it extra hard. After flying down a road behind my house, I yanked the clutch in and let go of the throttle. To Frank, I knew it sounded like his bike was flying and then suddenly stopped for some reason. I found it impossible to hold the devious grin from my face as I crept back up to my house. Frank was freaking out (as usual).

Unfortunately Frank only owned that bike for a month. After finding his father dead, he made the error of running out and jumping on it. In a matter of seconds, Frank had totaled his motorcycle. He lucked out and walked away with only bruises and scratches.

* * *

In the summer of 1989, Kristine and I were once again forced to separate by her parents. I went to live for two months with my buddy Alan in Imperial Beach, which is southwest of San Diego.

Living in California was just what I needed to get my head on straight and start living my life fuller. I returned home a new man, moved out of my mom's house, and in with my friend Frank, and his brother Phil (who we all affectionately called Chill).

While living with Frank, and Phil, I met a girl named Suzie and we hit it off quickly. Because Kristine and I were on and off, I started seeing Suzie. Eventually when Kristine and I patched things up I dated both of them for a while. *I know what you are thinking.* But, in fairness to me, I told them about each other. I think that since they never saw each other, it did not bother them.

* * *

Once again, I was moving. I ended up living at my dad's apartment for a while. One night my brother Scean, his buddy Edward, Paul, Marc, Scean's girlfriend Maurine, Maurine's cousin Yahna, and I were all downing shots of Tequila. I was asking Maurine about her cousin and Scean thought I was hitting on his girlfriend.

Storming down the stairs he came at me and punched me in the throat. I fell to the ground and was unable to breathe. I was gasping for air as Scean reached down with his hand. I grabbed it thankfully and was trying to ask, "Why?"

Before I squeaked a single word out, Scean belted me square in the nose. Blood splashed everywhere, and once again I fell to the ground. *Fade to black.*

As I look back on this, I realize that Scean was not only punching me to protect his girl, more to the point his anger was due to me being such a screw up. More than once he punched me for this very reason, and I believe that his aggression saved my life. *Thanks, bro!*

Needless to say, the contention was at an all-time high in my dad's apartment and I ended up moving out. I spent a couple of weeks at my friend Wayne's place then went back to Dad's for a short time before I finally moved into an apartment with some friends Mark and Jamie.

* * *

In the summer of 1988 a friend of mine, Henry, offered to get me a job delivering baby furniture. I accepted and ended up working for Lewis of London for two years.

This job had its perquisites and for the most part, I enjoyed doing it. Because it was expensive baby furniture, some of our customers were celebrities. I delivered Sugar Ray Leonard's children's bedroom sets, I brought Linda Carter a baby toy chest from Burt Reynolds, and I delivered Denise Austin's baby crib. I was also lucky enough to meet Art Monk. He was at the height of his career as a Redskin's wide receiver when I delivered his furniture.

* * *

One evening while John, George, and I were returning from deliveries, I mentioned how cool it would be to pop out onto the roof and surf on top of the truck. John and George thought I was just saying that and both dared me to do it. I told them I would do it and asked John to take my picture while I hung down over the windshield. George did not think I would really climb onto the roof while we traveled on the highway (otherwise he would not have let me do it). After John agreed to take my picture, I rolled the window down and climb out onto the top of the truck. We were traveling at around 60 miles per hour and the wind was extremely strong.

Due to the powerful winds and lack of holds on top of the truck, I had a hard time gaining purchase and hanging in front of the windshield. At one point, the wind nearly blew me off of the truck. Adrenaline started pulsing through my body as I regained my composure and clung to the window frame for my life. Finally, I was able to inch my body forward enough to hang over the roof and onto the windshield. As predicted, John snapped the photo and I climbed back inside. To this date, I still have that photo. Cats and their nine lives have nothing on me.

Another time, I was out making deliveries with Mike when he wrecked the truck into a tree branch. We were traveling through a neighborhood when I screamed at Mike to stop. Mike tried to react, but it was too late. We hit a large, low hanging branch from a giant tree. There was an extremely loud crunch and we came to an abrupt stop.

Jumping out, I looked to see how much damage there was. It appeared as though the entire top front of the loading area was crushed in. Deciding to get a closer look, I climb on top of the truck. After assessing the damage, I jumped down to the ground. Unfortunately, I landed with my right foot onto the edge of the curb. As my foot slipped, my knee popped out of socket, and I collapsed to the ground in severe pain.

I was completely incapacitated and had to rush to the hospital to get a factor VIII transfusion. I was laid-up on bed rest for a couple of weeks. Apparently, even though I have more than nine lives, they are filled with weakness and suffering.

Chapter Six

During the summer of 1989 I was driving my brother Laine home from Annapolis on a motorcycle he had borrowed from a friend. I only had a motorcycle learner's permit. During the ride home, we pulled over for a smoke. While sitting there, my brother must have dropped his glasses. We took off and continued riding home. Once on the Beltway, Laine realized he no longer had his glasses and asked me to stop. I pulled over on the left shoulder and asked, "What's wrong?"

He explained that he had left his glasses back there. I was leery of returning, but he said they were new and expensive. So, I agreed that returning would be the best thing to do.

As I started to cut across the grass median that divided the highway, I noticed a car approaching us on the shoulder. Since it was getting dark all I could see were his headlights. In a panic, I sped out of his way and started to head the opposite direction on the highway. Just as I took off, Laine flipped the guy the bird.

Suddenly, blue and red lights kicked on and I realized why he had been coming down the shoulder. Unfortunately, we had already made the U-turn and started the other way. He zoomed across the median and darted after us. I imagine Laine flipping the bird was also unhelpful. At the next exit, I pulled over and stopped.

As soon as I dismounted, the officer grabbed me and started screaming about fleeing. I was scared since I was riding with only a learner's permit.

After I explained that I was not fleeing, the officer told us to wait as he radioed in the situation.

While out on our escapades, one of my friends had given me a bottle of amphetamines. There were about a dozen pills and I was scared to have them found on me. So, while the officer was in his squad car squawking, I split them up and explained to Laine that he had to take half of them to hide the evidence.

Laine was shocked and exclaimed, "No way man!"

I immediately popped all of the pills into my mouth and swallowed them. Then I nonchalantly flipped the empty plastic bottle to the ground. I grinned at Laine's look of horror as the officer approached us.

He booked me and I spent the weekend in the "clink." When I arrived for processing, the pills I had taken were kicked into high gear. I was losing my grasp on reality and bright colors were flashing all around. As I spoke to the interviewing officer the walls started breathing deeply.

He asked me casually, "Have you been drinking or doing any other drugs?"

I was caught up watching the wall behind him expand and then contract. He sternly looked at me and repeated his question.

I turned my gaze toward him and found his face melting in a drizzle of vivid colors. I dug deep inside and pulled the words from somewhere in the pit of my stomach, "No, sir."

He moved on with his questions and eventually I was moved into a concrete room with a concrete bed.

Suzie showed up after the weekend and paid the fine to get me released.

The officer had given me 36 points worth of tickets including fleeing, reckless driving, speeding, and others. As the saying goes, you name it; he gave it to me.

When I went to court, the judge knocked my points down to twelve and said that my license would be suspended for three years. Being the naive boy that I was, I was unaware that you could reapply for a suspended license immediately. So, I went for almost three years without one.

* * *

I have always held a soft spot in my heart for fire. My love of fire includes fireworks. Of course since they were illegal in Maryland, my friends and I had to go out of state to get them.

My friend John and I had a particularly nice batch of fireworks without a place to light them off. After a few moments of pondering, we decided to launch them inside my apartment. Looking back at this, I still laugh my ass off, even though I realize how unintelligent it was.

We searched my apartment for tools to use. We dug up a 36-inch long cardboard tube and duct taped one end. The tube was fairly sturdy and we assumed it would be okay to launch bottle rockets out of.

After shoving the tube (duct taped end down) between two couch cushions, we commenced our insane pyrotechnics show. One after another we dropped lit bottle rockets into the tube. We watched in awe as they launched in a smoking ascent toward my ceiling. After hitting the ceiling, they usually bounced back to the floor, and up again. This bouncing continued until the rocket fuel finally ran out and the bottle rocket exploded with an intense bang. A couple of times we actually had to dive out of the way of these high-speed projectile attacks.

We were having the time of our lives until the fire started. Paying no attention to the tube, we sent more than a dozen rockets throughout my apartment. Minutes into this two-person celebration, John and I both smelled something burning. Looking around, we found that smoke was emerging from my roommate's sofa. We yanked the tube out and found that the duct tape had burned away leaving a molten opening.

After pulling the burnt tube out, I saw the couch was still smoking from where we had stuck the tube. Freaking out, we both yanked the cushions up in time to see the flames flick to life. Thinking fast, I sat on one burning couch cushion and John did the same to the other.

The couch was damaged badly, and we tried to hide the burns from view by turning the cushions over. Needless to say, when my roommate Mark came home, he immediately smelled the burning furniture, and started screaming. I think he was pretty pissed-off about his sofa.

* * *

In the fall of 1989, I started getting these itchy bumps on the left part of my forehead. Slowly, the bumps spread to the left half of my nose and around my left eye. They were getting painful. Before long, the pain was unbearable and I could not sleep. Finally, a family friend drove me to the metro so that I could travel to the hospital.

At the hospital, I was diagnosed with herpes zoster (shingles). Normally this disease is reserved for the elderly, but it also affects people with immune disorders (and in a few cases even people without immunity problems). The pain and irritation grew worse over the next week and the hospital could not do much for me except tell me not to itch. As the bumps grew larger they were followed by intense itchiness and severe pain.

Because shingles is based on the nervous system, the afflicting wounds were only on the top left quadrant of my face. It was bizarre how they started at my hairline on the left half of my forehead and crept maliciously down to my nose before stopping. The rest of my face was perfectly clear and normal.

After a weeklong rest in a hospital bed, I was released with huge, ugly scars on my forehead. If I was ever handsome, I no longer believed it. My face was permanently scarred along with my pride.

On top of the damage that the shingles had done, many friends and family members who saw me during this ordeal thought for sure that I was dying. Afterward, I ran into some old friends who had heard that I did die. Quoting Samuel Clemens, I coolly replied, "Those reports were exaggerated."

* * *

After living at the apartment for almost a year, I moved into a house with a new friend, Dave. That house was the biggest party scene of all time.

Near the end of 1989, on the evening before New Year's Eve, Suzie and I were partying hard. We drank a large quantity of alcohol and smoked a huge joint. We decided to go out and find something fun to do. When I was pulling out of my neighborhood, we noticed a bunch of police cruisers with lights flashing a couple blocks away.

As, I started to turn the other direction, Suzie begged me to go see what all of the action was about. I wanted to avoid those cops like the plague, but she kept pleading. Next thing I knew, we were on our way over to see what the commotion was about.

As we approached, my stomach turned and leapt up my throat. Suddenly, everything was pellucid. The police cruisers were lined up creating a blockade. We were approaching a sobriety checkpoint. Not only was I completely wasted; I did not even have a valid driver's license. At this point there was no turning back because they would surely chase me. Sotto voce, I cursed myself for listening to Suzie.

When we arrived, the closest officer was signaling me to put down my window. I rolled it down and asked, "Yes?"

"This is a sobriety check," he said in a torpid voice. "Please drive under five miles per hour by each officer," he continued. Finally, he hit me with the clincher, "As you pass each officer, turn and look him in the eye."

I nodded nonchalantly and followed with, "Okay." In the meantime, I was inwardly panicking. I eased my foot off the brake and edged the clutch out softly praying, "Please let me make it through this."

My hands were shaking as I approached the next officer. I turned and faced him. After a brief moment, I cracked half a smile and nodded. He nodded back as I continued. Sweat started to build on my forehead and I could feel my hands shaking more violently. This was an extremely difficult position for me.

As I closed on the next officer, I again turned and stared with my best poker face. Finishing with a nod and a grin, I grimaced as I imagined the last officer asking me to stop and get out of the vehicle.

I turned toward the last officer to look at him. As I did, my foot let the clutch out a hair and the car jerked. *Oh no,* my mind was screaming. I figured I was dead meat. I finally met the officer's eyes and smiled. With a double nod, I slowly passed him and crept out of the danger zone.

When we cleared all of the police cars Suzie laughed and exclaimed, "That was insane!" I felt like screaming at her, but instead I laughed and agreed with her.

To this day, I am no longer interested in police lights. If there is a group of officers with lights flashing, I avoid them.

* * *

My friends and I spent many evenings playing chicken by letting cigarettes burn down our forearms and occasionally our thighs. Usually you played against someone to see who would quit first. I was one of the reigning champions and the only person who had beaten me at this game of will was my friend, Henry.

Another "game" that consisted of burning flesh involved a red-hot marijuana *bowl* (pipe used to smoke weed) and a willing body part. Some of my friends had "bowl burns" on the webbing between their thumb and pointer finger. Others had them on their back or chest. I decided to partake of the ceremony and get one on my left shoulder. Never being one to put down a challenge, I decided to use a special bowl that we had that was more than an inch in diameter (most bowls are less than half an inch in diameter).

I rolled up my sleeve and asked my friend Mike to heat up the bowl. I watched in amazement as Mike and John went through three lighters just to properly heat the bowl to an angry red. The metal was glowing brightly before Mike finally turned and asked if I was ready.

"Do it." I firmly responded and watched in horror as Mike laid the bowl against the meat of my deltoid and the sizzling began.

Wanting to ensure that the burn was good and lasted, I asked Mike to keep it applied for a bit. We all watched with fascination as the heated bowl melted its way into my flesh. The burning smell was repugnant and the pain was immeasurable, but I remained stoic until I felt sure that my mark would remain for life.

Finally Mike pulled back stating that the mark was more than enough to remain permanent. My burned skin blistered immediately and was a purplish-red for weeks. Fortunately I did not get an infection, but looking back I realize how stupid this act was for someone with no immune system. On top of that, I will carry this adolescent mark for the remainder of my life.

* * *

Some friends told me about an abandoned rock quarry where we could do some high jumps into water. So, we all piled into a car and headed out into the sticks for an adrenaline filled day of mayhem.

When we arrived, the friend who had been there before took us on a winding path through the woods. As we passed one opening in the woods, he said, "That is the 15 foot jump. Wanna try that first?" My friends and I chuckled and kept walking.

A couple of minutes later he again stopped and said, "This one is 35 or 40 feet." Then he turned with a grin and asked sarcastically, "Do you guys want to keep going up to the 60 foot jump?"

Much to his surprise we all chimed in with a resounding, "Hell yes!"

So, we trudged further up the trail toward the highest point in which to jump. As we approached the clearing that signified this was the jump, my buddy Nick took off at a sprint screaming. He continued in this fashion until he leapt off the edge and we heard his shrill scream fade away moments before there came a loud splash. None of us could believe the fearless action as we carefully walked up to the jump area. Later Nick confessed that he probably would not have jumped if he went to the edge and looked, so he decided to jump without ever peeking. And they call me crazy!

We each took turns doing the tremendous jump and it was exactly as I had expected—exhilarating!

My brother Laine stepped up to do the jump and we explained that he needed to go in feet first with his toes pointed and his hands tightly beside him. He got the toes right—unfortunately, his arms were sticking straight out when he impacted with an echoing slap. He wore solid black bruises under his arms for several weeks after that dangerous mistake.

* * *

Another fun water related escapade that we used to do was the infamous rope swing located on Game Preserve Road. Imagine a backcountry road right smack in the middle of the city. A short walk into the dense vegetative forest brought you out to a picturesque creek with an immense oak tree leaning out over the creek.

On one side of the creek the land climbed quickly and allowed for a decent leap over the creek using a rope tied to the oak tree. We would try and out do the previous person by climbing further up the rocky hill to make our leap. Not wanting to be outdone, after I had reached the highest possible point with rope in hand, I asked my friend Marc to hold the rope for me.

Marc was curious and held the rope as I climb up a level on the rocks. Everyone was baffled, because I was six feet above and five feet behind the rope. I had no way of holding it to do my swing.

One friend thought I was making a joke and chortled while he asked, "How are you gonna swing from there?"

Before his question was finished I back pedaled a step and burst forward with a dive. Even Marc was caught off guard as the crowd watched in awe. I had jumped from at least 20 feet above the rocky shoreline without a rope. Next, midair, I caught the rope deftly and Marc let it go. I swung further than anyone had ever done before and I was the talk of the gang that day.

Many folks do not understand how a hemophiliac could put himself in so many dangerous positions. And, on top of that, I always seemed to come out okay (for the most part). Well, after 43 years of life, I think I have assembled a lucid answer to both queries.

First, I think that hemophilia has helped turn me into the adrenaline-seeking hound that I am. All of those doctors, parents and friends telling me that I should not do these things coupled with a protected childhood created the man with an attitude.

Second, I feel that many of things that I did were done with reckless abandon because I was not afraid to die at this point in my life (in some ways I fancied it). Because of this, I was able to totally commit to doing some of these crazy things. I feel that many times when people have doubts or worries they fail because they did not commit 100 percent.

Chapter Seven

In the fall of 1990 I was catching colds and things much easier than I used to. Since I was not taking any medication for HIV and I was drinking heavily, my body was starting to pay the toll. One night in particular I was extremely sick. I was coughing so hard and loud, that I started to worry for my life.

I spent the evening hanging out with friends at Kristine's sister Dawn's house for a party. I was so sick that I could not move from my seat on the couch. Kristine sat with me and clearly was worrying for my life.

I caught the looks of fear. People around me saw how sick I was and they clearly thought that I was dying. I was weak and barely able to throw smiles in their direction. When I would get a particularly nice grin going, a coughing fit would destroy it.

As I sat there, I noticed that two guys who showed up for the party were harassing my friend Lesley. Besides the fact that Lesley is my friend, I absolutely will not stand for men bullying women. I watched them as they continued to tease her and finally one of the men threw Lesley over his shoulder and quickly moved to the back of the apartment with her.

I grew suspicious since it did not look as though Lesley wanted to go with these guys. So, I forced myself up and lumbered down the hall toward a bedroom where they had taken her. Along the way, I asked my friend Brian and my brother Laine to come with me. I was dizzy and barely able to walk as I approached the closed door.

Knocking on the door I casually asked if everything was okay in there. No one responded so I tried the door and found it was unlocked. The opened door revealed Lesley sprawled out on the bed with the two men on each side of her. One of the two guys glared at me and said, "This room is taken."

I stood my feeble ground and asked Lesley if everything was okay.

Lesley looked scared, but she did not say anything. Just then the second guy leaned forward and said, "Everything is fine, dude. Close the door."

I stepped into the doorway and tried to appear tough as I asked, "Lesley? Is everything okay?"

Lesley nervously shook her head no but said nothing. Just then one of the guys stood up and he blurted out, "Hey man, everything is fine here." He started toward me as if to push me out of the door.

I drew in a deep breath and put on my strongest face before stating, "Lesley said it's not okay, so stop whatever you're doing and let her go."

By now the second guy was standing up and acting perturbed. It was at this point that I realized just how big the second guy was. My guess would be six foot three inches and 230 pounds. He appeared to be a solid wall of muscle. That may not sound huge, but back then I weighed 145 pounds soaking wet! I am sure that my sickened state was not helping matters, but it was starting to look like a dire situation.

Standing my ground I said with a look of finality, "Lesley, come with us."

The larger guy was stepping forward and saying something like, "She ain't goin' nowhere!"

I knew from experience that this was going to end ugly, so I quickly pushed Lesley out of the room and stoically stood my ground. As I prepared myself for the pain that was about to come, my brother Laine stepped in front of me and stood up to the looming danger. My pride grew as I proudly watched my brother get punched squarely in the face. His glasses flew off and he fell across the room like a puppet on strings.

Shock crossed his face, but he determinedly got to his feet and was preparing to take another beating. Knowing I was the oldest and most experienced, I once again started forward to take my brutal attack that would most definitely end with me in the hospital receiving factor VIII. This time Brian stepped forward and he was yelling something at the assailant.

Brian looked heroic following in Laine's footsteps as he took his beating with dignity. This guy was big and mean and he went through my brother and friend like he was running through sheets hanging on a laundry line in the backyard. I knew it was my turn to get punched in the face, so I started forward again.

At this point, the ominous bad guy was starting to realize that we were going to keep coming, and he pulled a pocketknife out swinging it in my direction. The knife sent shivers up my spine as I envisioned being stabbed and killed trying to protect Lesley's dignity.

Even though I felt like dying internally, I dug deep and tried to think of a possible solution to this desolate situation. I immediately turned and moved into the kitchen where I found what I was looking for. On the counter was a butcher-styled carving knife and I grabbed it making my way back to the would-be rapist. My head was spinning and I must have been swaying as I moved toward the big guy. I growled, "Pull a knife on me will you?"

By now the entire party was centered on the situation and people must have seen the determination on my face. I knew that I was outmanned and in a precarious position, but I was not going to go down without a fight. As I approached the knife-wielding attacker calm filled me. I believe that some things are worth dying for. This just happened to be one of those things. A smile cracked my lips as I stepped toward the now agape attacker.

It all ended in an instant as I was smothered by a mob of my friends. They all saw where this situation was quickly headed and they piled onto me to stop me from attacking back. I was pinned to the ground and someone removed the knife from my grip.

By the time that I was up again, the two antagonists were already out of the apartment and people were chattering about how brave Laine, Brian, and I had been. I collapsed on the couch with shivers and started coughing uncontrollably. I moved to the bathroom and continued my coughing fit until blood and bits of flesh emerged. I was convinced that I did not have more than a day or two to live. I looked at the blood and thought, *They should have let me have a shot at that guy with the knife.*

The next day, I traveled out to Annapolis to my mother's apartment. After another restless night, Mom decided to take me in for a check up. I had pneumonia and was immediately admitted to the hospital.

Over the next two weeks I lived in a hospital bed eating crappy food. I had been so close to death that many of the nurses and doctors did not know if I would make it or not. Doing my standard miraculous recovery I fought with death and overcame it once again. If there were sides to choose between death and me—you had better lay your money down on me, because I refuse to give up without a nasty fight. Take that to the bank and deposit it.

* * *

One afternoon at the hospital near the end of my stay, all of my buddies from home came to visit me. They brought a small ceramic bong and some highly potent marijuana. Here I was in the hospital with severe lung issues and pneumonia puffing away on a bong full of pot.

When my nurse returned to check in on me, she immediately recognized the smell and freaked out. She started screaming at my friends telling them to leave the hospital and was obviously deeply hurt by my blatant disregard for hospital rules. Up until this point, I had been someone she enjoyed visiting and after the "bong incident" she no longer found me appealing in the least bit.

After my stay in Annapolis was over I got home and was welcomed by my girlfriend, Kristine. She was playing nurse and making sure that I got the attention that I needed. She was lying in bed with me playing "kiss me where it hurts."

My roommate Kenny was a nice fellow, but you would never accuse him of being the sharpest tool in the shed. On top of that, he may have been a tad jealous of the fact that I had two girlfriends. Either way, he let Suzie in without thinking about the consequences. Suzie opened my bedroom door and announced, "Surprise." Needless to say, she was the one who was surprised. Suzie stopped coming around after that incident and we quickly faded our relationship.

* * *

One night, Dave, John, and I were driving around town in Dave's BMW. We were all three drunk and still drinking in the car.

At one point, John held up an empty bottle and asked, "What should I do with my dead soldiers?"

I reached back and grabbed it from his hand. In one smooth motion I threw the beer bottle out of the window and straight up in the air. Unfortunately for us, the car immediately following ours was a police officer and the bottle had landed on his hood. Dave was busted for driving while under the influence and the officers told us to walk home. I somehow managed to convince one of the officers that I had not been drinking. He let me drive Dave's car home. Not only had I been drinking, but I was also driving on a non-existent driver's license.

My brushes with the law were becoming more frequent and closer with each one. It was simply a matter of time and probability before I ended up behind bars for good.

* * *

The local police department decided to park a couple of squad cars with mannequins in them. They thought that by placing these vehicles in well-known speeding areas they could control the speeders. John, George, and I thought this was ridiculous and decided to play a prank on them.

I remembered a story about my parents when they were teenagers. Apparently they painted a large sign stating "Slow down, police ahead." They used to drive around looking for speed traps and they would sit a block or two away from them with this sign warning people.

We were on our way back to the warehouse from a delivery in Potomac and spotted one of the parked cruisers at Julius West Junior High School. Pulling one block past it, we climbed in to the back of the truck and crafted a sign. We carefully cut a bed box to a six-foot by four-foot rectangle and wrote on it, "Rockville City Police Are Dummies."

Once the sign was completed, we walked it over to the parked mannequin and leaned it up against the car. Laughing at the irony, we walked back to our truck and positioned ourselves for a view of traffic.

We sat and laughed hysterically as car-after-car drove by and looked on in shock at the blatant sign. Before long, an upstanding citizen came along and stopped to remove the sign. Our fun was over, but we did get a good giggle at the local authority's expense. The next day the squad car and mannequin were gone and we never saw them returned.

* * *

Kristine and I had again broken-up, and the drinking and drugs were getting worse. I knew that I was heading for a train wreck. Beyond that, I was also severely depressed and wished that this evil virus would take my life once and for all. Thoughts of suicide had drifted in and out of my head for the last two years, but my death wish hadn't come to fruition and I was tired of fighting this loosing battle.

My clash with life was coming to a head and I started planning my demise. I would daydream while working about the different ways to kill myself. Deep down inside I was fearful of the fact that I would keep living in this condition and could not stand it any longer. I spent hours debating different forms of suicide and trying to pick one that would allow me to go out in style. I had visions of fiery car crashes off of mountainous cliffs and leaps from the top of some skyscraper over Time Square. When it came down to it, I knew that my *kamikaze, seppuku, harakiri,* or more to the point *jisatsu* (all of these Japanese words translate to one form of suicide or another) would actually be a meaningless act that would hurt many people around me.

I decided that the simplest way to smoke myself would be with a straight razor and some warm water. So, I prepared myself mentally and did a little planning. I remembered that Paul had mentioned that slicing your wrist was goofy unless done properly. He had explained that you must cut your veins open lengthwise instead of across like so many people do. This was the surefire way to kill yourself, because there is no simple way to patch this damage.

I was so close to ending my life that I could taste it. I was actually starting to feel better knowing that my worthless life would end soon. I would put myself to sleep thinking about everything finally being over. Now it was just a matter of picking a time and place.

My depression was deeply motivated by the drugs and alcohol. I knew that I was going to end my life soon and it was directly related to the depressants that I was bombarding my body with.

I was ashamed of the life I was leading and I hated it. After serious consideration, I decided to pray for help. This was my last ditch effort before finally doing the unthinkable. God had never answered me in the past so why would he answer me now. Praying was something I had avoided for years.

I spent an hour kneeled beside my bed pouring out my heart. I cried nonstop and cursed God for putting me through all of this. I challenged him and asked why he had not already ended my life. I prayed until my thought process changed and I was whimpering for help. My prayer had turned from hatred to fear. Before long I was begging God to rescue me. I pleaded my case for life and how I would turn my pathetic excuse of a life around if he would simply save me from this sad state of affairs. After this troublesome night I collapsed into bed and slept better than I had in years.

My prayer was answered the next day. David was a childhood friend of mine from church. The morning after my tearful prayer for help, he showed up on my doorstep. He explained that he had just gotten back from his mission in Brazil and decided to look me up. He had actually been looking for me for weeks and had finally tracked me down at this house.

I could not believe the irony of this event. My testimony was instantly created on that morning. David had merely walked into my life while it was on the brink of disaster. Was this just a random coincidence, or was God answering my humble prayer? My heart was filled with understanding and love as I realized the true answer in the blink of an eye. God had heard me in my darkest hour and had sent a servant to save me.

Epiphany. My eyes were opened. I had spent my short adult life thus far wishing for a death that was not coming. I was wasting my talents by drowning them with drugs. I was wasting away like a coward. This realization hit me like a ton of bricks. Jaw held high, chest puffed out and eyes firmly set, I vowed to myself, *Never again.*

Overnight I quit doing drugs, drinking alcohol and smoking cigarettes. I have always been a big fan of cold turkey. I am an extreme man and I believe in extreme measures. Without another thought, I turned my back on those life-destroying habits and crushed them.

I started to attend the Church of Jesus Christ of Latter Day Saints (Mormon Church), as I did off and on growing up. I did not own a single suit or nice clothes at this point in my life. David gave me some of his slacks and shirts and helped me to attend church. I started leading as straight a life as I could. I truly believe that David saved my life that day, maybe my soul too.

At the same time that I started cleaning up my act, Kristine and I started seeing each other again. We had been through several break-ups and make-ups in the past, but this was the first one that I went through sober. My life was finally looking up as I fought to make something of myself.

* * *

After an incident, my boss George fired me. I had been working for Lewis of London for two years when this happened. I was playing in the parking lot making snowballs and chucking them. George came out of the store and was walking up when I targeted him.

After I pummeled him with the snowball, he cried, "You do that again and you're fired."

I instantly balled up another one and held it glaring. He looked at me sternly and his eyes said, *I mean it.*

I rarely accept such ultimatums, so I let it fly and hit him in the face. He yelled, "You're outta here!"

When I look back at this, I see that it was the best thing that could have happened to me. I was out of my drinking stage and was trying to make myself into a prosperous and upstanding citizen. I think George also saw the potential in me, and that is the real reason why he cut me loose.

Chapter Eight

After losing my job at Lewis of London, I immediately went out and started working again. This time, I worked for a temporary placement agency. They assigned me jobs working with computers. I finally felt like I had a job where I could actually use my brain.

Soon after getting my new job, I moved into an apartment with my brother Scean. Because we were both trying to improve our lives, living together was a good idea.

* * *

I started investing some of my time in thinking about life. One of my favorite ways to accomplish this is by playing the guitar. Music gives me time to ponder and enjoy myself. Some days I would walk for an hour or more carrying my guitar and playing.

One day while walking along playing to myself, a car stopped and the passenger addressed me. He explained that he was Alvin Garrett and that he would like me to teach him to play. Because I am and always have been a huge Washington Redskin fan, I knew who Alvin Garrett was. This person did not look like Alvin to me. I told him that I didn't think he was really Alvin Garrett. He grinned and said that he was. Next he turned to the driver of the car and asked him to confirm it. After the driver confirmed it, I decided to give him the benefit of the doubt. I asked why he wanted to learn to play the guitar.

Alvin went on to explain that he wanted to play the gospel blues for his church congregation. I agreed to help him learn, and spent the next couple of months dropping by his house from time-to-time showing him some bar chords and teaching him a little about the blues.

* * *

Ryan White, a famous hemophiliac who was barred from public school in 1985, died on April 8, 1990. The cause of death was massive internal bleeding which may or may not have been related to the AZT he was taking to fight AIDS. To this day, there is controversy over the cause of Ryan's death.

* * *

During the winter of 1990 I started working with MDIPA, a health insurance company. For the most part, I was doing data entry for medical insurance claims.

During my time working there, I also worked on creating documents and templates. It was at MDIPA that I started realizing my true potential as a professional computer operator.

While at MDIPA, I started taking AZT for my HIV. I also found out about some free counseling services offered to people with my condition. Unfortunately, I was the only hemophiliac at these sessions and I felt extremely uncomfortable being there. Shortly after starting them, I left my counseling sessions convinced that I could go this alone. Or, at least with Kristine's help.

* * *

Since my dad and my mom had separated, Dad started seeing another woman named Diana. I knew Diana from working with her years earlier at my father's land surveying firm, Rodgers and Associates. Once my parents were divorced, Dad and Diana started getting more serious. It was not long before they decided to take the plunge.

After they were married, I added three new siblings to my list: Diana's oldest daughter, Marcie, her son Quincy, and her youngest daughter, Becky. Since the marriage, I have grown closer and closer to Quincy. He is truly a close friend and brother to me. I have also bonded with Becky and become good friends with her. Because Marcie lives so far away, we feel more like distant relatives than friends, but I still love her like the sister that she is.

* * *

Scean and I were raised Latter Day Saints (LDS or Mormon), so we attended the LDS single's ward. The single's ward is comprised of single adult men and women. While there we each had opportunities to meet some nice women. Scean met a young lady named Monica and they immediately hit it off. Before I knew it, they were getting married.

The first night when they came home from their wedding (in Washington state), Monica made dinner for all of us. Scean asked, "What is this?"

Monica replied, "It's Cheeseburger Surprise." Then she proudly added, "Do you like it?"

Scean instantly shot back, "No. And, you will never make this again."

I was very uncomfortable as Monica started crying. I immediately started shoveling the Cheeseburger Surprise in to my mouth as fast as I could. With a packed mouth of food, I exclaimed, "Boy, this is really good."

Immediately after finishing, I asked Monica for seconds as nicely as I could.

I think I may have broken the ice a little, but I still felt a little out of place living with this newlywed couple. Soon after, Scean and I talked and we decided that it would be best if I moved out to give them some "space."

I was starting to get my feet on the ground, but I could not afford to move out on my own. So, I went back to my dad and asked if I could move in with him and Diana. They accepted me into their home and I had a roof over my head once again.

* * *

Shortly after Scean and Monica were married, my sister Raeghn decided to marry her college sweetheart, Mel. When Mel called to talk to my dad and explain that they were in love, Dad was a little perturbed. He thought they were too young, should finish college and were jumping into this entirely too fast.

Mel and Raeghn were only checking in with Dad to try and get his blessing, *not his opinion,* and they were married shortly after.

* * *

Soon after I moved in with my parents, they decided to move to a house in Poolesville, Maryland. I moved with them into one of their rooms there.

I was very sick and congested one day. In my delirious state, I thought that using a heating pad to clear up my congestion was a good idea. What I did not realize was that I was already extremely dehydrated. Minutes after applying the heating pad, I started feeling woozy. Soon, I was unable to move at all. I could tell that my heartbeat was well below normal.

I tried to call out to someone in the house to help me. Unfortunately, my voice was a mere whisper. Using all of my will power, I moved my arm to bang on the wall. My banging fell short, as I barely made an audible tap with my hand.

All these battles with death and I was on the border of being killed by a heating pad. *Poetic justice?*

Starting to panic, I struggled to cry out again. Finally, Kristine heard my whimpers and came to check on me. It turns out that the combination of the heating pad and my dehydration had slowed my heart rate to a dangerous level.

I spent the night in the hospital getting rejuvenated and healed. They hydrated me using an intravenous drip and helped me in recovering.

I learned a valuable lesson that day. Hydration is an important and necessary part of life. Especially when you are sick. Later in life, I learned that over-hydration could be just as deadly.

* * *

In 1991 basketball star Magic Johnson announced that he was HIV+. This was a groundbreaking announcement that shocked and rocked the world.

Finally HIV and AIDS were being recognized as the "normal" man's disease.

Chapter Nine

During the winter of 1991 I quit working for MDIPA and joined Hayes-Ligon Corporation. When I started at Hayes-Ligon, my job description was data entry person.

At the same time that I quit working for MDIPA, my doctor decided to switch my drug from AZT to DDI. DDI was a relatively new drug for HIV and it showed promising results. Unfortunately, it was a nasty tasting powder that I had to add to water or fruit juice to consume. I used to throw it up more than I kept it down. I battened down the hatches and stuck with this new medication.

* * *

After being without my driver's license for three years, I was finally able to get a new one. Paul's mom had an old Honda Civic and she offered to sell it to me. It needed a new clutch and some minor work. Cam was willing to let me buy it for an extremely reasonable rate. So, I decided to buy it and work on the clutch myself.

I had experience with clutch work in my old CJ Jeep. However, I had never dealt with a front engine, front wheel drive clutch. Needless to say, it was a nightmare. I had to lift the engine and support the transaxle on a transmission jack. After 18 arduous hours, Paul and I finished the transfer of the burned out clutch with a new one. While we were in there, we went ahead and replaced the flywheel and constant velocity (CV) joint boots.

I was proud of the fruits of my labor and merrily drove my new (used) Honda Civic all over the place.

* * *

I had my Honda for three months when tragedy struck. I was driving into work on a Friday morning and the streets were drenched from the rain that had recently been coming down in thick sheets. I approached "dead man's curve" at approximately 80 miles per hour. I slowed to 70 miles per hour (this is barely a sane speed on dry pavement) and started into the turn. The tires immediately broke loose and I steered into my slide. I slid completely out of my lane and into oncoming traffic. A delivery van was heading straight at me when the tires finally caught and slung me back toward my lane.

For a brief moment I thought I might make it out of this dangerous situation unscathed. Unfortunately, the traction only lasted long enough to shift the car into my lane. Once again I lost traction and my Honda slid off of the road.

Relief struck as I managed to keep the car relatively straight and was starting to slow it in the three-foot tall grass on the side of the road. I started contemplating what to do about a telephone pole that was 100 feet away. I figured that I could slow the car to around 20 miles per hour before the pole and at that speed I should be able to maneuver around the pole.

I had slowed to around 50 miles per hour when my car struck a massive object in the deep grass. Due to the tall grass, I had missed seeing a block of concrete that was approximately two feet tall.

The concrete met my vehicle on the right-hand side of the front bumper. It completely ripped the right fender off and tore the right-front tire away from the transmission by dislodging the axle.

After tearing the drivetrain apart, the concrete block then proceeded to launch my vehicle into the air. Unfortunately, because the block only hit the right side, my car started to flip while it was in the air. Before I struck the ground, my Honda was completely inverted. The car smashed into the curb and slid to a halt.

When the Honda landed, I hit my head on the roof and grayed-out for a brief moment. As I came around, I opened my eyes and saw that there was blood covering the windshield. As I peered around the car, I noticed that all of the windows were covered with large amounts of blood.

I immediately assumed that I was not going to make it through this accident as I thought, *No one can lose this much blood and live.*

My eyesight started to focus a little more and I soon realized that what I thought was blood was actually more of a purple color. Upon closer examination, I found out that the purple residue was actually on the outside of the windows. Relief hit me as I recognized that it was not blood after all. Apparently, I had landed right in a large patch of berry bushes and the berry juice was splattered everywhere.

Now that I had regained lucidity, I decided to climb out of my car. I opened the door and to my horror I found that I had a spinal injury and was paralyzed. There I was, a paraplegic created by own stupidity. Once again I was faced with reality as I noticed that my seatbelt was still intact and it was holding me in place. I was unable to leave the car since I was suspended upside-down by my seatbelt.

I quickly unfastened it and dropped like a sack of potatoes onto the roof of my car. After getting my bearings, I crawled out of the wreckage.

As soon as I appeared out of the wreck, a man approached and told me to sit still. He said that he had radioed his office and an ambulance was on the way.

After realizing that I would be going to the hospital, I quickly ducked back into my car to pull out my removable CD player radio that had been recently installed.

After getting my radio, I remembered that I had a new bowling ball, shoes, and bag in the back of my car in the hatchback. Walking back there I started to open the hatch. The man who had asked me to sit still was following me telling me that I was in shock and that I should not move. I tried to open the hatchback but it was jammed shut. I tried relentlessly to open the hatchback while the unknown stranger stood over me saying, "Son, you're delirious. You're in shock."

I did not pay any attention to the man (since I knew that I had all of my faculties). After finding the hatchback stuck closed, I started kicking it. This only maintained the man's idea that I was not all there. Finally, the hatch popped open and my bowling bag dropped out. I picked it up and held my head high as I moved away from the wreckage.

The man with no name who had radioed in for an ambulance offered to let me sit in his van. I took him up on his offer and sat in the passenger seat waiting for my ride to the hospital. Another person who had seen the accident came over with a suitcase-sized cell phone and asked if I needed to notify anyone. I decided to call my house and see if anyone was still there. My stepsister Becky was there with her boyfriend Sean. I told her that I had flipped my car and was waiting for the arrival of an ambulance to take me to the hospital. She did not believe me and I finally said goodbye saying, "If you don't believe me, than drive out to Dead Man's Curve and see for yourself." *Click.*

When the paramedics finally arrived, they asked to take me via the gurney from the van to the ambulance. I agreed and allowed them to put a neck stabilizer on me. Once in place, and on the gurney, the paramedics covered me with a sheet to protect me from the drizzling rain.

As they started to wheel me over to the ambulance, Becky arrived with Sean. I told the paramedic that she was my sister and he asked, "Do you wanna play a joke on her?"

I could not resist and said, "Sure."

He then proceeded to pull the sheet up and over my head. He told me to lie still. Another paramedic grabbed my arm and pulled it out of the sheet leaving it dangling. He said, "This will add to the effect."

Sean was ahead of Becky and he saw me covered and queried, "Is that Vaughn Ripley?"

Amazingly enough, the paramedic kept a straight face and somberly said, "It was."

Sean and Becky freaked-out at this statement. I could only hold the laughter in for a matter of seconds. I cracked up so hard that it felt like my side split. Poor Becky—I am not sure she ever forgave me for that terrible joke. But damn it was funny!

Chapter Ten

After wrecking the Honda, I was in desperate need to get a new vehicle. With some brief searching, I was able to find an old Dodge Aspen station wagon and purchase it. My friends all called it the "Grocery Getter." But, I affectionately called it the "Bat Mobile."

* * *

During the fall of 1992 I registered for college again at Montgomery College. I took English 101 and Elementary Algebra. I passed both classes with honors and made the Dean's list. I was continuing my journey to fulfill my constant need for improvement and adding to my knowledge.

* * *

My cousin Greg who is one year older than me was married on December 5, 1992. It was a festive wedding that I will always remember because it was performed in a Greek Orthodox Church.

Watching Greg get married was fun. It was another hint that I was now a man. Greg and I grew up together and were pretty close as children. Also, Greg was the first person to introduce me, innocently enough, to marijuana when we were 13 and 14 years old. I have many fond memories of our travels to manhood. And, because he was older, I often looked up to him for advice and mentorship on proper behavior.

Greg's wife Danae is a terrific person with a zest for life that is hard to find in most folks. I knew from the moment that I met her that she would be an excellent addition to the family.

* * *

On December 13, 1992 arguably the most famous HIV+ hemophiliac, Ricky Ray, died of AIDS related complications at the young age of 15. His brother, Robert, lasted eight more years before finally succumbing to AIDS on October 20, 2000 at the age of 22.

Five years before his death, when Ricky Ray was 10, he talked to his brothers and sister about problems with the local public school. Things were pretty bad for the Ray children in Arcadia Florida. Many of their classmates were frightened of getting near them for fear of catching the disease. And, on more than one occasion they were bullied and even beaten-up. They were considering dropping out of school and moving away. But, their parents consoled them and talked them into persevering.

Reading the stories about all that the Ray's had been through brought back strong memories and painful stories that hit too close to heart for me.

In 1988, someone set fire to the Ray family house. Fortunately the family was not at home. This forced them to finally move out of Florida.

The world can be a hard place, as hemophiliacs in the '80s and '90s are well aware.

* * *

While working at Hayes-Ligon, I created a timesheet using Microsoft Excel that employees could use instead of hand writing their time. I also wrote a macro that sped up some of the data entry processes at my office. Both of these developments got me quickly noticed by the President, Steve. Before I knew it, I was meeting with the Vice President, Bill, talking about how I could improve the current system.

The Vice President decided to let my friend Bob and me run the newly created Systems Department. Bob was quickly promoted and became my boss. I worked on creating a Novell network with IBM PCs. I was finally heading in a direction with computers that I longed for. If it had not been for the efforts of Bob, I may not have found the level of success that I have.

* * *

In the spring of 1993, I enrolled for another class at Montgomery

College. This time I took Intermediate Algebra and Trigonometry. Because I love math and it comes naturally to me, I made the Dean's list again.

* * *

There were many factors that led to my decision to stop taking AIDS medication. I would go through waves of depression that I never felt before. Also, the medication would make me throw up regularly. But, the biggest reason I stopped was because taking the medication reminded me five times a day that I was going to die. Yes, the medication was helping, but in my mind, it was only prolonging the inevitable. Instead of seeing the bright side, each time I took a dose of medication, I brooded over the fact that I was HIV+ and I would eventually die from it. I felt that this was causing some of my depression and thought that my immune system might do better if I would stop thinking these thoughts all day long.

* * *

Work at Hayes-Ligon was better than ever. I started reading every book that I could get my hands on about networking and system administration. I also enrolled at an expedited Novell CNE course and passed it. I was learning huge amounts of information about networking security thanks to Bob and Hayes-Ligon.

* * *

Kristine graduated Cum Laude from Lynchburg College in 1993. I was so proud of her and convinced that she was the woman for me. After talking, we decided to move into an apartment together.

* * *

While working for Hayes-Ligon, I got to go on my first of many business travel trips to Chicago with our sales manager Bill. While there a headache forced me to request a pain reliever. In Chicago, aspirin comes in a powder form. I had never seen anything (except cocaine) like this before. So, I dumped it onto the webbing between my right thumb and forefinger and immediately sniffed it. After the stinging subsided, I realize that everyone was staring at me agape. Apparently, you are supposed to ingest powdered aspirin by pouring it into a liquid such as soda or coffee. But, my headache diminished almost instantly and my face started tingling at my sinus cavity and it spread across in waves of tantalizing electricity. I think I found a new way to consume aspirin. *I like it!*

Also while there, Bill and I went to a White Sox game at Comiskey Park. We were sitting a couple of seats back behind home plate. Bo Jackson struck out three times and broke the bat over his knee as we watched in amazement. We also saw Frank Thomas hit a couple of homers. I believe I could grow to like this business travel stuff.

* * *

After completing the CNE class, reading many books and setting up the Hayes-Ligon Novell environment, I started taking tests at Orange Systems to become certified as a Novell System Administrator.

I spent many hours in the evening studying and preparing for each exam. Before I knew it, I had passed four of the seven exams necessary to get my Novell Certified Network Engineer certificate. The exams that I had already passed gave me a CNA certification. I was well on my way to becoming a very powerful man in the computer field.

* * *

A friend from work, Bonnie, introduced me to her boyfriend, Ralph, who collected old military jeeps. I immediately fell in love with his 1963 CJ-3B Willy Jeep. After a little bit of talking, he agreed to sell it to me for $1,500.

I fell head-over-heels in love with my newfound Willy and took it into mud everywhere. It was a formidable four-wheel drive vehicle and able to get to places where no other automobiles could.

I brought it over to my dad's house to show him what a great purchase I had made. His wife Diana came out and looked from the rusted-out floor, to the falling apart body and was immediately disgusted. She asked, "How much did you pay for this?"

I responded with, "Fifteen."

She shrugged and mentioned that it was *probably* a good deal.

A couple of minutes later, Diana overheard Dad and me talking about the price and I mentioned that it was fifteen hundred dollars. She turned pale and screamed, "Fifteen *hundred* dollars? As in: one thousand and five hundred dollars? I thought you said fifteen!" Dad and I laughed for several minutes when we realized that she thought I had bought this marvelous piece of machinery for a paltry $15.

* * *

On one of my many four-wheeling excursions, I found a nice construction site with tons of mud. This time out George, Melanie, Billy, Tom, and Steve were with me.

After nearly flipping the Willy a couple of times, I decided to take it a step further. Heading toward a three-foot drop, I yelled for everyone to hold on. Melanie did not believe that she would *really* need to hold on. We went over the embankment at 25 miles per hour. The jeep growled in the air as the engine, drivetrain, and tires all spun faster due to lack of purchase.

We hit hard and bounced mightily around for a bit. I heard whimpering and looked to the back. Melanie was sitting back there trying to keep us from realizing she was hurt. Clamping her hand over her cracked ribs, she held in the crying with all of her might.

Apparently, when we flew off of the jump, she went air born and came down hard with her ribs onto the steel wheel well. Unfortunately for her, the wheel well was tougher than her bones and they gave in an excruciatingly painful manner.

* * *

I have always been fascinated with Japan, Japanese culture and the Japanese language. My biggest lure to this country has always been the samurai. I am enthralled with chivalry and the samurai code *bushidou*. Bushidou is a Japanese word that encompasses the seven principles: benevolence, politeness, bravery, honor, justice, loyalty, and veracity. All of these principles were used to compose the samurai code. They were also principles that I found in myself.

Kaizen is a Japanese word that simply means improvement. But a deeper look into this complex word reveals its true meaning: constant attempts at improving every aspect of your life. Essentially it draws upon enhancing your personal life, spirituality, work life, health, and relationships. It is a single word with an entire world's worth of meaning. It is my belief that through kaizen and chivalry we can perfect ourselves.

Because of my love for this culture, I started teaching myself Japanese. I bought several books and computer programs to help me in this learning process.

I still consider myself a beginner, but I have never lost my love for this language, people, and way-of-life.

My favorite aphorism, "chiri mo tsumareba yama to naru" is Japanese and loosely translates to "even specks of dust become mountains."

I plan to continue my Japanese self-learning for my entire life. And I will never curb my appetite for kaizen.

* * *

My best friend Paul and his fiancé Dee had a baby girl and named her Alexandra. Shortly after having Alex, they decided to move to Phoenix, Arizona

Kristine and I did not get to see as much of them as we would have liked. The move was tough on us, but they seemed so excited about going. We miss being able to pile into the car and driving over to see them on a whim.

Shortly after they arrived in Phoenix, Paul and Dee were married in a small ceremony.

Chapter Eleven

In early 1993, I went to our bank and requested a signature loan to refurbish and restore the Willy. After I received the money, I was thinking about Kristine and how much I love her. It only took a short time of thinking before I decided to spend the money on an engagement ring for her instead of repairing my old jeep.

After selecting a beautiful heart-shaped diamond, I had it mounted in a nice fitting.

I decided to wait for her birthday to surprise her with the ring. But, similar to Christmas, my patience wore thin and I gave it to her four days early. Kristine's favorite animal is a panda, so I purchased a stuffed animal panda and attached the ring to it using a ribbon necklace. Stuffing the panda in a box, I wrapped it. I hid the panda and a rose under our couch in the living room and waited for her to return home from work.

Carefully planning everything out, I made steak Diane, and lit some candles for dinner.

When Kristine arrived home I surprised her with dinner. After dinner, we were sitting on the sofa talking about each other's day at work. I waited until the perfect moment, and knelt next to her reaching under the couch. Pulling out the gift-wrapped box I said, "Happy birthday sweetheart."

She opened the box and tears were building up in my eyes. I could barely hold in my emotions. She pulled out the panda and missed seeing the ring. She saw me crying and was perplexed.

Next, I pulled the rose out from under the sofa and as I did, she saw the ring. My tears were flowing freely as I said, "Kristine, will you marry me?"

She said, "Yes." We hugged and cried together. I was officially the happiest man on the planet.

We set a date for September 22, 1994

* * *

One day Kristine asked if I knew where my paternal father George lived. I explained that he lived an hour away in Virginia. She was shocked that George lived this close to me and we had not ever touched base. I guess I was so used to him not being a part of my life that I had never thought about it.

We talked a bit about meeting George and his wife Robin. After 26 years of not knowing my real father, Kristine and I arranged to drive down to Manassas to visit him. George and Robin were very open to meeting and hanging out with us. We grew a loving relationship that lasts to this day. If it were not for Kristine, I may have never gotten to know my biological dad.

Before we knew it, we were making weekly trips down to Virginia to stay with them for the weekend. It was hard to believe that I had spent all of my life thus far without even going to George's house and relaxing with him to philosophize about life. Kristine has done many great things for me, but this simple gesture takes the cake. I only wish I had found George earlier in life.

* * *

My work was going well, and Kristine and I were able to save some money. We were saving to fund our upcoming wedding and honeymoon. Our initially plan was to honeymoon in Japan.

After giving it some thought, we decided against traveling to Japan to use our money more wisely. We also wondered about saving money by not having a traditional wedding. We discussed this some and decided that buying a home would be a better use of the money. On top of that, we wanted to get me on Kristine's health insurance plan and an early marriage was a responsible decision. Shortly after we made this decision, our apartment building manager said they were becoming condos. We were given a choice of moving out or buying a condo.

We gave some serious consideration to buying one of the apartments, but in the end decided they were too old. So, our search for a new place to live brought us to a quaint place in Maryland called Germantown.

In Germantown we found some brand new condos that were reasonably priced. We worked out the details and used our wedding funds and a loan from my buddy Paul as a down payment.

Immediately after moving into the condo, we went car shopping. We were looking for a Toyota Camry and ended up coming home with a 4 Runner. My heritage as a four-wheeler was continued with this latest purchase.

* * *

A month after buying our condo, we decided to get married early. Since we were not going to be having the *big* wedding, we opted to use the justice of the peace to connect us in matrimony. So, on May 25, 1994 we were married at the Rockville City courthouse with only our close family members present.

The wedding was a joyous occasion and brought the different parts of our families closer. We had a nice lunch reception near Sugarloaf Mountain.

Looking back, Kristine would have preferred a church wedding. But, I think that we made a good decision buying a home instead. Perhaps sometime in the future we will renew our vows.

* * *

Our original plan for the honeymoon was a two-week trip to Japan. After some consideration, we decided to save money and do a drive across America instead. We took 17 days to drive from Maryland across the United States and back. For our drive out to the west, we drove the northern route hitting Ohio, Indiana, Michigan, Illinois, South Dakota, Wyoming, and then Idaho. Then for the return trip, we took the southern route going through, Utah, Arizona, New Mexico, Colorado, Missouri, Kentucky, and Virginia.

The trip encompassed visits to Yellowstone Park, the Grand Canyon, the Badlands (the South Dakota ones), Mount Rushmore, Devil's Tower, Rocky Mountain National Park, Four Corners, and the Tetons.

While in Yellowstone Park, we saw some buffalo. You do not realize how huge these animals are until seeing them up close and personal. At one point, Kristine climbed out of the 4 Runner to approach a buffalo claiming, "He looks so sweet."

I quickly got out of the truck and asked her to return, but she wouldn't.

Finally as we drew near, the buffalo lowered his head a bit, snorted, and stamped one foot.

That was all the notice Kristine needed as she sprinted back to the car leaving me to deal with the beast.

I cautiously backed to the truck without losing eye contact. I finally breathed a sigh of relief, as I was able to safely climb into the driver's side door.

After the "buffalo incident," Kristine and I continued through the park. Before long, we spotted a moose far out in a marshy area. Quickly pulling onto the shoulder we planned to get out and observe him. Unfortunately, the shoulder was soft dirt that immediately gave way and our truck slid into a ravine.

The truck finally came to a stop hanging precariously on the edge of tumbling over. Having been in situations like this before, I knew that the most important thing was that we remain in the vehicle to keep the weight distribution correct. This was old hat for me. *Is it disturbing that I am comfortable in dangerous situations?*

Fortunately a Park Ranger was driving by and I flagged him down. He offered to stand on my driver's side running board for additional weight and balance as I carefully drove the truck back up and out of the gulley. This was the first (but not even close to the last) time that I put our red 4 Runner into perilous danger.

While we were out west in Utah, we were able to visit Logan where my sister Raeghn and her family lived. We also stopped in Arizona to visit Paul and his family in Phoenix.

During one of our camping expeditions, we drove into Rocky Mountain National Park. Coming from the east coast, we were surprised by the sheer size of the mountains in the Rocky range. The mountains jutted out of the ground unexpectedly and climbed 10,000 or more feet.

All of my previous camping experiences (except a couple of Boy Scout outings) had been at campgrounds where you were assigned a tent site. So, I approached the ranger and paid for our overnight camp out. Then, I asked him, "So, what's our spot number?"

He looked somewhat confused and asked, "Your what?"

I repeated, "Our tent spot number. What is it?"

Grinning, the ranger replied, "Son, you pitch your tent anywhere you like."

I was filled with a sense of adventure as I hitched my pants up, puffed my chest out, and strutted back to the truck. *That's right, we're roughing it.*

Kristine and I pulled a ways up the dirt road and found a nice secluded (except for that park ranger, we were the only people within miles as far as I could tell) spot and we proceeded to pitch our tent. We cooked up some meat and hung out for a bit before finally retiring.

Once in the tent nestled in our sleeping bag, my head swelled with the idea that I was out here "surviving." I faded into sleep with a proud grin on my outdoorsy face.

Just before sleep overtook us, we heard a howling-type sound off in the distance. Kristine and I looked at each other with fear. Inside I knew that I had to show no fear to my wife, so I said, "No worries, it's just a wolf." Trying to look at ease, I followed with, "Harmless. Besides, he's pretty far off and alone."

Just as I had said that, another howl came from the opposite side of our tent, but equally far away. Then, the first howler replied. Kristine raised an eyebrow and said, "Alone huh?"

I soothed her with, "Sweetie, they are far away and have no idea we are out here."

Just then a third howl chimed in from another direction. We both cuddled and again tried to drift off to sleep.

Moments later, a fourth direction howled and the other three responded. It sounded as if the howling was getting closer. I did not want to alarm Kristine, but I remembered from my days as a Boy Scout that it is best to not leave out dirty dishes and scraps of food. So I explained that they might smell our bacon and such that we had cooked earlier. Climbing out, I told her that I was going to clean up.

Once outside the tent, I found a beautiful star-filled night waiting for me. I quickly gathered up the frying pan and our wares and stuffed all of them in a trash bag. After sealing it, I stowed it in our truck. *That should keep those nosey bastards away from us,* I thought.

I crawled back in the tent and much to my chagrin the howling was closer than ever. I squeezed Kristine tight and told her not to worry. We would be safe in our tent.

After a fitful fight with myself, I again started nodding off into la-la land.

I woke in the dark and found that the hair on the back of my neck was standing at attention. Quietly I lay there carefully listening for what had woke me.

I was about to drift back to my slumber when I was startled by a snort of breath in our campsite. This snort was big and loud and was not made by anything as small as a wolf. I sat bolt upright and tuned myself to the creature's sound.

Kristine spurted out, "Oh no. You heard that too?" She was thinking that it was nothing until I had shot into a seated position.

I could feel her shaking under the sleeping bag—*or was that me?*—As we listened to the heavy breathing only footsteps away from our tent.

Suddenly there was another creature approaching from the opposite side of the tent and breathing just as heavily. My mind wracked itself trying to figure this out. In the meantime, two more of the breathing monsters approached our campsite and we found ourselves surrounded. Obviously this beast was considerably larger than a wolf and yet it was in a pack type situation. I could not remember ever reading about bears traveling in hunting packs, but here we were, high in the Rocky Mountains all by ourselves laying in a tent listening intently to several large animals lurking around our campsite.

Kristine was getting considerably frightened and I was right behind her. As the creatures lumbered around we could hear the impact of each step and I was sure these were very heavy animals.

Just as I thought they might move on and leave us alone, one approached with loud footsteps near our tent and breathed so hard, I felt as if he was in the tent with us. I lurched backward in fear and Kristine was gripping my arm tightly.

Thinking, I desperately tried to find a solution to the predicament we were in. A light bulb went off in my head as I remembered that our new truck had a key fob that controlled the door locks. This same fob also had a little red button that was used in a panic situation. If this was not a panic situation, I did not know what was. So, I dug quietly around, found the keys, and pressed the panic button.

The 4 Runner's lights started flashing and the horn blared so loud it momentarily deafened us. In a stampede fashion, the monsters outside our humble abode stomped around in a panic of their own. It sounded as though they might be trampling each other trying to escape.

After a couple of seconds, I turned the panic alarm off and we were pleasantly surprised by the lack of any animal related sounds. Looking at each other, we realized that we were city folk. We both agreed that it might be a better idea to sleep in the truck. So, we carefully opened the tent door a portion and I peered out to find an empty campsite. We scurried out and into the truck.

Once in the truck, we spent 30 minutes trying to adjust and make ourselves more comfortable to no avail.

We finally agreed that I would pull the truck right to the front flap of the tent allowing us an easy escape route should we need it. Once the truck was parked, Kristine and I clambered back into our sleeping bags and went fairly quickly to sleep. The rest of the night was uneventful. Apparently the 4 Runner's horn and flashing lights had proven to be a good monster bane. *Toyota, the monster slayer!*

The next morning we woke and packed up our gear. I glanced around and tried to ascertain a mammal type by footprints. However, I was baffled by what I found and was unable to discern anything. *Some outdoorsman I am!*

On our way out of the campground, I stopped by the ranger's station and we walked in. Kristine and I wanted to query the ranger casually and see if we could find out what on earth had trampled through our campsite the previous night.

I was trying to think of a way to ask when the ranger asked, "Did the elk keep you up last night?"

Surely he jested. The heathen fiends from Hell that we encountered could not simply have been elk. For one thing, they were howling and breathing like demons. And they were huge and terrifying. Raising an eyebrow, I answered with my own drawn out question, "Elk?"

"Yeah." he threw this single word at me as if he were relaying the weather. Then he followed with, "It's their mating season and they call out to each other loudly with a wail." He looked from me to my wife and said, "Some folks find it hard to sleep with all of that ruckus."

I could not believe my ears. Kristine and I had been in utter fear and shock over a lowly herbivore that was out trying to get laid!

The ranger went into a little more detail and after he described how large they were, I realized with alarm that setting off the truck's horn had probably terrified them and sent them into a frenzied stampede. We were extremely fortunate that one did not trample right across our tent.

After getting home from the honeymoon, it was almost as if we needed a vacation from our vacation. Taking a long trip in the car like this definitely helped to build our relationship.

Chapter Twelve

One morning in mid 1995 I awoke early to a loud alarm noise. I turned to my alarm clock and pressed the snooze button. The alarm kept chirping, and I angrily pressed the snooze button harder. To my surprise the alarm was still ringing out. Finally, I threatened to slam my fist into the clock. Just before I swung my arm, I read the time on the clock to find that it was too early for it to be going off. As the grogginess started to wear off, I realized that it was the fire alarm that was screaming and not my alarm clock. At this realization, I sat bolt upright and then scrambled out of bed.

Creeping into the hall I stepped with a splash into freezing cold water. Not understanding what was going on, I continued down the hall, and into my living room.

The living room was covered with about two inches of water. I was dumbfounded as I sloshed around the room trying to figure out what was going on. When I reached the middle of the living room I saw that the water was pouring full-stream out of the electrical socket on the wall.

I started toward the massive leak with a stupid look on my face when full comprehension came to me. The water was dumping out of an *electrical* socket. And, the other socket plug was not leaking, because there was a plug in it.

The hair on the back of my neck stood on end as I followed the electric cord from the gushing outlet to the VCR, which sat there with the clock brilliantly lit. Realization swam slowly through my enervated mind as I deduced that the power was still on in the very plug that had a steady stream of water feeding into the pool of water that I stood in. I froze in my tracks as I tried to think this situation out.

Terrified of being electrocuted, I carefully backed away from the outlet and made my way back to the hallway. Once there, I scurried into the laundry room where the circuit breaker panel was and switched the living room power off.

Afterward, I started investigating the situation with a lucid and awake mind. I was able to deduce that the sprinkler system, which was built into the ceiling, had frozen and burst.

Moments later the fire department was banging on my door and I let them in. It turns out that our flooding had traveled down two floors and flooded the condos below ours as well.

When everything was said and done, more than 80 percent of our condo had been flooded. All of the carpet was damaged or destroyed and many pieces of furniture were also spoiled.

During the year our condo was built, our county had decided that all sprinkler systems should include the outside deck. This was a safety measure that was soon shot down when they realized that during the winter these same systems would freeze and burst. After the county reversed this law, all deck sprinklers were supposed to be removed. Somehow, our apartment was overlooked and our home flooded because of it.

The builder took responsibility and tried to right the situation by sending in a company with huge fans to blow-dry our carpets. Because the carpets throughout the condo were drenched, mildew had already begun and the drying was not working well. Kristine and I contacted the builder and explained that we wanted our carpeting replaced. The builder argued that it was not necessary and they tried to continue drying the deluged carpet.

We immediately started looking into getting this problem righted properly and decided that a letter to Consumer Affairs was in order. So, we wrote a letter to Consumer Affairs and included the president and vice-president of our building company. Before you knew it, the carpet company appeared and was literally rolling out the carpet for us.

* * *

My role as system administrator was growing and the workload was starting to pile up. The president approached me to design a customer contact database for our customer service department. With the work already at an overwhelming level, my boss Bob approached management asking for an additional person to help me. I knew one of the other data entry guys named David who was computer savvy and suggested we use him. Before I knew it, David was on my team and helping with the daily tasks.

Having a second system administrator on-board lightened my load and allowed me to spend time creating the contact database. I spent many long hours perfecting the system and finally turned the finished "Customer Service Database" (CSDB) over to the customer service department.

The CSDB was more than just a contact database; it also tracked any and all contacts that Hayes-Ligon employees made with our customers. I used Microsoft FoxPro to create the database and it was a robust first attempt at database creation if I do say so myself.

Once the CSDB was created and out of the way, management approached us again asking for a new database that would handle all of our "Mystery Phone Shop" information. David took on this assignment and did an excellent job of creating the database for them.

David showed extreme interest in databases and volunteered to spearhead the newest database project that was involving Oracle. This new system was going to transfer all of our current system information into a single database and was a big job to say the least.

* * *

Shortly after he arrived, David was so swamped with the new database creation and maintenance that he could no longer assist with the daily system administration tasks. Because our company was growing and the workload was piling on, Bob elected to get me another helper. This time, he selected someone from the customer service division named Shawn.

Shawn and I immediately clicked and I carried him under my wing showing him the proverbial ropes. With David already having extensive computer knowledge, he did not need any tutoring, but Shawn was fairly new to computer administration and was willing to learn. So, I spent several months mentoring him and showing him how to administer the networks.

Before long, our systems department was a smooth running, well-oiled machine. David was administering our Oracle database, Shawn was administering the network, and I was filling in the gaps. We had plenty of work, but we were efficient and proactive.

* * *

With time, our department was again being inundated with work. We recently had ordered new PC's for everyone to move them onto the new database system and the installations were taking the majority of our time. Bob, ever the diligent and effective manager, brought a new underling named Brad to our group. Brad was somewhat familiar with computer operations and did not require much training to get up to speed.

With Brad and Shawn helping me with network and system administration, we were able to free David up to become a fulltime database administrator. The company decided to send David off to Oracle for some intense database administration training courses. It was not long before David had built himself into a strong database administrator.

At the same time that David was training, I went to Sun Microsystems for my own UNIX administration training. Between David and me, we had logged enough training time to create a serious technology team.

During the Oracle training, David started realizing his potential and found that he could make considerably more money out in the computer world. It did not take long before he left Hayes-Ligon in pursuit of the elusive greener pastures.

After David left, I was stuck maintaining and managing the Oracle database. So, I started attending Oracle database administration courses. It did not take me long to gain two "masters" in Oracle knowledge and to build a powerful platform for my future ventures.

With David gone, it opened the door for me monetarily. Bob was able to leverage a higher salary for me by justifying it against the job market. Not to mention, the training I had gone through helped me to command a more respectable salary.

* * *

Kristine and I spent a lot of time discussing my lack of HIV-curbing medication. Without the assistance of life-prolonging drugs, it was only a matter of time before I succumbed to the HIV illness and eventually died. So, I started doing some soul searching for how I was going to deal with that issue. My principal concern was the fact that I bombarded myself with doleful thoughts of eminent demise when taking the medicine. So, I worked hard at coming up with a solution to this.

I literally woke one morning with the answer. If I could worry and stress each time that I took a pill, I could easily turn that into something positive by thinking the opposite instead. The solution was so simple that I kicked myself. Of course I could teach myself to use positive brainpower to redundantly think of optimistic things instead of pessimistic.

I decided from that day forward that each capsule that I popped, I would use affirmative incantations to strengthen my body and health instead of tearing it down with the negative thoughts. This turned out to be more powerful than I imagined, and my T-cell count climbed through the ceiling!

Later in life, I took this positive incantation session a step further by using it for other health issues. I became obsessed with mental healing. I used images of my favorite American Generals to command troops of cells to combat illness. I would spend time imagining General William Tecumseh Sherman crashing through my body tearing viruses and other bad elements to shreds like he did the South. My General Sherman shows no mercy for the enemies that had entrenched themselves in my flesh. Whenever I pulled him out of the air to use in my battles against sickness, he offered no quarter and cut a swath from shoulder-to-shoulder and head-to-toe.

This violent engagement is an important weapon in my overall war against the disease that plagues my corporeal self. As a matter-of-fact, I consider it as powerful a tool as the medicine that is prescribed to me by extremely competent physicians.

* * *

After I had been at Hayes-Ligon for nearly five years, our company was bought-out by Automatic Data Processing (ADP). The promise of things remaining the same was not powerful enough to overcome the lumbering behemoth that swallowed our corporation whole.

It was only a short time before the bureaucracy and red tape won out and changed most of our daily routines. ADP had big plans for Hayes-Ligon and they immediately started melding the little company into a profit machine.

During this time, ADP also absorbed some other companies who did related business. Some of these companies were not as lucky as Hayes-Ligon. ADP liquidated at least one of them.

I was dissatisfied with the direction that the company was going and I put my resume out in the market to see what kind of response I would get. The reaction to my resume was a pleasant surprise. I received an overwhelming amount of offers and I started seriously contemplating leaving.

In the meantime, I explained the situation to Bob and he told me that he would be happy for me if I found something at another firm. I was pleased that he was concerned about my welfare more than the corporation. This response helped to strengthen an already respectable relationship with Bob. Up until that time he had always been a mentor to me. With his latest gesture he created a friendship beyond what we already had.

* * *

My buddy Shawn and I had started toying with the idea of a TV show that would involve two ex-Navy SEALs that had become bounty hunters. The short stories started forming into powerful tales that wove together to create a fictional world of danger, intrigue, sex, and violence.

The more time that we spent on the stories the more engrossed with the idea we became. We came up with episode after episode of unique ideas for a weekly show. One of our dilemmas involved whether we approach syndicated broadcast TV stations or went directly to a pay channel like HBO. After a short time of debate, we decided that our show would be more robust and doable on an HBO type channel.

Over the course of several months, we came up with story ideas for 29 episodes. I started compiling the ideas into actual written format. Our next dilemma was, do we only write screenplays and shoot for a TV spot, or do we write books and hope that a station will pick up the ideas as a future show.

To this day, I still dabble in the stories and add a bit of content from time-to-time. But, the stories have mostly been shelved for other project ideas. My plan is to eventually release the stories as a nonstop series.

* * *

In addition to our story creation and general tomfoolery, Shawn introduced me to the game of golf. He took me out to manifold golf courses and started teaching me the ins-and-outs of the game. I was immediately attracted to this fun outdoor leisurely activity.

When I was younger, doctors and adults alike had suggested golf as one of the sports that I could safely participate in, but I ignored them. I did not realize how much fun you could have playing golf. Plus, the beauty of the courses and outdoor weather was an added benefit.

Before long, I was actually becoming fairly proficient with the clubs and really enjoying myself. Along with Shawn, my Uncle Dano, and Kristine's grandfather, Pop-Pop, helped me to become a better player and showed me things about the game that I had never seen before.

Golf has really helped to soothe my nerves and calm me down. It is a peaceful endeavor that brings joy to me each time I am out there participating. My retirement plans will definitely include some pleasurable days on multitudinous courses around the globe.

* * *

I already had sensitive skin before the HIV, but my medicines and the disease have attributed to more skin issues. I started getting this weird Rosacea type of rash on my face. One day, a coworker Jim asked, "What's wrong with your face? You got AIDS or something?" Of course, he was joking, but it hurt deeply. I cannot tell you how many times I have had to pretend to laugh at some sort of AIDS joke. It is hard to explain, but every one of those jokes steals a piece of me.

I immediately went to see a dermatologist to see about fixing this latest skin issue. He could not determine what was wrong, so he did a biopsy using a chunk of skin from my face. This test did not prove anything, so he asked to do another biopsy and I allowed it. The second biopsy still revealed nothing. But, I now had two scars on my face that would never completely go away.

After the biopsies, the doctor wanted to try an ultraviolet application, which was similar to using a tanning bed for your face. This did not work either, but it did leave me with nasty sunburn that lasted for longer than a month.

Finally, I gave up on my face and decided to just live with the acne type blemishes and blotchy rashes that flare up without any warning.

* * *

Many of my four-wheeling excursions happened on local construction sites. One of my expeditions in the mud included a trip to a newly created development that did not have any building happening yet. My friend George and I decided to go hit the gumbo mud on the day after a particularly vicious rainstorm.

George also had a four-wheel drive vehicle, but we left it behind and piled into my 4 Runner. We were having a blast ripping up and down the new construction site slinging mud all over the outside of my truck.

We approached a morass and I eyed the mud from inside the cockpit. It looked as though a little stream was cutting across this section of the site. George and I both agreed that my knarly truck would make easy handiwork of that mucky section of swamp, so I slammed the Toyota into gear and sped into the unknown mud.

Before we even reached the stream, the mud deepened and thickened. My Toyota was growling under protest but kept a steady line toward the stream. As we dipped into the stream, I realized that it was a little bigger and deeper than anticipated. As usual, my eyes had once again deceived my conscious.

To its credit, the truck slung mud and churned along for a good bit before finally coming to a sluggish halt. I immediately threw it into reverse and tried rocking back and forth to no avail. After about ten minutes I finally gave in to the truth that my precious off-road machine was savagely stuck in some deep mud. On top of that, I was stuck on private property that I had left grooves and ruts all throughout.

George quickly offered to get his pickup truck, which was named Pepe, and try to pull me out. So, we climbed out and into the muck to start our trek to a nearby phone booth. We called Kristine and pleaded with her to come pick us up and she graciously did. But, she was unhappy with our current predicament and especially the fact that I had gotten our expensive SUV stuck while doing something I should not be doing.

George brought his pickup back to the site and we proceeded into the mud field to get down to where my baby was stuck. As we approached the swampy area, we could make out my red 4 Runner sitting there abandoned deep in the stream. George started to approach the truck and was trying to position himself behind me when his truck suddenly started spinning tires viciously. It was only a matter of minutes before we recognized our newest plight. Now, not only was my truck stuck, but George's was stuck as well.

Our options were running out, but I recalled that my buddy David had recently bought an Isuzu Rodeo. Panicking, we jogged back to the pay phone and called Kristine. This time, she was a bit perturbed but came to get us none-the-less.

Fortunately for us, David was home and willing to get his brand-new truck muddy for our cause. He picked us up and we headed over to the spot where the two trucks lay in muddy graves. Unfortunately, David's truck did not even get into the swamp before he started having traction problems. Before we knew it, his truck was uncontrollably stuck as well.

Now we were in quite a pickle. We were illegally trespassing on private property with three of our vehicles. It was getting dark and our options were bleak at best. Once more, we called Kristine to come and retrieve us.

She was angry but hospitable. Once we arrived back at my condo, we put our heads together and tried to figure out the next possible move.

I had no choice now, but to contact my dad. Dad had a full-sized pickup with a winch mounted on the front, and he would have no trouble in the mud. The problem was that he not only was a surveyor, but this was one of his projects that we were stuck in. I called him and explained the situation. We both agreed that working in the dark was not a good idea, so we decided to wait for daybreak to go back and pull out our trucks.

Dad picked us up bright-and-early to head over to the construction site. We traveled in to the area where we were all stuck. As we approached David's truck, we could finally see where my truck lay at the head of the pack. Dad exclaimed that we were off-roading in an endangered plant reservation. He was angry that we had such disregard for the plants that we had blatantly driven through and over to achieve our mud excursion.

Shortly after getting there, we used Dad's winch to pull all of the trucks free. It was an adventure to say the least. After saying our thanks and goodbyes, we all headed our different directions. I slithered home with my tail between my legs.

* * *

I had been taking DDI and two other drugs for several months. The terminology for this combination was "triple drug therapy," soon to be replaced with "drug cocktail."

The DDI came in a powdered form and I had to mix it with water before drinking it down. This drug was particularly tough for me, because I had a hard time keeping it down. I would drink it in the bathroom at work and immediately throw it back up. It was a coin-toss as to whether I could keep it down or not.

Because it would make me so sick, I started skipping some of my regimented doses. This started happening more frequently, and I started seeing that I was missing my scheduled dosage more often than taking it.

It did not take long for my doctor to realize that this new "cocktail" was not working. We sat down and talked about it, and I agreed that I would try harder to take my medication.

Let the vomiting continue.

* * *

In September of 1995, Kristine and I decided to drive to Niagara Falls. We carefully planned our itinerary to include each state up the East coast via old Route 1. From Acadia National Park, we would cross Maine, and enter Canada in Quebec. The trip then went down through Canada to Toronto. From Toronto, we would cross back into the United States at Niagara Falls. This would facilitate us seeing the falls from both the Canadian and United States' side.

Our trip up old Route 1 was fantastic. The views along the shoreline were breathtaking. We dipped into Ripley, Maine and came across a large bull moose of all things! He was standing still in the middle of the street. He was quite a sight stoically standing there taller then our truck.

This was a quaint town with rich history. And, the namesake was appealing as well.

Once in Canada, we noticed a complete difference in attitude and environment. The people of Canada were friendly and yet somehow distant. But, the streets were so clean we could not believe it. The drivers were considerate and they had markings in the car lanes to keep cars the proper distance apart during travel. It was like a diorama in a museum, because there was no trash or homeless people. It was kind of amazing to think that this large of a populous area could stay spotless in the streets.

We went in the CN Tower, which was a bit pricey, but well worth the fee and time. The view from up there was amazing. And, the standing area was built on a glass floor one quarter of a mile in the air. Kristine could not bring herself to step out onto the glass. In the meantime, I was out there jumping on the glass trying to show her that it was sturdy. The funny thing is, the moment I jumped on the glass the crowd of people quickly got off the glass floor in a hasty panic.

After Toronto, we went to Niagara Falls. Neither of us had been there before. The falls were unimaginably beautiful. Simply trying to fathom the amount of water rushing by every second was inconceivable. Prior to our trip, I had seen many photos of Niagara, and they did not do the actual falls justice.

After our stop in Niagara, we made a one-day sprint for home.

* * *

In September of 1996 I went on a trip to San Francisco for an Oracle convention called, "Oracle Open World." This trip lasted a week and introduced me to the wonderful world of excellent food and a more diverse culture than I had ever seen.

While there, I was able to hook-up with my friend David who had recently left Hayes-Ligon. It was cool to hang out and travel around town with him.

I was able to increase my knowledge with Oracle by attending many informative seminars and speaking with experts who were there. I also was invited to a special event for Oracle Masters at the F.A.O. Schwartz Toy Store. That was a load of fun and a great way to connect with other Oracle Masters. The Oracle Master's night out was also an eye-opening experience for me, in that I finally started realizing how much money I was really worth.

While in San Francisco, I was able to drive on Lombard Street, eat at several fancy restaurants, and even take a drive down to Monterey Bay. During that trip South, David and I stopped by the Oracle Headquarters, which is known as "Emerald City."

My trip felt short-lived, as I headed back to home and my humdrum job.

* * *

ADP was scrutinizing one of the companies that it had bought. There was a widespread rumor that the small company was trying to sell its automotive software to outside sources after ADP had already bought it. A little investigating showed that it was a small group of developers who felt shafted for all of their hard work.

I was approached as a systems administrator to break into the computer systems that this company had and try to turn-up information pertaining to this software theft. Traveling with a private detective, I went down to Alabama and began investigating the situation.

The P.I. posed as a fellow employee and we were supposedly down there helping with the transition to ADP. Little did anyone know, we were down there trying to bust anyone who was stealing from ADP.

The P.I. managed to get a copy of the office keys and we waited until a late evening to do our surreptitious ninja work. We let ourselves in legally, since we were working for ADP and they technically owned the office space. However, it still felt borderline and the adrenaline flowed.

Inside the office, I commenced hacking into each and every machine. We located servers and specific desktops and I broke into several of them. Once inside, I was able to find some actual code that was being sold as a separate product.

Once we had located all of the substantial information, the P.I. and I started taking machines apart. We pulled hard drives out of several boxes and packed them up as evidence.

We were out of there before daybreak and we flew home to reveal the incriminating drives to our superiors.

That was a fun trek and I felt important helping to track down and uncover corporate espionage and embezzlement.

* * *

On Saturday, October 5, 1996 my cousin Katie married her sweetheart, Joe who was a U.S. Marine. The wedding was awesome and her brother Greg gave a heartwarming toast.

Joe stands six foot seven inches tall and his heart matches his stature. His Marine upbringing and stern disposition easily hides the fact that he is really a teddy bear on the inside. Kind of like an egg, Joe is extremely hard on the outside and soft and gushy on the inside.

Throughout the years, Joe and Katie have been there as a support system for Kristine and me. We are forever indebted to them for being there as friends and family.

* * *

Work at ADP seemed more onerous than ever. The politics and red tape associated with ADP owning our little company was nerve-racking. It is hard to explain, but I had an easier time when we were a little company. I felt that my salary was unfair and I also felt tied down by some of the office policies.

I finally approached Bob and explained to him that I was worth considerably more money and I had already received a couple of offers in this range. Bob was very understanding, but his hands were tied because upper management would not allow the kind of salary increase I was asking for.

I stayed at ADP for a bit longer before going to Bob again and telling him that I was going to have to take one of my offers soon if there was no increase in pay. Bob understood completely and was actually supportive explaining to me that ADP would not shill-out the money. So, I finally packed my bags and headed to the great wide open.

My next job was working as a consultant for Dyncorp. It was almost like my last gig, because the division I was working for used to be a small business that was absorbed by a large entity. But, the salary was commensurate to my skill set. After leaving ADP for Dyncorp, I received a 35 percent increase in pay.

The new job was full of red tape and politics as well, but I was getting diverse experience and enjoying the work immensely.

* * *

While working at Dyncorp, I became close friends with one of my coworkers, George. George and I started golfing together on a fairly regular basis. His game was well beyond mine, so he was a perfect golf mentor.

Before long, our creative juices started flowing in similar directions and George and I came up with some grand ideas for new businesses. Our greatest plan and scheme involved creating a multi-million dollar indoor golf restaurant.

The idea included using indoor driving machines and putting surfaces to accommodate many guests. In addition to the machines, we had the niche idea of having "beer girls" drive around the place in miniature golf carts serving drinks and snacks just like at a real golf course. Also, we planned to have a nice restaurant and bar area.

The original design was the inspiration for countless smaller ideas including a name for our resort. We decided to call our dream resort VirtuaLinks. I immediately went out and bought the domain name for our venture. Unfortunately, our brainchild slipped by the wayside as work overcame us. However, I maintained the web site and turned it into a climbing related web page instead. In the future, I am planning to use virtualinks.com as a hub for my entire web presence.

* * *

I started noticing that my toes were feeling tingly in the mornings, but did not realize that it was a problem. Soon, the tingling had spread to my entire foot and lasted longer than just the morning. The feeling is reminiscent of having your foot fall asleep with a little more pain involved. I tried not to pay any attention to this newfound problem, but some days it got so bad that my feet ached to even walk on them.

Finally breaking down, I went to see my doctor who told me about peripheral neuropathy and explained that DDI is known for this side effect. He immediately took me off the DDI because some cases have shown that continuing on the medicine after seeing the peripheral neuropathy can result in a lifelong problem.

After switching drugs, the pain and tingling did not go away in my feet, so my doctor sent me to a neurology specialist. Since that visit I have often wondered if one of the prerequisites of becoming a neurology doctor is being a sadist. The neurologist used long needles to probe different area of my feet and lower legs. The pain associated with this "probing" was considerable and I would not wish this problem solving technique on anyone.

Using the probes, he stabbed into sensitive areas looking for muscle contraction spots and nerve endings. Once the needles were in place, the doctor sent electrical pulses through them to see if my nerves and muscles were responding and working properly. The pain associated with this whole process was excruciating to say the least.

My test results showed that my nerves and muscles all seemed to be okay and the doctor determined that my tingling would go away. Of course, I now had the issue of being deathly afraid of neurologists.

After several months of numb and tingling feet, the peripheral neuropathy did start to slowly fade away. All in all, it took more than a year for it to heal almost completely. And, I still feel the remnants to this day.

* * *

Kristine's mother Kathy had been having on-and-off back pain and trouble over several years. During this period of pain and suffering, she was hospitalized for a minor heart attack. Her health insurance would not allow her to stay at the hospital that the ambulance initially took her to, so they told the family that she needed to be moved. Her doctor told the insurance company that if she was moved she would more than likely have a stroke. The health insurance company explained that they would not pay for one more moment in the current hospital and insisted that she be moved to one of their hospitals. Kathy was moved and as the doctor had predicted, she had a stroke.

At the beginning of April 1997, Kristine's Dad called us and explained that Kathy was not breathing. He had tried to resuscitate her and had already called an ambulance. He wanted someone to watch Kristine's baby brother, Jacob. Kristine and I rushed over. When we arrived, the paramedics were already there, trying to resuscitate her. I tended to Jake and made sure that he did not get a glimpse of his ailing mother. The paramedics were unsuccessful at saving her life and Kathy passed away. It was a difficult time for Kristine's family. Her mother was greatly loved and a very special loving woman. Kathy was only 49 years young when she died.

Because of her bad back Kathy was taking different types of pain medication. Apparently, one of these medicines interacted badly with one of her prescriptions and she was asphyxiated.

It's hard to put into written word how Kristine felt, but she was hit hard by her mother's passing. To this day Kathy is greatly missed and we often talk about how great it would be to have her here to enjoy many of our life experiences.

Chapter Thirteen

My stay with Dyncorp only lasted six months before the long commute got old. I started searching for new work and was lucky enough to find something comparable within a couple of minutes of my house. This company was called Acecomm. Acecomm was into telecommunications and had commercial and government work.

When I informed my boss that I was going to accept a job with another company, he had the division head, Joe, come in to try and talk me into staying. Joe sat down with me and discussed what I wanted out of life, and what my goals were.

He then baffled me with his next couple of comments. Essentially, he asked me if I would stay for a million dollars. I snapped back that of course I would.

Without batting an eyelash, Joe said, "Now that we've established that you're a whore, what will it take to keep you?"

I was dumbfounded by this comment and certainly offended. I decided to stick it right back to him, so I threw out a figure that was well above my offer at Acecomm expecting to knock him off guard. Instead, he coolly replied, "Done."

Again I was caught off-guard as he asked, "So, will you stay now?"

I explained that I would have to think about it. I went home to relay the message to my wife. She was baffled that Joe would treat me like that, and even more surprised at his counter offer. I was not sure what to do, because I had never received an offer like this before. On one side, I hated the idea of accepting Joe's offer after he called me a whore. On the other hand, we could really use the money and I appreciated how much they were showing their need for me.

Kristine and I decided that I could not pass up this offer, so the next day I called up my contact, Bob, at Acecomm and explained that I was sorry, but I could not accept the position. He asked why, and I explained that my current company had made me a counter offer that I could not refuse. Bob understood and he was about to say goodbye, when he asked, "How much did they offer you?"

I told him the figure and he said that he would call me back in a minute. Moments later, Bob called me back and told me that they could match the figure. At this stage I felt guilty about the whole situation. I was not trying to get Acecomm to pay me more money; it just worked-out that way. But, if they wanted me that bad and were willing to give me what Dyncorp was, I had an easy decision to make. I accepted Acecomm's offer and called Joe at Dyncorp to tell him so.

Joe was not happy, but it made me feel good to decline after his uncalled for comment. I realize that he was only using an analogy, but the smug nature in which he passed his idea on to me, was painful (even if it was true).

I picked up several friends at my new job that would last for the rest of my life. When I started with Acecomm I was the only database administrator and I shared my office with Greg and Doug. Both Greg and Doug were programmers and we immediately hit-it-off as friends. It did not take long for me to make additional friends outside of the programming group. I met Ben, John, Sean, David, Jeff, and Craig and quickly grew attached to all of them.

I was happy at Acecomm, because all of the employees in this small company atmosphere were cordial and that fit in with my personality. My boss Bob was quick to assist me in anything I needed to make my job more efficient and manageable. I approached Bob about adding some additional database administrators under my direction. He was quick to allow this and actually supported the move wholeheartedly.

With the assistance of the vice-president, I found a really talented and bright young computer-star named Joe. Soon after I brought Joe on-board, I also was able to move a couple of people from other divisions to assist in our database administration group. Before long, Joe, Sean, Craig, and I were all a part of the Database Administration Department.

At this stage, the group was shifted under a different part of the company and my new boss was Jeff. Jeff was a gifted boss with a flair for managing our group. He helped to mentor me and led me along the path that eventually allowed me to start and run a company of my own.

I never told Jeff how much he influenced my decision to go out and start my own company. In addition to the heuristic manner in which he helped me to improve my management skills, he introduced me to the world of self-help gurus and authors including Kenneth Blanchard Ph.D. and Stephen R. Covey.

* * *

My new group of friends and I were into similar hobbies and recreation, so we soon started venturing out to do things together on the weekends. Joe, Sean, and I all started to gravitate toward paintball. Before long, I had gone out and purchased a fully automatic paintball *marker* (gun) that was capable of firing eleven rounds per second.

Paintball was fairly expensive, so we found a local wooded area where we could gather and play without paying fees. Soon, we were all playing at a pretty decent level.

Occasionally we would invite other friends along to play. One day, Joe brought along a fraternity brother named Eric to join in our festivities. Eric made the mistake of showing up in gym pants. Because gym pants are not very protective of certain sensitive areas, this would prove to be a rather large gaffe. *Murphy's Law and all that.*

During one of our paintball matches, I came upon Eric hiding behind a fallen tree. I could barely make out the tip of his mask, which told me that his head was exposed to potential fire. Normally, it is unkind to take a headshot without first giving the player ample warning. Headshots can be extremely painful, so we usually will give an oral warning and ask the player to give up. If they choose to ignore the treatise, then their head is fair game.

I was hidden well and could see the apex of Eric's head. I decided to be fair and I called out, "Give up, I have your head in my sights."

Eric did not respond. But, he also did not move. This concerned me, because if you do not respond to a called headshot, you almost always immediately move your head to avoid the sting of the ensuing batch of paintballs. Eric did neither. So, I yelled again, "Headshot, do you give up?"

Again Eric refused to either move or cry out his truce. At this point I decided he must already be out by someone else's fire. So, I questioned, "Are you hit?"

To this question, Eric did not even flinch. I was worried that he was sitting there waiting to fire on me as soon as I stopped paying attention to him. So, I decided to move to a more commanding position. I got up and quickly moved to cover that gave me an even better angle on his head. This also allowed me to see more of Eric's face. Once again I queried, "Are you hit? I have you in my sights and I will fire if you do not respond."

Eric's stoic expression revealed nothing so I screamed, "If you don't say something, I'm gonna shoot you in your face!"

I thought I heard a faint murmur or whimper so I carefully listened and asked, "What?"

This time I was positive that I heard a soft cry come from him. With reckless abandon, I stood up and left my body open for a cheating shot and wandered over toward him. As I approached, the color faded from my face as I realized the situation. Eric was lying on the ground in a fetal position with both hands holding his nether regions.

Understanding hit me as I figured out that he had been shot and left for dead by someone. This well placed group of paintballs had hit him square in every paintball player's worst nightmare spot, the family jewels. Poor Eric was lying on the ground with tears streaming down his cheeks.

To this day, Eric refuses to play paintball. He has actually become the brunt of a horrible joke in which we all occasionally ask him with an ear-to-ear grin, "Hey Eric—wanna play paintball?"

* * *

My friend Sean and I started visiting the local Harley-Davidson dealership during lunch. We would "ew" and "ah" over these fine pieces of machinery. Both of us were exceedingly attracted to the many variations and styles of Harley motorcycles.

It did not take me long to decide that I needed a Harley. So, I placed an order for one. Unfortunately, there was a waiting list during this time. So, I put my name on the list along with handing over a $500 down payment. It was nearly a year before they finally contacted me and told me my Harley had arrived.

I asked the dealer to change the exhaust pipes and add saddlebags. During the three days that it took to do this, Kristine and I went out house shopping and found a new house that was perfect for us.

We immediately figured out that the money I was planning to use to purchase the Harley would be better used as a down payment for our new home. Also, with a large house payment pending, I did not want to jeopardize our credit with a monthly remuneration to the Harley-Davidson Motor Company. Together Kristine and I decided that it was smartest to drop the Harley idea. Unfortunately, they would not return my down payment. But, to this day I am extremely thankful that we chose the house over the motorcycle.

* * *

After nearly a year of working for Acecomm, my old workmates from Dyncorp, George and Cathy approached me with the idea of starting our own business. Basically one of the contracts that we had with our old Dyncorp job was unhappy with the current state of their system and approached George to ask if he would be interested in going out on his own.

George, Cathy, and I talked the situation over some and decided that it would be tremendously fun and lucrative to venture out on our own. So, we started forming a business plan and idea to form our own corporation.

It ended up taking us several months to hash out all of the details, but we were resolute in coming up with a surefire map to create and operate our own business.

We worked on our business idea until it became lucid and achievable. The only thing left to complete our design was to bring some customers on board. George and Cathy used their connections and started talking to different agencies about our new business. Before long they had several government agencies that were interested in our ideas and capabilities.

* * *

More than a year after I had left ADP, my old boss and friend Bob invited me to his wedding. As coincidence would have it, Bob was marrying Erica who is the sister of Roger another friend of mine from ADP.

Their wedding was quaint and filled with cheer. Afterward, the reception was held outdoors on a beautiful day.

Even though Bob and I were friends at ADP, our friendship has fallen by the wayside as we have both started families and moved around in the job world. I still think about Bob all of the time and wonder how he is, but I never seem to find the time to pick up the telephone and say, "hello." Unfortunately for me, I rarely if ever talk to, let alone see, many of my past friends like Bob. Life and work have separated us. Friends like Bob do not come along that often and it hurts to think about the special few that I have left behind in my search for success.

* * *

On July 9, 1998 my cousin Michael married his betrothed, Anne. As is usual for that side of the family, their wedding was fabulous. It was a memorable occasion with plenty of fun people and fine spirits.

Like his brother Greg, Michael and I had a lot of fun growing up together and I still remember the boy that he had been. It is weird watching everyone grow up, but rewarding at times like these.

Anne is a darling girl with a heart of gold. She is sincere about her thoughts and has a giving personality that is only bested by her beauty. Michael became a luckier man on that wonderful day.

tamashii no tomo - Soul mates

The beast ... Vaughn's Suzuki Hayabusa

The boys–Dan, Chris, Vaughn, and Ben

My SV-650

Racing around the track

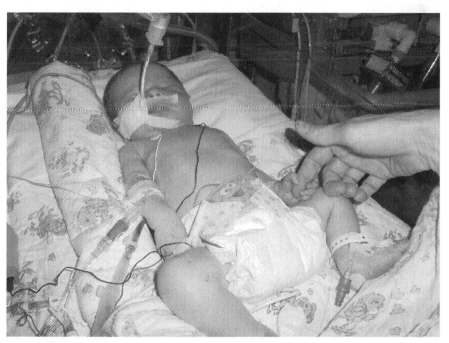

Trinity is literally hanging on for her life

Vaughn showing off his nuts at Seneca Rocks

This is how I trained for my Rainier climb

Roy, Paul, Mike, Vaughn, Scean, Charles, and Scott
(Sky-high Mike is busy taking the photo)

Self-portrait in whiteout conditions

Peering down a very deep crevasse

Vaughn and Trinity leaving footprints in the sand

Vaughn's FJ Cruiser at Assateague Island

Vaughn showing off the Gretsch at his 40th birthday

Vaughn in a nutshell

Does this look like the body of a 42 year old man
fighting AIDS for nearly a quarter of a century?

Andrew, Vaughn, and Pete at mile zero
during our C&O Canal adventure

Vaughn, Pete, and Andrew after 190 miles on the C&O Canal Towpath

Samson, Vaughn, Trinity, Kristine, and Xander

Vaughn, Scean, Sarah, and Mike about to tackle Rainier

Vaughn applying Titanium Dioxide sunscreen

Vaughn relaxing at Camp Muir, notice Mount Adams in the distance

Vaughn on the Ingraham Glacier with Little Tahoma behind him

Vaughn worn out and frozen to the bone

Kristine and the Harley are my two beauties

Chapter Fourteen

During August of 1998 George, Cathy, and I finally decided to take the plunge and start our computer consulting business that we had been discussing over the previous few months. We started our company with only the three of us, plus my friend Larry as our system administrator and our mutual friend Dee as our office manager.

We found and leased a small charming office space in downtown Annapolis. At the same time, we were communicating with business startup consultants and additional resources. Together, we came up with the corporation name, Bay Technologies Consulting Group, Incorporated. We started Bay Tech as an S-Corporation.

Before long, Bay Tech was booming and we were bringing on additional employees. Our work was streaming in at an alarming rate and we quickly grew to twelve employees and several consultants. Our customers were extremely satisfied and everyone was having a good time.

Starting my own company was a life changing and business savvy growing experience. I was making leaps and bounds in my understanding of the business process. On top of that, I was adding many tools and talents to my resume including front-end application development in Powerbuilder.

We spent a lot of our time traveling to Chicago, San Diego, and Atlanta to appease our growing customer base. It got to the point where each week at least one of the three company owners was on the road visiting a distant state.

* * *

I had quite an adventure on one of my many trips to Chicago for

Bay Tech. I traveled to Midway airport to meet with a client. One of my consultants, Carol came with me. After finishing up our meetings, we were heading back to the airport. Because our rental car return was not located at the airport, we had to take a shuttle bus.

Carol and I were settled in our seats when an elderly couple came on board explaining that their flight was leaving in 20 minutes. They pleaded with the driver to hurry the ride and get them there on time. The driver explained that during this time of day, they would be lucky to get to the airport in 20 minutes. The couple continued to plead and the driver shrugged and said, "I'll see what I can do."

As the conversation came to a close, one more passenger climbed onboard the bus. Everyone on the bus had heard the tête-à-tête between the driver and the old couple except the newest arriving traveler. As soon as the new guy had both feet on the shuttle, the driver slammed the door and punched the gas. Immediately, the new guy flew backwards and flopped onto the floor. This was obviously very disturbing to him as he picked himself up and exclaimed, "What's the rush, buddy?"

None of the other passengers bothered to explain the situation to him. If the others were half as enticed as I was, they were keeping quiet enjoying this hilarious situation.

Just as the new guy was throwing his bags onto a shelf, the bus ran off a curb and slid sideways into heavy traffic. He once again flopped onto the floor. I was having a hard time keeping in the laughter. At this point, the new passenger was getting deeply annoyed. He picked himself up and moved into a seat.

The funniest part of this whole situation was this new guy looking around the bus for affirmation about the erratic behavior by the driver. He was shocked to see that everyone else on the bus was quietly minding his or her own business and acting as if this was perfectly normal.

We started approaching some heavy traffic and the bus driver instantly shot into the incoming traffic lane. Cars were blaring their horns and screeching as they swerved out of the way of this maniac. By now, the new guy was clearly confused and looking from person to person on the bus intently. I wonder if he thought he was on *Candid Camera* or something. It was the funniest thing I had ever experienced. I felt like I was on an episode of *Jerry Seinfeld*.

Finally, the driver ran a red light (in the opposite lanes of traffic flow) and illegally turned into a parking lot. Zooming across this parking lot, he drove over a curb and once again slid sideways into traffic. This time, the shuttle bus nearly tipped on its side with the force of the turn.

We pulled up to the drop-off point only five minutes after leaving the rental car agency. That was the single fastest and most entertaining shuttle ride I had ever experienced. The moment the bus stopped the new guy ran off ranting as if he had gone mad.

I turned to Carol as we exited, and we both broke into huge grins about the situation. To this day, I wonder if the new guy still tells the same story from a horrifyingly different *Twilight Zone*-type angle.

* * *

Since my buddy Paul moved out to Phoenix, Kristine and I would travel out there occasionally and visit them. On one occurrence, Paul asked if I wanted to try rock climbing again. It had been a minimum of 13 years since I had been on the rocks, but I was interested.

We traveled out to a nice climbing area with Paul's friend Scott. Scott had extra gear and we rented what he did not have.

Scott took us to a *single-pitch* (tall climbs are broken into pitches and each pitch is approximately 100 feet of climbing) climbing area made up of needle shaped rock formations. All of the climbs required someone to lead the climb initially and then setup top rope anchors.

After Scott led the climb and placed the anchors, we climbed the rest of the morning and into the afternoon. It was a fantastic time and really stimulating for me. Once again, I had the climbing bug. This time, I was hopelessly addicted, because it was even more fun with all of the advanced gear that protected our lives.

When I returned home from Arizona I immediately told my friend Joe about the level of excitement and feelings of success associated with rock climbing. I explained how it challenged me on a personal level that was hard to imagine in any other sport or hobby.

Joe was instantaneously fascinated and agreed to join me for a beginning climbing class that was locally taught. We signed up for a one-day class that taught us the basics of setting up top-rope anchors and climbing.

The most important aspect of the class was teaching us how to belay. A belayer is the person who stays at the bottom of the climb and uses a belay device to feed and bring-in the climbing rope that is attached to the climber. The belayer's job is simple: *do not drop the climber.*

Essentially, when you top rope climb, a rope extends all of the way up to the top of the climb and passes through an anchor (think pulley), from there, the rope goes back to the ground. The belayer has one end of the rope in his belay device, which is attached to his harness and the other end of the rope goes up through the anchor and comes back down and then it's attached to the climber's harness with a knot. As the climber starts up the rock, the belayer shortens the rope length by pulling-in some of the slack rope. Once the climber reaches the top of the climb, he signals his belayer and then lets go of the rock face. The belayer than allows the rope to slowly pass through the belay device, lowering the climber. The climber's life is literally in the hands of the belayer and this is why I considered it the most important aspect of the training that we took.

The class was enthralling to both of us and we went out the next day to purchase some of our own gear. Together, Joe and I became obsessed with rock climbing.

After we had done some initial climbing, we realized that some additional training was going to be necessary. So, we signed up for another class and learned even more about our all-consuming hobby.

After visiting all of the local crags and doing many of the lower level easy climbs, Joe and I started advancing and climbing on more complex rock faces. Joe's brother, Larry, was also interested in climbing and we finally arranged to have him come out. After a short period of time, the three of us were going from crag to crag in the Maryland area trying to conquer tougher levels.

* * *

Even though climbing was consuming most of my attention, I still found time for golf. George and I decided to try and attend the 1999 U.S. Open of golf. Unfortunately, these tickets are hard to come by and you can only purchase them through a lottery. As fortune would have it, we won a spot at the open. We were able to get three sets of tickets, so George's friend Dave went with us.

The event was located in Pinehurst, North Carolina. We decided to drive down there. Along the way, we stopped at several extremely nice golf courses to play some rounds of golf. The most memorable course was Tobacco Road. Tobacco Road was a unique course and excessively tough. George managed to play a fairly decent round, but Dave and I were all over the place trying to locate our balls.

Pinehurst was a quaint little town with several world-class golf courses throughout it. The first night there, we hooked up with one of Dave's friend's JB who happened to be working at the Open for Lycos. We all decided to visit the local tavern and drink some beer. So, I offered to buy the initial round of Guinness laced with Chambord.

Instead of starting a tab, I elected to pay immediately. The bartender brought me a bill and it read $120. I innocently leaned in pushing the receipt back and said, "Excuse me, you gave me the wrong check. I was the guy with the four beers."

The bartender quickly slid the receipt back to me and retorted, "That's the bill for your four drinks."

Needless to say, we moved on after the first round.

The rest of our trip was not nearly as costly (if you do not count the passes to the actual event). We had a great time wandering around and checking out the professional golfers in action.

During the week, we had gotten fairly close with one of the course security guards. On Saturday, she let us place folding chairs inside the spectator ropes at one of the tee boxes. So, we spent the morning drinking heavily and being within several feet of many golfing specialists.

Before long, the alcohol was catching up with us. We started getting a little on the rowdy side as our three sheets were fervently being placed to the wind. On certain occasions, one of us would start laughing as a golfer would approach the tee and this triggered a myriad of chuckles and giggles at the least. It did not take long before we were leaving the area to vent our haughty laughter.

At one point, one of the golfers was addressing his ball and preparing for a backswing while we waited with bated breath. Unfortunately, Dave's chair could no longer bear his load and it collapsed with a loud crackle, some crunches, a bang, and final harrumph from Dave. Dave lay there for a moment bewildered and wild-eyed. George and I were both stricken with the dilemma of being aghast with shock and horror and the downright human reflex of laughing our butts off.

The golfer stood in shock and the crowd around the tee was appalled at our blatant disregard for spectator regulations. Silence filled the air and blanketed all of us in blushing solitude. Finally, George broke and let out a snicker. This was all it took to burst my dam and let the guffaws inundate the serene moment. I was laughing so uncontrollably that I had to leave the scene in an awkwardly embarrassing moment.

For Sunday's final Open day, we went directly to the eighteenth-hole bleachers. We were the first people to arrive, and we had to sit in those hemorrhoid-generating seats for five hours before the first of the final golfers would come through and finish their round. But, at the end of the day when 3,000 or more people were gathered around the general area trying to get a peek, it paid off tenfold to have front-row seats to an amazing finish.

We decided to curb our drinking to a minimum. So, we limited ourselves to three mixed drinks per hour. Fortunately it was raining all morning long and it was easy to restrain ourselves from getting out of our drenched bleacher seats to retrieve colorful beverages.

The day finished with a three-way battle between Tiger Woods, Phil Mickelson, and Payne Stewart. Since Phil is my favorite player, I was obviously rooting for him. Besides he had yet to win a major and was primed to win this one. In the end, Payne triumphed. This would prove to be a Godsend, as it was the last U.S. Open that Payne would compete in because he died a couple of months later in a freak jet accident.

As usual, our trip was an exciting success and it was the most fun I have had at a sporting event.

* * *

My brother Scean and his family decided that a move out west to Washington State would be a boon because my sister in-law Monica's family lived out there. They settled close to Monica's parent's home in Tacoma. It was heartbreaking for me to see them go, because we were a big part of each other's lives. Scean was my best friend. On top of that, he has four lovely daughters and Kristine and I felt that we would not see them grow up if they were across the country. And, Monica was becoming close with both Kristine and me so she would be sorely missed as well. This westward reposition was going to be hard on my entire family.

We lugubriously helped them pack and load a rented truck. Tears flowed freely as we said our goodbyes and sent them on their way. Since they left, there is a void in my life that will not be filled without them. We do fly out to Tacoma at least once a year to see them, but it is not the same as when they lived three miles away and we could visit on a whim.

* * *

On an impulse I decided to build a homemade rock climbing gym in an unused portion of our basement. I started by choosing exactly what I wanted of my climbing cave. After a clear idea was formed, I spent hours drawing different designs on paper. Once I had created a final sketch of my desired outcome, I started planning how to accomplish this enormous task.

I made a list of all of my hardware and lumber needs and went out to Home Depot to seal the deal. I also started ordering plastic climbing holds online. Along with holds, lumber, and hardware, I also needed to have special mats made to prevent injuries in the event of a fall. So, I found a gymnastic mat manufacturer online and special ordered mats to fit in my climbing cave.

One of the main reasons for building this wall was for climbing specific workouts, so I also ordered Eric Hörst's H.I.T. (Hypergravity Isolation Training) Strips from Nicros. The H.I.T. Strips required a 50-degree overhanging wall, so my gym design incorporated this.

Many of my friends participated in this project. And, without them, I would probably have never finished. Out of all of the help I received, my friends Joe and James contributed the majority of the assistance.

For starters I nailed pressure treated 2 x 4's to my concrete floor as a base. From there, I built the gym by attaching 2 x 4's from the floor to the ceiling. Once the framing was completed, I pre-drilled and mounted T-nuts on the plywood walls. The T-nuts are used to attach the plastic climbing holds to the wall. After the T-nut installation, I mounted the plywood on the framing to finish off the structure.

With the edifice done, all that was left was to pick locations to place the climbing holds. I meticulously laid out the holds in patterns that would create intense climbing lines all over the climbing cave. After the holds were placed, I laid out the mats for protection and immediately jumped on to my spectacular creation.

* * *

On March 12, 2001 my dad's cousin once removed, S. Dillon Ripley died. Dillon was the secretary of the Smithsonian Institute. He headed the museums for 20 years before retiring. He was 87 years old when he died of pneumonia.

While Dillon was secretary, the Smithsonian founded eight new museums and seven new research facilities. Among the new museums was the Air and Space Museum, the capitol's most popular with more than 9,000,000 visitors each year. And, with his guidance, the number of annual visitors increased from 10,800,000 annually to more than 30,000,000.

He studied at St. Paul's School in Concord, New Hampshire and in 1936 he graduated with a bachelor's of art from Yale University. He then studied zoology at Columbia University and obtained a Ph.D. in 1943 from Harvard. As you can see, extreme collegiate values have trickled throughout the Ripley family.

Dillon was secretary of the Smithsonian Institute from 1964 to 1984. And, the S. Dillon Ripley Center (known simply as the Ripley Center) was named in his honor.

During World War II, Dillon joined the Office of Strategic Services, which was the predecessor of the Central Intelligence Agency and was in charge of American intelligence services in Southeast Asia. After the war he taught at Yale and was a Fulbright fellow in 1950 and a Guggenheim fellow in 1954. He also became a full professor and director of the Peabody Museum of Natural History.

In 1985 Dillon was awarded the Presidential Medal of Freedom (the highest civilian award). He was also awarded honorary degrees from 15 universities, including Brown, Yale, Johns Hopkins, Harvard, and Cambridge (United Kingdom).

On top of all of his astounding achievements, Dillon was also an accomplished writer and published three books.

I had only met Dillon once, but I feel the kinship and loss. Men like Dillon and the phenomenal things they accomplish are fantastic inspirations for me. Because he is a relative only strengthens this fact.

* * *

After a decade of not owning a motorcycle I finally went out and bought a 2001 Kawasaki Concours. It is a sport/tour bike based on the Ninja 900. This bike is both very comfortable and agile. Alas, it weighs over 600 pounds and was a bit bulky at times. It was especially hard to get back on two wheels after it had been dropped. Unfortunately, I dropped it twice and found out just how hard it is to pick back up.

I joined the Concours Owner's Group and started taking occasional rides with the gang. Many of my rides included trips down Skyline Drive and the Blue Ridge Parkway. Both of these are beautiful country road rides through some of the most thrilling curves on the East Coast.

My friend Dan bought a little sport bike and we started riding together. We spent many fun afternoons pushing our bikes to the limits. Because of the enormous saddlebags and trunk, my bike was not really made for the *twisties* (windy sections of road), but I somehow managed to keep up with Dan and even sporadically drag my foot pegs.

Soon I was testing the top-end of this bike as well as its handling. I was sorry to find that it was only capable of doing 124 miles per hour. Of course for any normal person, this kind of speed would be more than enough. However, I am anything but ordinary.

* * *

My buddy, Larry, started dating this girl who was into skydiving and it was not long before he was talking me into doing it. I had always dreamed of jumping out of a perfectly good airplane, so of course I agreed whole-heartedly.

As a beginner you normally have three options for your first attempt. These options include static line, tandem, and freefall with a group of instructors. The third option is not always available and is more expensive, so we really only had the first two options. Static line jumping is normally done only a few thousand feet off the ground and does not include any freefall time. Essentially, your parachute is connected to the plane via a static line. When you jump, this static line pulls the ripcord for you and the parachute immediately deploys. A tandem jump is performed with a certified *jumpmaster* (highly qualified and certified skydiver) connected to your back who is only there to ensure you will pull your ripcord. The tandem jump allows for a freefall; which is the time you are falling before the chute is opened.

Because we thought the majority of the thrill would come from the freefall, we decided to jump tandem. The place that we used was going to take us up to 14,000 feet before we finally leaped. This would allow for nearly a minute of freefall before the parachute would finally need to be called upon.

The ground school consisted of several hours of explaining the logistics and importance of the parachute (there was no need to tell me that it is important). We were carefully shown exactly how to use our altimeter watch and at what altitude to pull our ripcord. We also went over the tandem jump in detail and learned how to properly "step" out of the airplane.

Our plane was a King Air. It is a powerful and large twin-prop plane that was able to lift a large group to our jump altitude in a very fast time.

As we approached our jumping altitude, each of us hooked ourselves to our assigned tandem jumpmaster and formed a line at the door. After the door was opened, the instructor that was attached to my back waddled with me toward it.

My instructor explained that we would stop in the doorway and he would count to three while we rocked back-and-forth. On three we would leap out and start our terminal velocity descent. When our turn came, I anxiously wobbled toward the open door. I overlooked the fact that there was a one-inch tall lip and as I prepared to get my feet on the threshold I tripped. Instead of patiently counting to three, we tumbled instantly out of the airplane with a whoosh.

The freefall was intense and gratifying. I was taking it all in with extreme exhilaration when my instructor tapped me on the shoulder. I casually looked back with a grin and saw that he was pointing to his altimeter wrist unit. I quickly looked at my altimeter to find we had surpassed our ripcord area. Shock gripped me as I tried to find where the ripcord was. All of my shuffling and looking was preventing my instructor from pulling the cord and now we were both a hair uneasy. Finally, my fingers found the cord and I tugged. The chute opened and we breathed a collective sigh of relief.

Once in the dawdling parachute glide, we were able to calm down and enjoy the ride. My heart was beating so fast I could feel the pulse against my throat. My instructor nonchalantly asked me if I was a queasy sort. I explained that I was not and he asked if I wanted to do some spinning. I immediately replied, "Yeah!"

He explained that if I tugged on only one of our steering lines we would spin. And, the harder I pulled the faster and tighter we would rotate. So, I pulled with all of my might and he was correct, we twisted so fast that our legs flew out with centrifugal force. It was an adrenaline-filled blast.

When we finally hit the ground, he unclipped from my back as I was whooping with glee. He quickly told me that he had never been jumping with anyone who just leapt out of the plane before his count to three. Even though my manly side wanted to keep him thinking that I carelessly flung myself out at my first opportunity, I had to admit that I had tripped on my way out the door. We both laughed a good bit afterward about our maniacal trip.

Since that experience, I have not been skydiving again, but I am interested in returning. One thing I have not done yet that I plan to try is bungee jumping. W00t!

* * *

On September 20, 2000 my stepbrother Quincy and his fiancée Kim married. I was in the wedding party and had lots of fun. It was a beautiful wedding filled with good times. Quincy's best-man Eric gave a great toast and the festivities were among the best I have ever seen.

Quincy and Kim make an adorable couple that is straight out of a romance novel. They are both loving people with lots of caring friends and their union has brought together people and created life long friendships. In a few instances, they even helped create couples including two of their best friends, Jackie and Billy, who ended up getting married.

* * *

In November of 2000 my cousin Susan died of Marfan's Syndrome. Unfortunately, I never had the opportunity to meet her. It turns out that my aunt Francis, who died from a ruptured aneurysm in the early nineties, also died of Marfan-related complications.

Susan had the most significant signs of Marfan's Syndrome in our family. She had severe scoliosis, and eventually heart complications that required surgery. The first was in her mid twenties the second took her life at the fledgling age of 35.

The main concern for people with Marfan is with the development of dissecting aneurysms. Marfan's Syndrome is an autosomal dominant disorder. Unlike hemophilia, which women can carry and not have, if you have the gene for Marfan, you have the disease. If you have children, you will pass it on 50 percent of the time. It is not a recessive trait that skips generations. However, Marfan is also a disease with multitudinous manifestations that can range widely within a family.

My other cousin Carol has the physical characteristics of Marfan's Syndrome. She also has Mitral Valve Prolapse. Because of this, she takes preventive medicine to slow down the stress on the heart (beta blocker) and to try to slow the development of possible aneurysms. Due mostly to technological advances, life expectancy today for people with Marfan, that is properly monitored, is well into their seventies.

It is very unlikely that I have Marfan's Syndrome, because my father would also have it. At this stage in his life, it is extremely unlikely that he would have it and not have displayed any of the telltale signs. Since I am a magnet for illness, this simple fact is a breath of fresh air!

* * *

Shortly after Scean and Monica moved to Washington, Kristine and I were itching to visit them. So, we packed some essentials and flew across the country for a visit. It felt so good to see them in person. All of Scean's daughters had grown so much and we felt out of the loop.

While visiting them, I got my first glimpse of the mountain that would forever be engrained in my mind. Mount Rainier is the most awesome natural creation I have ever seen. I was captivated by the sheer size of it. And, my mind started spinning gears that would eventually lead to my many attempts at climbing it.

I explained to my brother my primal urge to climb this beastly rock jutting from the ground only 90 minutes from Scean's house. Scean casually responded elucidating that he would *never* do something as crazy as climbing Mount Rainier.

I spent the better part of an afternoon trying to change his mind, but he firmly stood by his sane decision to stay on or near sea level. A quick bit of research showed that Rainier's summit is 14,412 feet above sea level and this did not bode well with Scean. He also explained that people die every year attempting to climb this mountain. Secretly I started plotting my intricate plan that would eventually have us far up on that beautiful mountain. I knew deep down inside that Scean's sense of adventure was larger than his fear of dying during a leisurely hike up a hill on the horizon.

I continued to bug him about climbing the mountain for the remainder of the time that Kristine and I were out there. At the same time, I did some investigating at the local climbing stores and purchased some books and maps. After a bit of exploration, I found that this climb was not only attainable, but it was easily within our reach. If Scean was going to live so close to this magnificent feature, the least I could do was chip away at his will and convince him that together we could conquer this goal.

Chapter Fifteen

Kristine and I have always loved children and have spent many hours discussing our different options. In the past, our options included adopting, having Kristine inseminated by someone else, or just getting pregnant the old-fashioned way. The third option would put Kristine at risk of getting HIV and would also place our unborn child at risk so this was not a viable choice. Kristine wanted my baby as a legacy because she always worries about how long I have to live. My legacy wouldn't happen with the two options that we considered practical. So, for the most part, we accepted the fact that we would not be parents.

One day Kristine found an article on a new in vitro fertilization procedure that was being performed in Italy. Apparently, they had huge success with inseminating women without transmitting the virus to them. They were doing some form of "sperm washing" before fertilizing the embryos. Kristine investigated this route in more detail and found that there were no cases of women becoming HIV+ during this process.

We immediately started planning our trip to Italy to have this done. Our excitement was beyond description, because we both wanted to have children so bad.

Our preparation revolved around going to Italy and spending our life savings to try to get pregnant. Unfortunately, there was no guarantee that we would become pregnant. We would only be able to afford one trip and attempt. And, this one trip was going to put us in debt for a long time. But, we both decided that it was what we wanted.

Then one afternoon, without warning, Kristine came to me with some very good news. She had heard that this "sperm washing" technology was being tested in America and that we would be able to participate. This was groundbreaking expertise and it was happening in Boston. We cried in each other's arms as we realized that our dream was getting closer to reality.

It did not take long for us to collect information and find out that we were eligible to be a part of this leading edge technology. It was going to cost approximately $20,000, but this was a pittance compared to what Italy would have cost. Without question, we started preparing and within weeks we were on our way to Boston for this attempt.

They would perform the "sperm washing" procedure ICSI (Inter Cytoplasmic Sperm Injection), pronounced "ixy." Essentially, the doctors would pick up a single sperm in a micropipette and actually inject it into the egg to get fertilization. Before the actual fertilization happened, they used a small portion of the sperm to test for infection. After finding no HIV in several tested sperm they used a single one to fertilize an embryo. They did this for two or three embryos and then re-implanted them in Kristine's fallopian tubes. This process is supposed to be close to foolproof in preventing the spread of HIV to a partner during pregnancy. We both knew that this was our key to starting a full-fledged family.

Boston was a great trip and educational for both of us. We learned a good deal about the entire procedure and how it worked.

I must admit that it was not fun leaving behind sperm. I assumed that it would be easy. After all, this was a process that I was intimately familiar with. I simply needed to masturbate with a condom on and voila. It turned out to be much tougher than expected. Fortunately they allowed me to go back to my hotel room for this. But, the condom was two sizes too small, and it was harder than I ever imagined (no pun intended).

I was finally able to "finish." And, a great weight was lifted from me, as we were able to pack up and head home from Boston only leaving behind a tiny, albeit gooey part of me.

* * *

As if it was not already enough of a pain the first time, the Boston medical place that had us out for my "deposit" wanted me to return to leave another "donation." So, we packed up our things and drove up to Boston again. This time, we took my stepbrother Quincy and his wife Kimmy.

We had an enjoyable time vacationing in Boston and between Kristine, Quincy, and Kim; they were able to keep me cheerful about the whole process. They were not all in the room mind you, but they did cheer me on. I was still unhappy with the way I had to leave a batch of sperm behind, but it was easier each time I did it. I was hopeful that this would be the last time I would actually have to go through this procedure.

* * *

Joe, Larry, and I were becoming more engrossed with climbing and I decided it was time to step it up a notch. Up until now, we had only been climbing top rope style, which meant we could not take a fall of more than a foot or so. And, we could never climb higher than about 90 feet. After doing some research online, I found a rock outcrop located in West Virginia called Seneca Rocks that was well over 200 feet tall. And, the local rock jocks offered instructional classes on proper lead climbing techniques.

When you lead climb, you no longer have an anchor on the top of the rock (which is how top roping works). Instead, you place your protection along the climbing route. You start at the base with your belayer and just start climbing. In *trad* (traditional) lead climbing, you place a piece of protection by gently jamming it into cracks that exist in the rock. Then, you clip your rope into this protection piece (called pro) and continue to climb on. With this method, you could potentially fall all of the way to your last placed piece of pro and then the same distance below that piece. So, with lead climbing you could potentially fall 20 or more feet. Because climbing rope is dynamic, it stretches a little bit similar to a bungee cord. This "stretching" absorbs the majority of the shock from the fall instead of your body. And, the absorption of shock is directly proportionate to the force of the fall. In other words, the longer you fall, the more stretch and give the rope has to lessen the damage to your body.

I tracked down a local climbing legend, Tony, who gave instructional classes at Seneca Rocks and reserved all three of us a slot for training in early April. Joe and Larry were nearly as elated as me and we drove down to Seneca Rocks with immense grins plastered on our faces.

We camped at a local campground and woke the morning of our class to freezing weather. We dressed for the cold morning and headed across the north branch of the Potomac River in our hiking boots with backpacks filled with climbing gear on our backs.

Once at the base of the rocks, we realized the scope of this adventure. Unlike rock climbing areas we were used to, that stood maybe 40 feet tall, this rock face towered above us at over 200 feet. On top of that, we had already hiked up out of the valley, which was another 300 or more feet below us. So, in actuality, the exposure on the rock would feel like 500 or more feet.

Tony took us on a beginner's route named, "Conn's East." This route was rated a 5.4. And, Tony planned to take us on a 5.5 variation if we felt up to it. The way that the climbing rating system works is like this: Level 1 would be considered walking on a sidewalk. Level 2 is like walking on a dirt path. Level 3 is similar to hiking off the beaten path. Level 4 is clambering across rocks frequently using hands along with your feet. A Level 4 climb is frequently referred to as a "Billy goat path." Finally, 5 is where technical climbing begins. At the fifth level, a fall would almost certainly result in broken bones and possibly death. For this reason, once you reach 5, it is normally necessary to use a rope for safety. Once you are in the "5" range, it is broken down even further by difficulty ratings. So, a 5.0 (pronounced five-oh, not five point zero) is a very easy climb that would be considered about as easy as climbing a ladder. From there, it goes up decimally in tenths until you reach 5.9 (five-nine). Originally this system, called the Yosemite Decimal System (YDS) only went to 5.9, because it was thought that 5.9 was the toughest possible climb anyone could attain. But, with the advent of stickier rubber soles on climbing shoes and technically advanced climbers, the 5.9 realm was surpassed. So, the system was adjusted to allow climbs above 5.9 by adding 5.10 as the next level. And shortly after 5.10, 5.11 came along. With the realization that technology and abilities were skyrocketing, climbers decided to further break the 5.10 and above ratings into four divisions per level. So, 5.10 was broken into four levels by being called 5.10a (five-ten-A), 5.10b, 5.10c and 5.10d. From there, every new rating followed this system, so a tougher climb than 5.10d was called 5.11a. When I started climbing the toughest climb that had been done was a 5.14d. Currently the toughest achievable climb is 5.15b. It is only a matter of time before the next level is conquered.

Since it is normally understood that you are referring to a climb in the 5 range, many climbers simply say "ten-A" instead of "five-ten-A." When someone says, "I climb nines," they mean that their normal ability allows them to climb up to 5.9.

But, I digress.

So, with a rating of 5.4 to 5.5 you can see that this was a relatively easy climb comparably. Since Larry, Joe, and I had top rope climbed up to a 5.9 at this stage in our climbing careers, we felt that this would be simple. Surprisingly, it was considerably tougher than expected. With lead climbing there is an added mental game that constantly tugs at the back of your mind. This subconscious demon whispers into your ear about painful possibilities such as a fall. The more you focus on this whisper the tougher the climbing becomes. In addition, you are now spending time looking for pro placement areas and actually placing pro. This all keeps you hanging on the rock in precarious positions for longer periods of time. In turn, this all wears on your muscles as they fill with lactic acid and start to pump. It all becomes a vicious circle as your mind now starts to scream about the pumped muscles and potential falls that will result from your weakened forearms.

Long story short, lead climbing is a different monster entirely from top rope climbing and is considerably harder to master and do.

On top of all of that hoopla, when you lead climb, you climb higher than ever imagined while on top rope. The way this is achieved is through pitches. A pitch is a section of rock, which is normally around 100 feet tall (it could technically be nearly as tall as the length of your rope, but this is not normally the case) that you climb before setting up a belay station and preparing to climb another pitch. This is how people climb extreme climbs like El Capitan at Yosemite, which is a 3,000-foot tall rock face!

The climb that Tony took us on went somewhat diagonally up the rock face, so we did four pitches and climbed over 300 feet even though we never were more than 200 feet off the base of the rock face.

After the training session with Tony, all of us agreed that lead climbing was awesome and we were more enamored with climbing than ever before. This new angle of climbing had opened a new world to us that would again tug us deeply into the addicting world of rock climbing. It also added a dangerous edge that was easily overlooked by the adrenaline that was created while doing it.

Chapter Sixteen

Kristine and I had been searching for a local fertility solution for over a year before we found a clinic in Fairfax, Virginia named the Jones Institute. After doing a little investigating and meeting with the doctors there, we found out that they would be willing to work with us and our unique situation.

My trips to donate sperm became considerably easier, because the donating bank was located in Norfolk, Virginia instead of Boston.

Even with the proximity, there was a drawback with using the Norfolk site. Where I "donated" my essence of life was in a small room. And, they had plenty of smut material to help me along in this area. As usual, I was freaked out by "the couch" and did not get anywhere near it, but I was getting more used to this procedure and was actually finding it fun.

I was not forced to use an under-sized condom at this clinic. So the trial of forcing latex over my precious member and pinching its life out was gone. However, a new difficulty arrived as I realized that I would have to make my shaky shot into a small cup. Suddenly, my mind was filled with the vision of countless others before me with a similar task and I was petrified of the floor, walls, and furniture. Nervously glancing around the room, I continued my charge. Reading this, I assume you giggle (as I am while typing), but being there was a tad tougher than I can convey on paper.

Just as I found myself on the brink of Shangri-La, I noticed that I could see doctors through a crack in the revolving shelf that was designed for me to anonymously hand over the vial of semen. This was disturbing to say the least and it deflated the situation as it were. I managed to overcome this obstacle eventually but the lingering thought of doctors being right there and within view (if you were willing to lean in and stare through a crack) was tough to get rid of.

After I was done with that fiasco, Kristine and I laughed about it jovially. *Ain't life grand?*

* * *

Kristine started her fertility medication on May 20, 2001. She had to give herself a 10cc subcutaneous (which means, introduced under the skin or tissue) shot of "lupron" (leuprolide acetate) each morning for 13 days. Leuprolide acetate is a synthetic nonapeptide analog of naturally occurring gonadotropin releasing hormone. Obfuscation aside, it will increase her estrone and estradiol levels. Basically, it is used to trick her body into believing it's pregnant.

Then she had to give herself gonal in the evening for the last five days before the operation.

She finished up with a shot of Avidril hCG as the final subcutaneous shot two evenings before the retrieval operation. All in all it was a bunch of shots and Kristine was a trooper!

The egg removal procedure happened on June 11, 2001 at 7:22 a.m. and everything went well. The operation lasted about 22 minutes and 9 seconds. Afterwards, Kristine was pretty sedate and adorable. We first heard that they thought we had seven eggs available for fertilization.

That evening she started taking Doxycycline orally.

Then she started giving herself an intravaginal medication called prometrium, which is projesterone. Getting pregnant is not as easy as I thought!

On June 12, 2001, we found out that only three of the original eggs were properly fertilized and ready to be put back into Kristine. Since we were only planning on using three eggs, this number worked out pretty nicely.

We traveled back out to the Jones Institute on Thursday, June 14, 2001 to have the fertilized eggs (which are called embryos) put back into Kristine. Our doctor performed the procedure in about 11 minutes. It went smoothly and we were excited with the ease of the transfer. We received a "report card" which told us that our embryos were all mature and the Jones Institute rated them a two on a one to five scale. A one is considered the best possible rating, and the doctor said he rarely sees an embryo with this rating. Afterwards, Kristine had to stay on the table for 90 minutes.

This is a restful time designed to assist the embryos as they find their way home in the uterus.

Finally, on June 25, 2001 Kristine had a pregnancy test and we found out that we were pregnant. WOOWHOO! We (mostly Kristine) had undergone all kinds of painful procedures. But, it finally paid off and we were successful.

The baby's due date was set at March 6, 2002.

* * *

In celebration of Kristine's 30th birthday, I decided to surprise her with a tubing trip on the Antietam Creek with 60 of our closest friends. I had planned the trip months in advance and had everyone's invite out early to assure his or her attendance. It went over terrifically, because Kristine loves tubing and all of her friends had so much fun.

We spent the entire day drifting down the large creek at a snail's pace with all of the beer we could manage to drink. We stopped in the middle of the trip in a quaint field to eat some lunch and relax, and then we got back in the creek and continued our leisurely drift.

A couple of days after the tubing party, my friend John called me and asked who the cute blonde girl was. I explained that she was, Lesley, a friend of Kristine's since elementary school. John was enamored and asked if I could talk to her and find out if she was interested in seeing him again.

So I told him I would do what I could. I called Lesley and told her that my friend, John, from the tubing party dug her and was wondering if she wanted to go out with him sometime. She sounded interested and asked with some excitement, "Was he the cute one with the bandana on his head?"

"No." I replied and finished with, "That was my buddy Steve."

Lesley queried, "Well, which one was John?"

After a pause and a couple of "um's" I came out with it, "John was the drunk one that couldn't keep his head out of the water."

Lesley giggled for a bit and then realized that I was serious. After a bit of persuasive talk, for which I am famous, Lesley agreed to give John another chance.

John and Lesley dated for a little while and before you knew it, I was the best man at their wedding. My toast, which was inspired by and included the entire story of how they met, was greeted by some hearty laughter.

As silly as it sounds, this is one of the most romantic connections I have ever witnessed.

* * *

On August 7, 2001 Kristine woke with a slight cramping feeling. We were ten weeks into our pregnancy. She became scared when she found a pinkish discharge while going to the bathroom. We tried not to let it bother us, but both of us were concerned.

After speaking to her doctor, Kristine set out for a trip to get a sonogram. I met her at the sonogram appointment and comforted her as best as possible. The sonogram technician was able to locate our baby, but was unable to find a heart beat. I felt my heart sink as the reality started to settle.

We both wanted a second opinion before believing that we had experienced a miscarriage. We traveled to her obstetrician and he confirmed the diagnosis.

Needless to say, this information hurt us deeply. The doctor suggested that we get a dilation and curettage (D&C) operation to remove the unborn fetus. He was hoping to get some information from the surgery that might tell us more about the miscarriage.

Losing the baby after all we had been through was devastating to both Kristine and me. We would spend long hours crying and holding and comforting each other. Regardless, we knew that we would try again soon.

* * *

I was driving into work on September 11, 2001 thinking about the bout with bad luck that had befallen Kristine and me. I do not believe in bad luck, but I was becoming depressed (which is very unusual for me) thinking about the countless odds I had against me.

Kristine called me and explained that she had just heard on the news that a small aircraft had wrecked into one of the Twin Towers in New York City. I quickly turned on my radio and tuned to the Howard Stern show to see if they had any further information. Howard said that a small plane had wrecked into one of the World Trade Center buildings. That was an odd thing to happen, but I figured it was no big deal, because I knew that those buildings were designed to take the impact of a commercial airliner.

I felt a moment of sadness for the miserable pilot that had made a wrong turn and listened to the show a little more carefully.

Pulling onto the DC beltway, I thumbed the volume and listened with horror as Howard announced that another plane had hit the other tower. *This is not possible,* I thought to myself as I became engrossed in what was being said. Two planes wrecking into buildings in Manhattan within minutes of each other is not an accident. I listened to Howard intently as he relayed what he was hearing and seeing.

The traffic had come to a complete standstill, which did not stand out as abnormal for me, because 495 often backed up in the morning during rush hour. Sitting in this veritable parking lot, I continued to listen.

After five minutes of not moving, I started to worry that there was more going on with the traffic than normal. I decided to make my way over to the shoulder and try to exit at Connecticut Avenue. From there, I would find my way a little further east and resume my fight with daily traffic.

By the time that I had gotten over to the shoulder, Howard was announcing that there was an explosion at the Pentagon. This was unreal and my mind was swirling with all kinds of thoughts. I tried to call Kristine back at work and found that all circuits were busy.

The Pentagon made three and I wanted to be home instead of at work. When I finally got off on Connecticut, I turned around and headed home. Before getting back onto the beltway, I noticed that Connecticut Avenue was completely stopped as well. I was starting to be unnerved as Howard announced that the two planes that wrecked into the twin towers were commercial airliners.

I listened to the radio in shock for the remainder of my trip home. Just as I was pulling into my neighborhood, Howard was screaming about one of the towers collapsing. The entire group on the radio was crying out and talking over each other in confusion and shock. I was reeling as I pulled into my driveway imagining how many thousands of people must have just died.

I walked inside my house and immediately flipped on the television. I stood agape with a look of horror plastered on my pale face. I could not avert my eyes as I watched with shock and awe while the devastating scene of the twin towers crashing to the ground unfolded.

Every year little things take away a piece of my innocence and harden me to the world. This day in particular did more damage to my innocence than any of my prior life experiences combined.

I was seeing red, and retribution was all that I could think of. Suddenly, my puny existence and paltry problems no longer seemed to matter.

* * *

During routine blood tests, in early 2002, my doctor discovered that I had the hepatitis C virus (HCV). Hepatitis C has been referred to as a "silent epidemic." Millions of people have the disease, but many of them are not aware of it because the symptoms can remain dormant for decades. Chronic hepatitis C is the most common reason for liver transplantation and the leading cause for developing liver cancer.

"Hepatitis" is a Latin word and translates to "inflamed liver." There are five known types of viral hepatitis, but only A, B, and C are common. Hepatitis C is the most common chronic blood-borne infection in the United States. To date, there is no vaccine against hepatitis C.

One out of every four people with HIV also has hepatitis C. "Coinfection" with hep C and HIV is common because both come through exposure to infected blood. However, unlike HIV, hep C is rarely transmitted during sexual activity. Thus, different people may be more or less likely to have both infections. HIV/hep C coinfection is more common among intravenous drug users and folks with hemophilia.

Because people are living longer with HIV, a condition like hep C has time to gradually attack the liver. Due to this fact, many HIV+ people with hep C coinfection die from liver disease related to HCV infection.

People infected with both HIV and HCV normally have more of the hep C virus in their blood, and develop liver disease more easily and quickly. HCV takes advantage of weaknesses in the immune system due to HIV. There is also speculation that people with hep C experience more rapid progression to AIDS.

Suffice it to say that the HIV HCV coinfection is very bad.

I was briefed about how many hemophiliacs get HCV because of the constant transfusions that we receive from so many different donors. I also learned that it was a liver debilitating disease, so I decided to stop drinking for fear of further damage.

I was sent to a specialized doctor and found out that there was a new medicine that had a 50 percent chance of successfully removing hepatitis C from an infected person's body. The doctor also explained that few people are able to stick with the regiment of excruciating drugs for the 10-month period that it takes to complete. This latest development had challenge written all over it, so I opted to try it.

Unfortunately, I found out that there was a waiting list and I would be notified when I could participate. In the meantime, I stayed off of alcohol and started reading up on this harmful disease.

* * *

Kristine accepted an offer to work one of the American Red Cross first aid booths at the Winter Olympics in Salt Lake City. We decided that I would fly out to join for some of this time to attend some of the events and to visit with my sister Raeghn's family.

We purchased tickets to freestyle skiing and hockey. Both sporting events were fantastic and we felt like we experienced a once in a lifetime thing by attending them. The hockey was a special treasure, because we saw Canada play the Czech Republic. My brother-in-law Mel, who is Canadian, and Raeghn, came with us rooting for Canada. And, because Kristine's ancestry is Czechoslovakian, we both cheered for the Czechs. The hockey match ended in a tie after a fierce battle.

Seeing the Olympics with my wife, sister, and brother-in-law was definitely a fun-filled experience that will always remain in my memory as a blast!

* * *

Kristine and I decided to try to have a baby again. She got her Rubella booster in March of 2002 and we made our attempt in June of 2002.

Unfortunately, politics was starting to interfere with the in vitro procedure, and the medical group was beginning to question if it was safe for couples like us to go forward with the procedure. We continued our battle to go forward with this, but we were finding many hurdles along the way.

I have known from an early age that worthwhile things are most often hard to obtain. Having a baby is no different. Kristine and I realized that we would have some skirmishes ahead of us. But, we both wanted this more than we have wanted anything prior. And, our fight abilities are up there with the best of them.

* * *

After sitting on a waiting list for two months, I finally received my PEG-Intron and Rebetol. These drugs work in conjunction to possibly cure hepatitis C. I needed to take them for nearly a year and the side effects were considerable. The PEG-Intron is taken subcutaneously (injected into fatty tissue just beneath the skin). Mixed with the Rebetol, which is taken orally, the two combine to offer a 50 percent chance of defeating the hepatitis virus.

I started taking these new medications on May 18, 2002. The first night of my medication, I woke every hour or so with nausea and a sinus-like headache. In addition to those side effects, I also had severe chills, which made my entire body shiver, and kept my teeth chattering for some time. When the chills subsided, they were followed by a wave of heat. I was sweating pools and felt like my body was on fire.

The second day of my medication was filled with massive amounts of gas and hourly bouts with diarrhea. Also, I had muscle aches across every inch of my body. My nausea was much stronger on the second day.

By the third day, my nausea was starting to subside and the muscle aches were fewer. However, I still had a rough night's sleep as I sweated up a storm once again.

When the fourth day finally came around, my nausea was all but gone and my aches were nothing but a dull sensation. Most important to me, the diarrhea and gas had gone away also. However, I still had an occasional headache.

On one occasion, I was attempting to mow the lawn and I suddenly started sweating profusely. Before long, my vision was blurring and I realized with a start that my mowing pattern was erratic. I decided that if this did not clear up, I would move inside for a breather. The only problem was that I had only been outside mowing for about 15 minutes and I was a tad disconcerted that I could be this weak and sick. Moments later the world darkened and I collapsed onto the ground next to my lawn mower.

I woke a few minutes after passing out and managed to get myself inside to drink some fluids and get my feet up. Unfortunately, I could not finish the mowing job and I was reduced to calling my dad to ask if he would be able to come over and do it for me. My pride was dented, but I had no alternatives as this simple task was beyond my grasp.

According to my doctor and nurse, the first couple of weeks are the worst. And, most of the suffering only happens after the shot, which I inject only once per week. This is doable!

* * *

After several years of begging Scean to climb Rainier with me, he called me one afternoon and exclaimed, "I can't spend another day looking at the mountain without knowing that I at least made an attempt at climbing it."

I could not believe my ears! Had my brother gone mad? Or, had my incessant chipping away at his will finally broken him? He explained that it was neither. It truly was the simple fact that he saw that wondrous peak every day of his life and he could no longer look at it without trying to climb it.

I was elated and immediately broke out my dusty guidebooks and started rebuilding my knowledge of the routes, equipment, and training that we would need to go through.

Scean and I decided to climb Mt. Rainier in June of 2003. This would only give me two solid months of good training, because my hepatitis medicine had drained all of my energy and I would not get a truly descent workout while on it.

* * *

Fighting through the sickness and weakness of injecting myself with the hepatitis C medicines was becoming harder with each day. By August, which was less than three months in, I had already lost 25 pounds and I was weaker than ever before in my life. I did not know how I would be able to continue this regiment for seven more months. Many mornings I worked harder at lifting myself out of bed than anything I had ever tried to do.

The medicine was really starting to bring me down and I fought harder than I thought possible just to go through each day with a smile on my face. All of my friends and family kept commenting on my weight loss and appeared worried about my physical state. With a forced smile, I explained to them that I was fine. I said this each time even though I was terrified on the inside.

I started calling into work and eventually was rarely able to make it to the office. When I did make it in, it was after 11 o'clock in the morning. One of my saving graces of owning my own company was the fact that the other two owners were caring enough to help carry me through this dire time of need. Without George and Cathy and their undying support I would have been forced to quit taking the medicine. I owe a great debt to them, and I am afraid there is no way to repay it.

* * *

After resolving the politics, our fertilization doctors informed us that we would be able to try the procedure again in October.

We had plenty of concerns with my current medical condition and all of the poisons that I was pumping into my body. We felt that it would be best to trust the doctors and their opinions when it came to our decision to proceed at this time.

* * *

This little adventure starts on Monday, November 11, 2002. I suppose I should start by describing the little problem Kristine and I have with a flooding basement. Every time it rains hard, and our gutter has a couple of leaves in it, our basement floods. Because the gutter backs up, the water drains over the edge and into our basement stairway entrance. If so much as three or more leaves reside in the basement stairwell, the sump pump drain clogs (at least partially) and starts to fill the area with water. This water eventually creeps to the level of the basement door and floods into the house. ARGH!

With this in mind, it is imperative that I keep the basement stairs and the gutter free of leaves. So, here is where my tale begins—

Since a ton of leaves fell during the previous weekend and we were due for some heavy rain, I decided to clean my gutters out. Because it was raining already, I preferred not to climb on the ladder. However, given the choice of allowing my basement to flood or climbing a ladder in the rain and cleaning gutters, I would take the ladder any day (pun intended).

So, I carried that bulky, pain in the ass ladder out of my garage and brought it around to the deck in my back yard. This would not have been such a tough task if I had not been having all of my strength drained by the medication I was currently subjecting my body to. The rain was temporarily subsiding so this might not be too bad after all. After placing it and climbing up top, I started emptying the gutter of the evil leaves.

After a couple of minutes of cleaning, the ladder, having a mind of its own, decided to slip on the deck. To make a long story short (or shorter at least) the ladder dropped out from under me. Now, I am not one to be frightened of heights or falls, but a little adrenaline did course through my body as the ladder slid away below me.

In an instant, I grabbed the gutter with both hands. As I did this, I remembered someone once telling me that a gutter would never support a person's weight. I am here to tell you, that a gutter most certainly can support a man's weight, at least if he only weighs around 145 pounds (thank goodness for my cursed medication that had trimmed me down). In actuality, the only thing that happened was the gutter bent out at a severe angle. Perhaps it was able to support me, and consequently save me from an overnight stay at the Hospital Motel, because I grabbed on near one of the huge nails that holds it on.

Anyway, I was dangling by the gutter with a single foot on the ladder, which had stopped at an unstable angle about six feet down after it slid into the railing on my deck. Fifteen feet below, the deck ominously looked up and said, "Com'er boy." I was not worried about the drop to the deck. That is to say, 15 feet would be bad (probably end with a broken leg) but not terrible. The problem was that I hung precariously over the basement stairwell also. This would add nine feet to my fall and it would end on concrete instead of wood. To top it all off, I would probably fall onto the rail that splits the deck from the stairwell and break my body in half. It was this vision that kept me clinging to the gutter with more finger strength than I thought I had.

During this episode my neighbor from two houses down was in her backyard attending to chores or something and she noticed this spectacle. She calmly queried, "Is everything okay?"

Hiding my trepidation I casually responded, "Oh yeah, I'm fine."

She quickly responded, "Well, be careful up there."

No shit, Sherlock!

Momentarily after this exchange, my wife Kristine popped her head out of the door and asked, "What the heck are you doing?"

I did not want to tell her that I was in dire need of assistance. But, I did not have any choice. After a squeaky plea for her help, she made her way out and supported the ladder at the base. I finally built up the courage to let go of the gutter and drop onto the ladder. After crawling down (as close to a horizontal angle as vertical) I thanked her and put the ladder back in place to finish my job.

Kristine did not like the idea of me going back up, but she agreed to keep the ladder stable for me as I completed the necessary work.

Somehow, I seem to temp fate at every turn and manage to walk away with only sore biceps and stretched finger tendons.

Chapter Seventeen

Following our doctor's advice, we attempted the in vitro fertilization again. After the entire process of giving Kristine tons of shots and jumping through more hoops than an ankle biting mutt at a trick show, we found that only two of her eggs were usable. Normally, we get eight or more good eggs. Kristine was fairly disappointed with this, but we had the two eggs implanted anyway. After a little bit of time, we found out that the eggs had not taken and we were once again left barren.

Both of us were depressed with this whole process. And, I was also bringing us down with my weakness and broken will during the hepatitis medication period. Our life together had definitely reached the nadir and we wondered how we could rebound.

Together, we huddled and supported each other. Taking one step at a time, we trudged on wearily. We knew that this was just a trying time and we would get past it, but sometimes it is easier to think good thoughts than to see the light at the end of the tunnel.

* * *

After years of dabbling in Japanese studies on my own, I decided to take the class at our local community college. So, I signed up and started attending Japanese classes.

I found that my previous reading and studying helped considerably, because I was leading the class with my erudite knowledge.

I flew through the class with flying colors and received an A at the end. I also walked away with some enhanced understanding of the Japanese language. This class helped to build a strong base for my future of Japanese speaking and writing.

* * *

Knowing that the only path to success is to climb back in the saddle, Kristine and I sought to try our luck at the baby making again. This was our third time. We both worried that we might run out of time and money before actually having a baby.

Kristine is headstrong and she knows what she wants, so we pooled the funds and gave it another shot. One of the many things that I admire about my wonderful wife is her perseverance. She likes to grab the bull by his horns and the fertilization process is no different than anything else. If I have learned anything from her, it is that where there is a will, there is a way.

* * *

Because my Rainier climb was coming, I decided to start training and preparing for a successful ascent. My workouts felt like they were impossible, because the hepatitis medicine was taking its toll on me, and sapping my body of any strength.

I forced myself with more willpower than is imaginable to workout with weights and go on long hikes. Since I literally had no energy, my hikes result in plenty of rest stops. I found myself out of breath and weakened with each step. My training consisted of hiking with a 25-pound backpack and hiking around a local molehill called Sugarloaf Mountain. The problem was that I was barely able to carry that pack with me, and on Rainier it would be double the weight. My hope was that when I finish with the Godforsaken medicine I would immediately leap to a new level of bodily performance.

In the meantime, I needed to settle for barely being able to bench press 65 pounds (which is a third of my normal range) for a couple of repetitions before complete failure.

* * *

In April, I was finally able to stop my hepatitis C medication. I could not believe the cloud that lifted from me merely days after I stopped taking this poison. My entire outlook on life improved and my strength returned in leaps and bounds.

My headaches and pains drifted away as if they had never existed. And, my entire body felt like I had spent a week getting massages and pampering. I could not believe the enormous vitality that I felt surge through me as the medicine cleared out of my veins.

I went in for blood work and the results were no hepatitis in my body. The doctor warned me that this might not be a true reading and that we would have to test again in six months to find out for sure. But in my mind, I was cured and it was cause for celebration!

As a celebration for finishing the medicine, Kristine and I decided that I could buy a new motorcycle. I had always been enamored with the Suzuki GSX-R line of crotch rockets. But, I wanted something a little more comfortable because my commute to Annapolis was about an hour each way.

After doing some investigation and searching, I finally decided on the Suzuki Hayabusa. At the time, the Hayabusa was the fastest motorcycle in the world. And, it is a sport-tour, which is considerably more comfortable than many of the racing-styled sport bikes. With a top speed of nearly 200 miles per hour, the Hayabusa was potentially a death trap for me, but I knew that I could control myself and keep the beast tame.

I joined Hayabusa.org days before buying my bike. Hayabusa.org is an online forum and community of Hayabusa riders and aficionados. Around the same time that I joined so did some other folks from around the country. Andy, Bill, Keith, and Ben all bought a Hayabusa at about the same time as me and they ended up joining the forum during that time. We all quickly became online friends. These friendships have lasted well beyond when the Hayabusa was gone. On top of that, Ben has become my best friend and someone who has added so much to my life. It is impossible to explain with written word. *Wipes tear away with a sweep of his ragged sleeve*

When the time came to pickup my motorcycle, it was raining. I had ridden countless times in the rain, but never with such an extreme torque-to-weight ratio. I was fearful of accidentally flicking my wrist a hair too far and breaking the rear tire free, which would in turn smack me into the ground. The combination of respect and fear of this extreme machine got me home safely.

I rode the Hayabusa every day and was starting to get used to its quirks and idiosyncrasies by the end of the first week. I had only gone 120 miles per hour, but that was more than enough speed for me. I could not imagine going much faster than that. Besides the motorcycle was in the break-in period and I was not supposed to wind the engine up over 6,000 revolutions per minute (RPMs). Of course, this motorcycle has six speeds and is capable of going 89 miles per hour in first gear.

I was quickly learning how instantly this brute could snap to attention. It is hard to explain the exhilaration that you receive from a slight flick of the wrist, but suffice it to say that I have never felt anything quite like it. A professional drag racer can take a stock Hayabusa right off the showroom floor and run a 9.6 second quarter mile at over 145 miles per hour. It puts things in perspective when you consider that a Ford Mustang GT (which many folks consider a quick car) takes about 14 seconds to perform the same feat.

I was riding faster than ever imagined by the time I was in the second week of ownership. I now had the bike up to 140 miles per hour. The thing that started to scare me was the fact that I no longer feared the faster speeds. I would be riding casually and look down to find myself doing 110 or more miles per hour. To top off the danger factor, I started splitting lanes (riding the white line between cars to pass *through* traffic) at harrowing speeds during rush hour. One of the nice features of the Hayabusa is its ability to pass with authority. I would find myself behind a line of slow cars and easily pass all four or five cars in a single sweep during passing zones.

My friend Dan and his cousin Chris wanted to go out riding with me and I felt that I was ready to hit the twisties with them. So, we left out of Germantown and headed to Poolesville via the back roads. We were taking it pretty easy, because Chris was a new rider and I was still feeling the Hayabusa out (or, was it feeling me out?).

Occasionally I would partially open the beast up, and show-off to Dan and Chris. We would be riding in a pack at 80 miles per hour and I would turn with a sneer and hit the throttle. This momentary flick of my wrist would get my bike to 120 miles per hour in fewer than two seconds. And, the force that I pulled away at was mind-boggling.

I finally decided to really open her up and show us all what this monster was capable of. We were on a particularly windy section of road and I wanted to blast some. So, I tucked in and aired it out a bit. I was flying through a turn at 80 miles per hour in second gear and I hit the throttle a little early to see if I could break the rear tire loose. Unfortunately, this road was not in the best of shape and it was riddled with potholes and bits of gravel. I chose to hit the gas right over a nasty pothole. As I dipped into it, the front-end popped up and the rear followed right after as it hit the lip of the pothole. Imagine me leaned over for a high-speed turn in a partial wheelie with no tires on the ground. Just like I had experienced countless times in the past, everything around me slowed down as adrenaline pumped into my body.

The bike came down hard in the lean and my front wheel touched down instantly after the rear. I was still in the turn, but both tires were sliding with a loss of traction. Because it was a curve to the right, my slide was taking me into oncoming traffic; which was absent fortunately. On top of that, the handlebars started vibrating madly, which evolved into a full on "tank slapper." I started trying to stand the bike up some, but the tank slapping handlebars were making this simple task nearly impossible. The side of the road was quickly approaching me.

The bike was finally standing upright and the tank slapper was actually coming under control. But, the edge of the road had an eight-inch drop into a muddy field. There was no way to avoid going off the road, so I sat upright and prepared for the worst. Because the slide and commotion had skimmed a bit of speed, I rode off the road and into the mud at about 50 miles per hour. The bike was still vibrating with the remnants of the tank slapper, but it quickly stopped this in the mud. Knowing that the brakes would drop me like a sack of potatoes, I carefully steered the Hayabusa back toward the road. Hitting the eight-inch edge of the road nearly parallel, my bike soared right back up onto the pavement. From there, I moved over to the proper side of the road and started to control my breathing. I shook off the icy feelings I had and continued on my journey with a good bit less speed.

A couple of more nice curves and I was back to riding at higher speeds. When we arrived at the next stop sign, I turned to Dan with a smile and asked, "Which way?"

Dan's eyeballs were enormous and he shouted, "Are you crazy?" He was talking rapidly as he said, "I shit myself back there. Are you okay?"

Perplexed, I thought for a moment and realized that he was behind me during that entire procession. Grinning, I replied, "Yeah, I'm okay."

It was in that moment that Dan realized that all of my talk about loving adrenaline and being a hair on the crazy side was not just some fancy embellishment that I made up while casually sipping a beer.

From there, we slowed it down a bit, but in the weeks to come we would be right back up at that mad breakneck pace.

Chapter Eighteen

Along with racing my Hayabusa motorcycle on the local winding roads, I was continuing to get out and climb. On one occasion, Larry and I were at Sugarloaf Mountain doing some top roping and enjoying ourselves greatly. Shortly after we started climbing I saw another couple of people approaching our area. I immediately recognized one of the advancing folks as a famous local climber named, Mark. Mark, also known in these parts as Indiana Mark or just plain Indy, was picking a spot to climb just down from us. I called over to him and asked, "Mark?" To which I followed with, "Man, I have been using your web site, and now your guidebook for years."

Indy is very humble and does not think that the fact that he has climbed everything in the area over the last 20 plus years and documented the majority of it is anything special. I, on the other hand, beg to differ. I think it is something special and I was very excited about meeting him, and years later I am proud to call him friend.

After some small talk, we all decided to share our top rope anchors. We climbed together most of the afternoon before I got onto a tough 5.9+ climb called, "Blood Guard." This climb starts out hard with little to hold onto and even less to stand on. I tried it a few times before popping off one time and slamming into the rocks on uneven feet. My ankle buckled and I immediately felt the familiar feeling of an oncoming bout with internal bleeding.

Not wanting to disappoint Indy with my weakness, I stood around for a little while sharing stories and laughing with him. Before long I was motioning to Larry that we needed to bolt. I limped back down the approach trail and climbed into the car. Once in the car, I explained to

Larry that I was having a bleed. He was concerned, but we had talked about this before and he trusted in my judgment.

I ended up in the hospital to receive some factor VIII. But, my bigger concern was the fact that I was due to fly to Washington in less than a week to climb Mount Rainier with my brother. Long story short, I was still in a soft cast in Washington and did not make my attempt at the mountain.

Vaughn—zero; Mount Rainier—one!

* * *

After five years of running a company, I decided to move on to work with Oracle Corporation. Managing a company has countless benefits, but it also has some downfalls. One of the downfalls that are commonly overlooked is the fact that you are no longer just supporting your family. At Bay Technologies, George, Cathy, and I were supporting as many as a dozen families at a time. This weighed heavily on my chest when I tried to go to sleep at night.

Another problem that I was encountering was the fact that I was so busy with running the company that I was no longer getting my feet wet in the trenches. I love to roll-up my sleeves and work directly on projects.

I talked to Cathy long and hard about my decision to leave. She understood completely and was very thoughtful with her advice. After negotiating a commensurate selling price, I sold my shares of stock to Cathy and moved on.

Oracle was a 45,000 employee company and working there was a good bit different than running my own company. I lost my political pull and say in how things were done. However, I quickly worked into a smooth routine and was able to add to my growing skill set with databases.

At Oracle I bounced from project to project putting out fires and meeting lots of new people. I love working with people and found the constant change refreshing.

* * *

On October 26, 2003 my wife, my buddy Dan, and I packed up and flew to Atlanta to take a two-day course at Kevin Schwantz's road racing school. The class takes place at Road Atlanta racetrack on rented Suzuki racing motorcycles.

Before I get into the meat of the story, let me start by introducing you to our riding instructor—

Kevin Schwantz was a motorcycle Grand Prix World Champion. By the time he retired, Schwantz had accumulated 25 Grand Prix wins, 21 lap records, 29 pole positions, and the 1993 World Championship. When he retired, his racing number, 34, was retired with him. It was the first time in motorcycle racing history that a rider was honored in this fashion. Throughout his professional career, Schwantz always rode a Suzuki and never settled for second place. He was the perfect mentor for someone trying to get into motorcycle road racing.

Chris and his girlfriend Kimberly were not able to come down, so they agreed to watch my Labrador retriever, Tyler. Tyler ate something funky while we were gone and he proceeded to leave the largest piles of diarrhea and vomit that you have ever seen (it was like ten or more *HUGE* piles of diarrhea). They ended up staying up all night cleaning up the house, floor, and walls and taking Tyler to the 24-hour animal hospital. Eventually, Tyler had to have surgery and has since recovered.

Dan and I could not stop laughing about poor Chris and Kim not only missing a most excellent trip, class, and fun time. But, also having to clean up massive piles of doggie doo (wet ones mind you)! So, Dan asked Kevin if he would make a special picture and sign it for our friend. Kevin loved the idea and was laughing and telling the story to all of the other instructors. So, we took a picture of me and Dan on either side of Kevin and he signed it, "Chris, sorry you missed it. Thanks for picking up the poo! Kevin Schwantz #34."

The class was broken into two sections: Street and Advanced. Dan and I went street, because we had no track experience. The street class was then broken into three groups on the track: slow, medium, and fast. We elected medium for the majority of the two days. During the class, we had 20 minutes of class time while the advanced group was on the track. Then, we switched to the track for 20 minutes while the advanced group was in the classroom. It continued like this for the entire two days. Twenty minutes equates to approximately ten laps around the track once you factor in preparation.

On day one, Dan and I were pretty slow, even though we were going as fast as we ever had on the street. The day started with rain, so we had to be slower anyway. I am actually glad it started this way, because we got a little "slow" practice in before getting busy. We both started on SV-650's, which are slower than the other option, GSX-R 600's. But, the SV's handle and brake very nicely and are a fantastic track bike.

Just before lunch, our instructor (you get one instructor per three or four students on the track) signaled me to pull ahead of him and lead the way around the track. I was stoked! But, it was at this point that I realized that I knew nothing about the track. I had been following the instructor's line around the track and not looking for reference points to keep my line proper. Anyway, I went through turn two wrong and ended up on the wrong side of turn three's entrance. Turn three is blind, because you come over a big hill during turn two. I almost went down slamming the brakes on and shifting to get around three. The instructor passed me in turn four and once again asked me to follow him. That was my big lesson for the day. You absolutely must learn reference points and remember the turn directions!

When lunchtime came around, we sat at the table with Kevin Schwantz (as a-matter-of-fact, I sat beside him). We sat for an hour talking and laughing with one of the greatest motorcycle racers of all time! It was like a dream-come-true.

After lunch we got back on the track and now it was completely dry, so we were able to kick it up considerably! We switched bikes to the GSX-R 600 (nicknamed Gixxer), which is substantially quicker with its higher horsepower and redline. The SV topped out around 125 miles per hour and the "Gixxer" was about 150 miles per hour. With the GSX-R we were getting a rhythm and were going much quicker. After each session on the track, our instructor took us aside and talked about all of our ups and downs on the track. This was very essential to honing our skills.

When the class ended for the day, we noticed Kevin and the other instructors heading down to the track. We ran down to the bleacher section and for the next half hour watched the coolest display of sheer madness I had ever seen. Kevin was on an SV650, an instructor named Michael was on an SV1000 and the others were on GSX-R 750's. Unbelievably, Kevin was in the pack during many laps around the track. He was so fast, that even though it was impossible for him to keep up with the big bikes on the straights, he managed to hang because of his speed around the turns. This is pretty amazing when you consider that the back straight is nearly a mile long! And, on top of that, his instructors are all world-class racers!

After day one, we met at Kevin's favorite restaurant (Mexican) and had dinner with everyone. It was a blast. We sat with two instructors and had the time-of-our-lives listening to heart-wrenching stories about Kevin.

By day two I was going considerably faster around the track and leaning further than I had ever leaned before. I actually dragged my right knee one time (barely scraping it against the ground) and Dan was able to drag both of his. Halfway through the day, I decided to move to the faster (of the three) groups and was flying around the track at speeds I could have only imagined the day before.

This may not sound like much to many of you reading this. But to a hemophiliac who was barely allowed by his physicians to ride bicycles as a child, it was like a science fiction novel!

All in all, I would chalk this up as the single most exciting learning experience of my life. As far as inciting exhilaration goes, it was only second to the day my wife said, "I do." I would strongly recommend this class to anyone who is interested in motorcycles.

After finishing this class, I decided to buy a track only motorcycle and start doing days at the track!

* * *

I spent long nights researching track bikes and the technologies available. After countless hours, I decided to go with the Suzuki SV650, which is what I rode at Kevin Schwantz's school in Atlanta. The main reason behind my decision was the fact that tons of aftermarket parts and accessories were available for the SV and it was a veritable tank. On top of that, it was a nice handling and braking machine that was right at home on the track.

I started searching online for this particular bike and found many of them available. I also remembered that George (one of the co-owners of Bay Technologies) had purchased an SV two years earlier. I called George and asked if he still owned the bike. He explained that he still had it but did not ever ride it and was considering selling it. After a couple of minutes of discussing this, I became the proud owner of a perfect track bike.

I immediately went to work stripping the bodywork and lights off and replacing them with a special fairing designed for the track. I changed the brake pads, tires, exhaust, suspension and foot pegs. I also altered the shifter by reversing the shift pattern (this is common in the road race community).

After my modifications were completed, I had the bodywork painted and I applied some nice stickers. My bike number was 922, which is an amalgamation of Kristine and my favorite numbers.

The bike was complete and I was ready to hit the track with it. I had also convinced my friends Dan and Ben to do some track racing. So, they were both finishing up their bikes at the same time.

* * *

I started having severe pain in my mouth due to pressure from my molars, so I decided to visit the dentist. Because of hemophilia and my lack of cavities I had not been to the dentist in more than 20 years. Most folks, including my dentist, freaked out when I revealed this fact.

The dentist confirmed that my molars were starting to push my other teeth around and that they would need to be removed. I caused quite a stir among the dental community with my hemophilia and HIV. Eventually I was able to find a qualified oral surgeon who would do the procedure for me.

I warned my dentist and oral surgeon that I would have some pretty hefty bleeding from an operation like this, but they both felt that it was minor and should not promote a problem. For safety's sake they decided to consult my hematologist who agreed with them and decided against giving me factor VIII before the procedure.

The operation was fairly simple and was extremely entertaining. After being gassed, the surgeon went to work using a hammer, chisel and pliers. I was happy to find that I could watch the entire procedure through the reflection in his glasses. I sat in awe at the archaic way that he performed this tooth extraction. I figured there would be lasers, ion cannons, and even photon torpedoes. Instead, he placed a chisel on my tooth and banged away with a hammer until it shattered. Then he went in with the pliers and dug around removing all of the tooth and bone fragments. Occasionally a piece of tooth was so hard to pull that he had an assistant hold my head and he propped himself holding my jaw with one outstretched arm while yanking with the other. It cracked me up to see that dentistry had not changed much in thousands of years (or, perhaps that was just the laughing gas).

After the molars were gone, the oral surgeon stitched my mouth up and sent me on my way. Before this ordeal would end, I spent time at four different hospitals on seven different occasions even missing Christmas day while receiving factor VIII. It turned out that the lowly hemophiliac knew a thing or two about his personal bleeding experiences and the highfalutin city slicker doctors were once again incorrect.

Four months after my surgery my teeth were still sensitive to cold foods. But my gum line had healed.

* * *

Riding the Hayabusa was becoming crazier with each outing. Before long, my buddy Ben was riding nice long wheelies and I attempted to mirror him. When you first start to try to ride a wheelie, you imagine the front is coming off the ground each time the suspension stretches open a little. But, when the wheel really leaves the ground, it is an exhilarating feeling.

Riding wheelies is a sensitive business that includes managing to give enough throttle to stand the bike up, but not too much to *loop* (wreck by flipping over) the bike. After this initial leap of faith, you must then alter the throttle control in tiny increments to keep the bike at a steady balanced level. The problem with the Hayabusa is that due to the long wheelbase the "balance point" is at a seriously high angle. In order to obtain the balance point, you need to nearly stand the bike straight up. Many people overlook the fact that this is not the end of the wheelie. After you are done riding a one-wheeled freak show, you need to bring that front tire back to the ground. This sounds easier than it is sometimes. Essentially, you need to ease off the throttle and float down. When you get near the ground, you blip the throttle just a touch to lighten the landing. If you hit the ground too hard, you will bounce and risk damaging your front forks. Not to mention jarring your teeth and even slamming your jewels on the tank (which ain't fun). On top of that, your front tire must be precisely aligned with your travel direction to avoid a tank slapper.

Before long, Ben was riding some terrific wheelies including ones where he sits on top of the gasoline tank or stands on the foot pegs. I managed to lift the front-end a good bit and ride out some one-wheeled extravaganzas, but nothing like Ben was doing. After the standard first gear 45 mile per hour wheelie was becoming old hat, Ben started experimenting with gear switches. This proved to be a daunting task and he was unable to keep the bike standing through the shift. But, he did find that he could lift the bike up in second gear at over 90 miles per hour and ride this out past 120 miles per hour.

Both Ben and I decided that some training was in order. So, we talked to our friend Dan and decided to head to Tampa to take a wheelie school. This is a Keith Code class called "On One Wheel." It turned out to be lots of fun. The instructors put you on a tricked out Triumph motorcycle that has a fabricated wheelie bar on it. This bar acts as a safety mechanism by killing one cylinder in the engine if you stand the bike up too far. After that, the rear brake is put on if you pass beyond the first safety setting. The coolest part of the whole setup is that the bar is adjustable. So, you start with the wheelie bar in a position that only allows the wheel to be pulled a tiny bit off the ground to get you comfortable feeling the wheelie. Before long, they adjust the bar and allow a taller wheelie.

By the end of the day, all three of us were riding out nice tall wheelies at the balance point. We were very happy with our progress and found that this training was going to easily transfer to our motorcycles at home. As we had thought, it did transfer. But, Dan and I were both still fairly leery of riding wheelies on the street. Ben on the other hand was improving in leaps and bounds, and before long was riding 125 miles per hour on one wheel for two miles and longer! You can view some of his more spectacular ones on www.youtube.com by searching for my name.

* * *

Dan and I decided to attend Kevin Schwantz's racing school again. This time, we were able to talk our friends Ben and Chris into joining us. We all booked our class and hotel rooms. We decided to drive down this time, because Ben and I would both be bringing down our built track bikes to ride instead of using the class provided motorcycles.

We loaded up the trailer and headed down to Atlanta for our class. Because it was early in the season, there was a smaller turnout at the class and they combined us into one group composed of street and advanced. This combination worked nicely for us, because we were essentially at a middle ground.

While there, we were bragging about Ben's wheelie shenanigans to some of the instructors. Jamie, a professional road racer, was particularly interested in Ben's high-jinx. They explained to us that we were not allowed ride wheelies during the class, but they were enjoying our stories of long wheelies none-the-less.

During one of our sessions, Dan and I were following Jamie on the track. After we pulled out of turn seven and entered the back straight, Jamie looked back at us and nodded. Before we knew it, he stood his bike up at attention. While it was up, he shifted gears two times. His bike was now going about 140 miles per hour. To add insult to injury, Jamie then stood up on the bike and rode into the wind like a banshee. As if this was not enough, he then shook the bike and started it into a one-wheeled gyroscopic frenzy. The entire bike was vibrating viciously. Before he finished the wheelie, Jamie had the bike up around 150 miles per hour and nearly shaking out of control. He brought the motorcycle down with the calm hand of a rodeo rider and continued on down the track. Dan and I could not believe our eyes!

Later in the day, another of the instructors named Trey heard about Jamie's feat and decided to one-up him. While heading up the front straight after turn five he stood his bike up and rode a wheelie down the entire straight right in front of us. This would not be such a great feat if it had not been for the fact that there was a pack of students and instructors in front of him. Trey proceeded to weave his way through the group on one wheel. He set the bike down with barely enough time to jam the front brakes on and stuff the bike into turn six at a hairy speed that skittered his bike nicely through. It was the most fantastic feat of motorcycle control that I had ever seen.

By far, this was the most exciting class that I had ever experienced. Not only was I able to walk away with some mad track skills, also I was able to see some of the country's best racers do things that I would not have believed had I not seen them with my own eyes. If I did not properly pass it on with my recollection of the first time I took this class, I would highly recommend this class to all thrill seekers.

In the end, Chris, Dan, Ben, and I got more than our money's worth. We made friendships with world-class racers, experienced things that many only watch on television, honed our track related skills, and above all else had loads of fun. The amount of learning that you receive from this class is unparalleled and would take months, if not longer, on your own.

* * *

My first day at the racetrack with my brand new beautifully painted motorcycle ended in a pretty serious wreck. I was getting pretty used to the nice curves of Summit Point Racetrack, when I went into turn one too *hot* (faster than I should). Attempting to scrub a little bit of speed, I ended up shifting my suspension just a tad too much and breaking the front tire loose. The bike quickly went into a *lowside* (a slide where the bike is on its side and the tires are out front). I slid like this all of the way through turn one thinking about how silly it was for me to brake that hard during a lean. Mentally I was kicking myself and already preparing to pick the bike up and march back out with some improvements when the bike lurched as it bumped over the outer rumble strip.

Excruciating pain shot through my body as my ankle spanked the rumble strip with splintering shock. Next, my knee banged into the bumpy edge of the track and finally my hip slammed into the concrete bumps. Pain was starting to issue throughout my body when the bike suddenly stood up. As the bike slid off the track and bounced around, the tires had snagged a piece of the rutted grass and dirt and forced itself into an upright position.

Since I was still straddling the motorcycle during this process, I was thrown upward for an airy *highside* (where the motorcycle violently throws you up and over itself). Painful realization impacted me as I was flung from my comfortable seat.

Flying through the air in slow motion, I watched in terror as my bike tumbled along below me. I did not have to be a rocket scientist to see that my trajectory was going to land me with a high impact into my somersaulting motorcycle. A split second before the impending collision, the bike took a bounce off to the side and I landed on the hard ground narrowly missing getting tangled up in my flipping piece of metal.

Sitting up, I looked around and assessed the situation. I did not appear to have any broken bones, and I felt fairly okay. So, I stood up and waved an "okay" symbol to one of the closest corner workers. I patiently waited for the "wreck truck" to come out and help me remove my scrap metal and plastic from the area.

By the time I had gotten back to the parking area and my trailer, I realized that I was feeling pain throughout my entire body. My elbow, hip, knee, and ankle were all already starting to swell with the internal bleeding that only a hemophiliac can feel and intimately understand. Besides my aching body parts, my right thumb was really throbbing and turned out to be dislocated.

A quick trip home and then to the hospital resulted in a couple of days of receiving factor VIII. I visualized how lucky it had been that I had not gotten tangled up with my tumbling motorcycle. I also felt that I had gotten off easy with minor scratches and bruises compared to the possibilities. However, I knew that I would be back on the track in a week or two.

Kristine and I milled over the finer points of my wreck and talked for some time about how dangerous it was for me to be out there. Explaining that the track is many times safer than the street did not bode well with her considering that I was still riding on the street.

We both agreed that it was not smart for me to keep this perilous activity up and for now, we decided that if our latest venture into becoming parents came true, I would give up the motorcycle racing for good.

* * *

Amid my motorcycle mayhem, Scean and I decided to take another crack at Rainier. Since my last attempt did not even leave the comforts of Tacoma, I agreed to avoid all dangerous activities (including rock climbing and motorcycle racing) for two weeks prior to our attempt. I started my arduous training and was quickly improving my endurance and stamina in no time.

Since my training included hiking and climbing, I would go to Sugarloaf Mountain as often as I could. On one occasion I was top rope climbing a fairly easy route with Larry. I noticed that the rope was starting to get some slack in it and I asked Larry to pull the rope in a bit. He responded by telling me that he had me tight. I looked up and found that the rope was jammed in a crevice between two rocks. I told him the rope was stuck and that I would try and get it out from my end. Grabbing the rope while I hung on to the overhanging rock with my other hand, I tried to tug and shake it free. The rope was stuck pretty snugly in this crack and I could not break it out of the rock's grip.

Considering my situation I could only see three ways out. I could continue climbing through a tough part of my climb and get up to where the rope was stuck about 15 feet above me and try to pry it free. This option would leave me with a pretty nasty fall and pendulum into a jagged rock wall and did not look very promising to me. Plus, hanging in that position for a couple of minutes and tugging on the rope had started to burn my forearms a bit. I was looking at a stout climb that would be loads tougher with swollen forearms and pumped muscles.

The second option was to just let go and hope that weighing the line would pop the rope out of the snag. This option was a tad scary because the rope was over and through a fairly sharp edge where it might be cut once weighed. On top of that, if the rope didn't come unstuck I would be left hanging in the air 20 or more feet off the deck swinging without a way to get back to the rock. This option could potentially turn into more of an epic than my current predicament.

My third option was to untie and downclimb the way I had come up. This option was a bit disturbing to me, because I was already starting to feel worn out and downclimbing an overhang tends to be considerably tougher then climbing up. Not to mention the fact that I would be sans my rope and therefore could possibly fall 20 feet landing on my back. On a good day, 20 feet is a long way to fall. Falling 20 feet onto a jagged rocky floor is a death sentence for a hemophiliac.

Weighing my options, my arms were getting more pumped and I was wasting time. I asked Larry for his opinion about letting go. He responded letting me know that the rope was on a sharp edge and might break under the added pressure of my body weight and swing. He didn't like that idea.

By this time, my arms were actually aching and I was getting *sewing machine leg* (this is when your calf and thigh get so burned out, that they start to shake uncontrollably). I decided that my best option was to untie and attempt to downclimb. My pump was getting worse and I had to start moving.

I yelled down to Larry, "I'm gonna untie and downclimb."

Larry blurted back, "You're gonna do what?"

I calmly explained to him my predicament and that I was planning to untie and downclimb. During this discussion I started working on untying my knot from my harness. Larry tried talking me out of this course of action and was attempting to come up with a better (read: safer) way to achieve this goal.

Horror started to creep in as I realized that my knot was tight and my pumped hands couldn't work properly to untie it. Unfortunately for me, I found this out after getting part of the knot undone. I could feel the edge of panic creeping in as I twisted and tugged one-handed trying desperately to get the tenacious knot free. I envisioned popping off the rock with a partially untied knot that would surely slip and drop me to the rocky ground. Sweat was creeping into my eyes and I found myself taking time to wipe it out with the back of my arm. It was during this wiping procedure that I noticed how perilous this assignment was. My arm was completely pumped and my hands were shaking from the adrenaline that was coursing through my body. *Simmer down now!*

Digging deep inside myself, I made a last ditch effort to finish untying the knot. My arms and legs were barely able to keep me on the rock as I finally got the knot undone. Now I was faced with the difficult (to say the least) job of downclimbing without the safety of a rope with completely blown forearms.

Just as I had freed the rope, Larry told me again that he didn't think it was a good idea for me to untie. He was still trying to figure out a way to help me as I made the first backward move to free myself from this precipice. I cut him off by yelling down that I had already untied and was coming.

I slowly worked my way back down to an easier section and finally off the rock wall. My arms screamed with relief as I was finally able to leave the rock and shake them out. I was so pumped that I could not untie my shoelaces or even hold a bottle of water.

My hands shook uncontrollably as I turned to Larry and said, "That was a close one."

We both laughed and moved on to another climb.

* * *

Over the next couple of months, I traveled to ride on the track eight times. During this time, I managed to wreck four more times and run off the track on seven occasions. I was starting to realize that I was either going to have to change my aggressive track behavior or give up this sport. In the meantime, I somehow managed to convince myself that it was okay to have these accidents, because I was giving it my all out there.

Needless to say, I was riding like an idiot and was not giving it my all by any means. I was out there endangering myself as well as others. However, at least one of my wrecks was to avoid running someone else over, so I comforted myself with this chivalrous act.

If I did not start learning to control my adrenaline filled track days I would have to give up this crazy sport once and for all. The most aggravating part of being out on the track is that my buddies were not wrecking nearly as often as I was. And, in Ben's case, he was not wrecking at all and managing to improve well beyond my skill level at the same time. Perhaps this sport was not for me after all. I needed to sit-down and have a serious heart-to-heart chat with myself and decide on some priorities.

On top of the track sessions, my days on the street with the Hayabusa were becoming crazier as well. I found myself riding 150 miles per hour on the highway in traffic on a regular basis. I was starting to realize that this "way of life" was exactly the opposite (more like a "way of death") and would result in my untimely demise if I did not get it under control.

When I was off of the motorcycles, I rationally figure out that I must stop riding like that. But, when I got back in the saddle, I defenestrated rationality and once again became a bozo. The Japanese have a saying for the person that I am. It is *yama otoko*. This literally translates to mountain man. But, ironically it is often used to mean "wild man." Before long, I attached this name to myself and have even considered getting it tattooed in Japanese characters on my back. My hematologist says that I cannot get a tattoo. *Decisions—*

Chapter Nineteen

There is a saying: "four times the charm"—well, there is for Kristine and me. On our fourth attempt to have a baby, the fertility exercise stuck and we became pregnant. This attempt was easier for us, because we found a fertility place that was willing to work with us in our local area.

Now that we were pregnant, Kristine decided to retire from the American Red Cross and work from home. Also, as promised, I agreed to sell my crotch rockets and be done with the dangerous motorcycles once and for all.

The due date for our little baby was February 4, 2005. Once we were able, Kristine and I categorically agreed to find out the sex of our unborn child. We felt that this would help us with preparation of its room and initial clothing selection. In addition, it would help ease our weary minds with the fact that we really were having a baby.

* * *

Riding downtown on the subway gives me time to sort out my thoughts. One particular morning in July was no different than any other. I sat there pondering life and asked myself, "What shall I do next." This question comes to me often, because I am constantly looking for ways to improve and outdo my last feat.

Literally moments after asking myself this deep internal question, I noticed a sign on the wall advertising the AIDS Marathon in New Orleans. Tilting my head a little, I thought to myself, *I could run a marathon.* This thought was fleeting and was immediately followed with negative things like, *don't be ridiculous, your joints cannot withstand such an arduous task, and this is far too tough for you to accomplish.*

173

I noticed that the marathon was scheduled for February 27, 2005. Since it was currently July, this would give me slightly more than six months to train. With this in mind, I realized that the marathon was actually doable with a proper training regiment. I made a mental note to visit the AIDS Marathon web site.

Once I arrived at the office, I was again uplifted with the idea of running a marathon. I did not even know what a marathon would entail or how long of a run it would be. So, I did a couple of cursory searches on the web and found that a marathon was a run that extended for 26.2 miles. Twenty-six miles! Damn! That is a long distance to run. More searching uncovered the fact that Oprah Winfrey had run one. I greatly admire Oprah and many of the amazing things she has accomplished in her life. I thought to myself that if Oprah could turn herself around and become fit enough to run a marathon (in a very impressive time no less) than I could do it too. What I failed to notice was that Oprah had trained with a world-class fitness trainer for nearly two years to accomplish this feat and I was looking at six months with the joint debilitating hemophilia against me. But, I have never been one to let hemophilia hold me back and affect my outcome. So, I decided then and there that I was going to run the 2005 New Orleans Marathon.

I immediately signed up for the program and gathered information about running such a long distance. The task was daunting, but I knew that perseverance was going to pull me through. I started formulating a training plan based upon information that I received from the Whitman-Walker Clinic who would be coaching me through the training process.

Before long, I had setup a web site and was asking friends and family for donations. On top of the grueling task of training my body to run four times further than I ever had in my life, I also needed to raise $2,500 to support AIDS victims. I felt like this was a huge undertaking, but one that must be done. I knew in my heart that I was capable of both raising the money and completing the marathon. This feeling was quickly comforted by the love of my friends and family who donated more money than I would have imagined. Not only did I reach my goal of $2,500, I surpassed it by more than $1,000.

This was a life-changing experience that was helping me to grow in new areas. The support that I had from all of the people around me in my life showed me how much I meant to them. It was an unbelievable feeling to have them donate so much to my worthy cause. And, because I was afflicted with this horrendous disease, I knew that their donations were indirectly for me. This simple notion brings a steady stream of tears to my eyes. People love me.

My training was fairly straightforward. I ran three days per week, increasing my mileage each week by a mere 10 percent. When I started my training, I was only running one or two miles per day. Before long, I was running further than I had in my life on a regular basis. I am utterly amazed at how resilient the human body is. This training was ingraining the pure fact that my body would adapt to anything I threw at it.

Now that my mileage was increasing, I started to split my running week into two maintenance days of about three or four miles each day and one long run day that increased each week. My long run day was on Sunday and I would go downtown to Washington, DC to run with 100 other runners all training for the same event. This experience was building me in many ways that I never thought possible. It was a wonderful experience that made me want to become an even better person. I love to follow Tony Robbins' simple rule: "Constant And Never-ending Improvement." And, this training was detailing this rule in ways I never imagined feasible.

During one of my long run Sundays, I was going for a new record distance of twelve miles. As our group reached the eight-mile mark, my left heel started complaining. It was merely a tingling sensation, but it stood out as a different feeling than I had felt prior to this point.

One more mile passed and suddenly I felt an eruption of pain just above my heel along the length of my Achilles tendon. The pain was shocking and it nearly knocked me off my feet. Limping slightly, I sucked in air through my clenched teeth and told myself that this was merely a cramp and that it would subside shortly.

Trudging through the tenth mile, I worried as the pain continued. I casually asked the others if they had experienced pain in their Achilles tendons before. No one had, but they started querying me about my current pain. I explained that I was going to keep on trucking as long as I could and I pretended that the severe pain was trivial.

Sweat built at the corners of my eyes and I was starting to feel the affects of the problem in my lower calf. The pain was so sharp that I nearly yelped with each new step. By the end of the tenth mile I realized I would not be able to finish this run at our current pace. One of the guys I was running with named Duane was toying with the idea of slowing down due to a hamstring issue, so we slowed and vowed to stick together until the end of our run.

Unfortunately my tendon was worse off then I had originally thought and I was unable to run at all. I was doing a medium paced walk and wincing with each and every delicate step on my left foot. I managed to limp back to our starting area and crawled into my car with a ringing headache and an excruciating emanation from my left leg.

I ended up having a rupture in my Achilles tendon. Essentially, the tendon is double surrounded by tissue and I burst the outer layer. This resulted in severe pain and a reddened lump on the exterior. It was nearly impossible to walk, let alone run. My vision of running a marathon was quickly being clouded by the fear of failure. One of my running coaches, Allie, gave me some suggestions of proper rest and recovery procedures. For the most part, she instructed me to ice the area for 20-minute periods every two hours. I followed this regiment, but I had become extremely disheartened with the fact that I might not compete in this race.

People around me started suggesting that I change to the half marathon instead of the whole one. They justified this by stating that my body could not handle an entire 26.2-mile run. This notion invigorated me to show the world exactly what I am capable of. It is weird how I tend to improve the greatest when challenged, but it is so. And, I digress (as usual). I followed my coach's advice to a tee with the rest and recuperation period. I stopped running for nearly two weeks and was careful to rest the entire time.

My marathon was fewer than three months away, and I was extremely nervous when it came time to run again. I carefully went out and ran very delicately for the first two runs. I was feeling my Achilles tendon with every step and it scared me into believing that I was a moment away from a complete rupture and utter failure. I read every article I could find on running with this kind of injury and found that if I landed more on my heel (instead of my toes as I used to run) and then rolled along my foot, I might improve my chances of abstaining from additional injury. I followed this advice and found that it was helping.

Before long, my confidence had returned and I was not nearly as concerned with my tendon. However, the fear played a pivotal role in the back of my mind.

I was back to running the long runs with the group downtown and my running and endurance levels actually improved with the two weeks off. Now more than ever, I felt that this marathon was within my reach!

Chapter Twenty

On February 9, 2005, Trinity was already a week late and the obstetrician told us that she was breach and Kristine would need to have a Cesarean Section (C-Section) the following morning.

Oh, did I mention that we found out we were having a girl? And, we decided to name her Trinity Viola?

The middle name came easily, because it comes from Kristine's Great Grandmother Viola. The family affectionately called Viola "Mama."

Trinity however came from an odd amalgamation. The name first came to us through Kristine's brother who thought it was a beautiful name. On top of that, Kristine and I liked it because of our Christian background and the relation between this name and the Father, Son, and Holy Ghost. Finally, my favorite movie is *the Matrix,* and one of the main characters (my favorite heroine) is a woman named, Trinity.

* * *

A bitter wind and freezing air threatened to detriment the beautiful day, but failed to wipe the ear-to-ear smile off of my mug. During the C-Section, I was in the room and able to watch the operation happen.

At one point, after the major incision was made, the nurse hooked a tool to Kristine's upper abdomen and attached a bandage to the end. After hooking this inside Kristine's rib cage, the nurse yelled, "Incoming." Immediately after this announcement, she pitched the roll of bandage over the operation table. The anesthesiologist caught the roll at the head of the table and placed it over his shoulder while he turned away from the table. Once it was tightened the nurse said, "Okay." He leaned into the tug-of-war and pulled the bandage taut. As he did this, Kristine's upper abdomen opened wider.

When the nurse explained that he had pulled it far enough, the anesthesiologist tied off the bandage on a machine. This entire process only took a moment, but I felt like I was in an 1864 Civil War operating tent during this part of the procedure.

Trinity was born (removed) on February 10, 2005 at 2:40 p.m. When she was born, her cry was weak. In addition, Kristine appeared to have some bleeding problems.

Trinity looked fair skinned and a little water logged. I held her in my arms and brought her to Kristine so she could see her. After this, Kristine was wheeled to her post-operation room.

After Trinity was taken away, I spent my time traveling between visits to the post-operation area to be with Kristine and the nursery to see Trinity. I was bringing Kristine progress reports on Trinity and letting her know how she was doing.

Bubbles of foam were coming out of Trinity's mouth and she was having trouble breathing. Her chest was sucking in painfully as she appeared to struggle to find enough oxygen. The nurses informed me that they thought there might be a problem. Kristine and I had already been through so much just trying to have this little baby and it was starting to take a toll on me.

I wandered back to see Kristine to talk to her about the problems with Trinity and I found her covered head-to-toe in electric blankets. Apparently Kristine had lost more blood than originally thought and the doctor was worried about her decrease in body temperature. At this point, I was starting to get a severe upset stomach and my mind started to reel as I thought about the problems with both my wife and my daughter.

My father, George, showed up to visit us at the hospital and he recognized that I was having a hard time. So, he offered to take me down to the cafeteria to get some food. I went with him and relaxed a little bit while eating some dinner.

When George and I returned Kristine was crying. She explained that Trinity had a more serious problem than we thought. She was born with esophageal atresia. Apparently when Trinity was born, there was a problem with her lungs being full of mucus and maconeum. The lungs being full of maconeum is normal for a c-section, because the baby does not go through the birth canal, which compresses the body and squirts the fluid out of her lungs. She seemed to be having more problems than normal, so they moved her to the Neonatal Intensive Care Unit (NICU) for examinations. Soon after she was there, an X-ray revealed that she had a problem with her esophagus. Further examinations divulged that part of her esophagus was missing and her throat did not connect to her stomach. This condition known as esophageal atresia / tracheoesophageal fistula is a serious circumstance that requires major surgery. So, she was transferred to Children's Hospital in Washington, DC that evening. We were told that she would remain there for as long as six months to receive proper treatment.

* * *

Because of the C-section, Kristine had to spend the night in the hospital, so I went home alone. I felt that there were a bunch of problems stacked against us, but I had faced unbelievable odds before. I put on my happy face and continued through life one step at a time,

I decided to take a shower and go to bed. I undressed and climbed into a steamy hot shower and was instantly calmed and comforted by the hot water. As I washed and relaxed, images popped into my mind of my new baby and my wonderful wife both in the hospital with questionable issues. I slowly came to the realization that for the first time in my life the outcome of a certain situation was completely out of my hands.

Darkness started edging in around the corners of my vision and my chest was constricting. I had never felt this kind of suffering before. Up until now, each problem I had faced in life was my own personal one. Previously, I had looked my tribulations in the eye and smiled. This was a new kind of problem that affected me dramatically but there was absolutely nothing that I could do about it.

Suddenly my knees felt weak and my vision darkened further. Gravity sucked at me as I collapsed under my newly found weight. I slammed into the shower stall floor with great force and fell forward. I caught my head with my hands and started to cry deeply. I was kneeling in an extremely hot shower with goose pimples all over my body. I started shaking uncontrollably as if I were freezing. The crying continued and came out in scary bursts of energy.

I do not know how long I stayed glued to the stall floor crying. But, when I emerged from the shower my body was prune-like from being in the water for so long. I had cried for at least 20 minutes and probably longer. Facing the steamy mirror I felt like a rejuvenated man. It had been a decade or longer since I had truly cried. Facing the fact that there were things in life that I couldn't control, I finished my ritual and climbed into bed praying for rest.

Sleep captured me quickly and easily and I slept undisturbed for the first time in a long time. I guess my body needed to expel that negative energy in order to start the slow healing process.

It is funny how you know that you should not let things outside your control affect your emotions and yet how powerfully this threw me on my knees. Here I was at nearly 40 years old learning something that pride did not allow me to learn until then.

* * *

Trinity's operation went without a hitch. They were able to connect her esophagus to her stomach and make all of the associated repairs. The surgeons were very happy with the success of the procedure and told us that her esophagus was close enough to the stomach that it did not have to be stretched very far. They expected her to heal and be out of Children's Hospital before two months. This was a great relief to Kristine and me.

The doctor mentioned that, as expected, she had gastroesophageal reflux disease (GERD) also loosely known as acid reflux. And, it would probably be a lifelong issue for Trinity. Fortunately it is not a big problem and is cared for with a daily dose of medicine.

Along with Trinity's good news, Kristine was already starting to get better. Her doctors explained that she would heal completely and in a timely manner. With Trinity and Kristine only a day away from catastrophe and looking so good, a great burden was lifted from my heart.

* * *

Only two weeks after Trinity's birth and it was time for me to travel to New Orleans to run my marathon. I was a little concerned since Trinity was still in the hospital and we had been visiting her every day. Kristine has always been very supportive and told me to go run my race. She saw that I wanted to go and that I had been through six months of torturous training to accomplish this.

Together we decided that I would make the trip, run my marathon and come right back to my family with a new challenge completed. Ben and my sister-in-law Dawn also traveled down there to cheer me on.

New Orleans was more of a party town than I had imagined. Of course our trip was right around the time of Mardi Gras, and the partying was still going strong. Doing the tourist thing, Ben, Dawn, and I traveled around the town and took in the sites.

February 27, 2005 came quicker than expected. I woke early in the morning and prepared myself mentally for my run. Checking the weather and finding rain and cold brought a moment of despair to me. I quickly used my will to overwhelm the feelings of doubt and stuck my chest out with pride as I marched out of my hotel room on my way to run with thousands of others.

In order to allow my body a thorough warm-up, I walked the two miles from my hotel to the Super Dome; which was where the race would start and finish. The walk was brisk due to the cold weather. Fortunately, the rain had started dying out and a light mist was replacing it. I was wearing a poncho during my warm-up walk and the plan was to ditch it just as the race began.

I arrived at the Super Dome with time to spare and found my friends with whom I had spent the last half year training. We were all psyched and ready to get out there running. Our coaches went over some last minute details including starting out slowly and gradually increasing our pace.

Quicker than I had expected, we were called to form up and get ready to begin. There were so many people running this race that I felt more like a cow being herded than a runner taking a jog. The race began and I started jogging with my group of six friends.

Waving as I passed Ben and Dawn I realized the enormous challenge that was before me. I was starting a run that would go on for more than four hours and surpass 26 miles! The sudden understanding left me momentarily agape.

It did not take long for me to get into a nice groove. As our coaches had mentioned, I was feeling as if I could run faster. I held those feelings back and worked a steady rhythm to match my associates. As a team that had spent countless days training together, we ran like a well-oiled machine.

At the first water station I noticed that the folks were also handing out beer. I gladly grabbed a small paper cup of Budweiser and chugged it in early celebration of my marathon. The beer went down a little rough and I started to question my weird hydration tactics. Inwardly I promised myself that I would only accept water and Gatorade for the remainder of my run.

We passed the five-mile mark without any problems and I was feeling antsy about picking up the pace. I asked some of the others how they were feeling and there were mixed emotions about increasing our speed.

Subconsciously I knew that if I still felt strong after the eight-mile mark, I was going to make a break and pull ahead of the group.

Sure enough I was feeling like a million bucks as I passed eight miles and I explained to the group that I was planning to turn it up a notch. Most of them were happy with the current pace and wanted to keep it. But, a couple of folks were actually excited about speeding up and they joined me in the faster jog.

Our group was a tight-knit one that encouraged each other and helped to carry us through tough spots. I cannot imagine what it must be like running this type of challenge without friends along to support you. I was extremely thankful for this throng of friends who were crazy enough to run with me.

At twelve miles I felt extremely strong. I held my head high as I again passed Ben and Dawn who were screaming my name. Occasionally someone I did not recognize yelled my name out also. This was because I wrote my name in large clear letters on my tank top before starting the race. The funny part is that some of the folks I was running with did not write their names, so people cheered them on by calling out, "Good job, Vaughn's friend!" This cracked us up as we continued our run with chins high in the air.

I had just passed mile marker 16 and felt better than ever. I actually picked my pace up a hair and felt strong and able. Throughout the race, my partners had split, come back, and split again. We found that it was tough staying together through potty breaks and the like. Speaking of potty, at one point I needed to go pretty bad and there was not one portable john in sight. I scanned the area and saw that some men were relieving themselves on the side yard of a local house. I knew this was not a kosher thing, but I needed to go so bad that I felt like I would burst. So, I jogged away from the crowd and joined the guys in a line of urination that could only happen during a marathon type event. And, did I mention that we were in New Orleans?

Back in the swing of things with an empty bladder I ran with a reckless abandon and easily got past the 20-mile point. Random people were still screaming my name and cheering me on. I was growing fond of having the crowd chant my name as I passed certain areas. It was invigorating to come around a corner panting and chugging along to hear a crowd singing your name in unison. This writing your name on your shirt thing was the bomb!

Mile 24 just passed (or did I just pass 25?) and I was no longer a part of the rational world. I was officially pushed beyond anything I had ever done. My mind shutdown normal thinking and had me in autopilot. Everything blurred as I continued my autonomous gait. I could not figure out how much longer I would be running, but my body was starting to complain in a serious way. There was a mutiny coming on and I was not sure if I could control it.

I heard someone scream, "Only one mile to go!" and my body let out a sigh of relief. It literally felt as though I had been running for days. My hamstrings had been cramping for quite a while and every possible muscle was aching with pain. I was surprised to find that even my neck and wrists were sore. I never realized how much of a toll this task would wreak on my body.

Suddenly my coach Steve appeared from out of nowhere and started jogging with me. His lips move, but I can't hear what he's saying. I smiled and nodded my head at appropriate times and then lucidly heard his last question, "Why don't you sprint in for the last half-mile?"

Clarity rang in and pushed all nebulous and negative thoughts away. My will took over for an insane second and agreed, *Yes. Why don't I sprint in!* I turned to Steve and smiled in agreement.

Digging deeper into myself than imaginable I commanded my inner banshee to complete this task with a level of dignity by running the last section of this Godforsaken race at full pace. My body screamed back a determined negative answer, but it was too late. My mind was back in the driver's seat and was going for broke. I felt exhilarated as my legs pump beyond pain and into the next level of surreal attack. I was running with all of my might at a dead sprint. I approached the Super Dome for two minutes as if I was running the 40-yard dash.

Surprisingly, my legs and body were able to keep up this insane pace as I entered the tunnel and rounded the last corner before the finish line. In a full out run, I crossed the finish line with steam to spare. I slowed my pace to screaming cheers from the gathered crowd.

Remembering the advice of my coaches I eased into a brisk walk and continue to walk around for five minutes. During this time, I noticed Dawn and Ben and approached them for a sweaty victory hug. After some more walking and easy stretches, I finally sat down and felt the heavy weight slip off of my back.

I finished the marathon with a time of 4:38:17. I was a little disappointed that I did not beat my 4:30 goal, but was grateful to cross the finish line in one piece.

Four days of sheer agony and muscle pain reminded me of the daunting mission that I had completed. I ran a marathon and nobody can ever take that away from me.

Check one more thing off of my long bucket list.

* * *

Back home, Trinity was continuing her battle to survive at Children's Hospital and the doctors informed us that she had gotten methicillin resistant staphylococcus aureus (MSRA). MSRA (pronounced "mersa") is a form of staph infection that is a tougher strain to heal. This infection is prevalent at hospitals and affects many babies in situations like hers. The hospital put her on antibiotics to fight it and they were hopeful that it would not affect her in any prolonged way.

Apparently, other babies in the hospital had MSRA and nurses transfer it by walking between areas. Kristine and I found this a tad bit disturbing, but understand that there are relative risks and complications involved with hospital stays.

Finally after more than three weeks of torment and despair, we were able to bring baby Trinity home. She was, and is, truly a marvelous gift and wonder. Kristine and I felt so fortunate after all we had been through to have this gem living at home with us.

I melt internally every time that twinkling set of eyes catch mine and hold my gaze. Each day brings new discoveries and fantastic revelations. I never fully understood what others meant by the magic of a baby until I experienced it firsthand.

* * *

After my marathon, my body weight had gotten down to 150 pounds. So, I quickly adjusted my workouts to include muscle mass and weight gain. Before long, I gained ten pounds and felt eons stronger.

The mass training was short-lived though because I needed to adjust my training to incorporate aerobic capacity for my Mount Rainier attempt in the upcoming summer. I adjusted my training yet again to reduce the amount of time-spent weight lifting and started concentrating on heavy burdened hiking. I also had started utilizing my VersaClimber to put some oomph into my climbing ability and body endurance.

It did not take long for my body to adjust to these strenuous activities and my aerobic capacity was surging forward to unfound areas. My neighbors probably started to wonder about the weird guy that put on severe weather plastic hiking boots and mowed the lawn with a 50-pound backpack on.

As my training intensified, I realized that I had spent the majority of my life doing some form of exercise or another. I started looking into and investigating possible personal training avenues and found that my experience fit nicely with many certification programs available. Then I hand selected a couple of certification programs and carefully scrutinized each of them considering getting a personal trainer certification.

I spoke with my cousin, Danae, who is a Certified Conditioning Specialist (CCS) and found that her program from the National Strength Professional's Association (NSPA) was a comprehensive program that was well suited to my style of training. I e-mailed their office and requested more information on the program.

Deciding on the NSPA Certified Personal Trainer (CPT) program, I ordered the training materials and scheduled my class time. Before long, I was learning more about anatomy, muscles, and body strength then I had ever imagined. I quickly absorbed all of the knowledge I could and then attended several classes.

Feeling that my skills and knowledge were at a high point, I planned a time to take the CPT test and took it. I passed with room to spare and felt very accomplished with this tough task. My plans include additional training and further certification, but for now I intend to grow my knowledge the old fashioned way; through practice.

Chapter Twenty-One

Having a baby gave Kristine and me the seven-year itch. That is the seven-year house itch. We had lived in our house in Germantown for seven years and were ready to move on to something new. The little girl was incentive to find a place and get nestled in to a nice new home.

We searched far and wide, before finally finding a cute new development in Brunswick, Maryland. We talked it over and decided it would be a good idea to move. Knowing that I was planning to take a job with the federal government in Washington, DC, we opted for Brunswick, because of the commuter train.

We happily picked our lot, house and options. From the time the builder broke ground until our house was completed, Kristine, Trinity, and I faithfully drove out to Brunswick each weekend to check on progress.

* * *

After working in the commercial world for my entire life, I finally decided to take a stab at government employee work. I found a fantastic group of efficient and highly intelligent people that worked together in a cohesive fashion that I had only dreamed of prior to now.

The director of this tight-knit group, named Ashok, quickly became my friend and we instantly saw where I could fit into his organization. We spent a little bit of time figuring out how I could be best utilized and decided in tandem that it would be beneficial to have me come on board. So, I applied for the position and quickly found out that I was accepted.

After submitting my resignation to Oracle, I started work for the United States government in the esteemed Department of Justice. My coworkers and I quickly hit it off and they welcomed me into their arms.

I have built many friendships with some wonderful folks. In addition to my immediate friendships, I also have meaningful amity with countless other people that I work with day in and day out.

Working with this extremely efficient group of people has grown my business sense in ways that I had not imagined possible. I am adding technologies and skills to my resume every day. I feel a kinship and connection with each of my coworkers that is hard to explain. Suffice it to say that I found my niche and I think that I will hang around for quite a while.

* * *

On May 19, 2005 my stepsister Becky and her fiancée Bill were married in a great ceremony that brought several families together and built lasting relationships. I had the distinct honor of reading a bible verse during their ceremony and it touched my heart as well as hitting home.

During the festivities I was dancing and ended up breaking my finger. Somehow, my hand got caught under my shoe while I was performing the splits. I am such a klutz!

Since their marriage, Becky and Billy have grown even closer with Kristine and me. They are wonderful people with high expectations and aspirations.

Chapter Twenty-Two

My elbow was starting to cramp up along with my neck and lower back. I shifted my body around in the tight quarters for the third time in fewer than five minutes. My elbow has a tendency to give me trouble because of the cartilage damage from the many bleeds it sustained when I was a child.

As I shifted to find a more comfortable position, *Self Rescue* (a book I was reading), fell off of my thigh and thumped to the ground. I sighed with displeasure as I reached to retrieve my book. The confined space kept me a mere two inches from touching the paperback. Finally, with a grunt and stretch, I was able to pick the book up and return to an upright position.

Leaning back I closed my eyes and tried to think happy thoughts. My neck was aching more than ever and I turned my head to the left as I tilted it slightly to try and crack the pained vertebrae. Opening my eyes I peered out the oblong airline window. Glaring back at me was Mount Rainier. *Insert eerie music here*

The hair on the back of my neck stood on end as Rainier sat menacingly in the middle of nowhere calling my name. The summit of Rainier is 14,412 feet above sea level and the base is approximately at sea level. The elevation change from base to top is a longer distance than a climb from base camp to the summit on Mount Everest! Rainier is also one of the deadliest mountains to climb in the 48 contiguous states.

Dreamily staring at the crater on the top of the mountain, I envisioned standing up there. If my plans succeeded, I would be up there in fewer than four days.

It was Sunday, June 19, 2005. My wife and daughter were with me at the end of our last leg of a flight to visit Tacoma, Washington. Our plan was to stay with my brother and his wonderful family for a week. The true meaning behind our trip was my summit attempt on the challenging Mount Rainier.

Smiling, I turned away from the window to face Kristine. She was white with worry as she stared past me at the lone mountain that threatened to take her husband away from her.

I comforted her with a pat on the arm and a quick, "Nothing to worry about, honey." Minutes later we were on final approach to Seattle-Tacoma International Airport. *Nothing to worry about.*

$$* * *$$

Our party consisted of eight men from all over the country. My experience stemmed completely from rock climbing so it amounted to rope use skills and fancy footwork. Because I lived in Maryland, I had no glacier experience. Not to mention the fact that I have lived at nearly sea level all of my life. My brother Scean lived in Tacoma and also had no glacier experience. Scott (a true outdoorsman) had been up Rainier three times before this attempt and had climbed most of the peaks in the Cascade mountain range, not to mention doing a lot of rock climbing in the area as well. Paul lived in Phoenix Arizona and had no glacier experience. Charles (AKA: the Machine) and Mike (AKA: Buzz Saw) were also from Phoenix and had lots of hiking experience, but no glacier experience. Another Mike (AKA: Sky-high) was from the Tacoma area and was a small aircraft pilot and aerial photographer with some glacier experience. I met Mike a week earlier via the cascadeclimbers.com Rainier forum. Roy was from Oregon and was a commercial airline pilot. By the end of our summit bid, only three of our eight-man party actually made it to the summit.

Six of us left Scean's house at 4:32 a.m. during a typical Tacoma mild drizzle. The two others in our group had camped the night before at Cougar (in Mount Rainier National Park). Our packs were loaded in an open trailer connected to Scean's minivan. The trip to the Longmire Entrance took about 90 minutes, and the drizzle turned to a slight rain during this time. From Longmire, it was nearly a 30-minute drive through the park to Paradise. Once we arrived in Paradise, Sky-high Mike and his friend Roy were already waiting. We checked in at the ranger station and changed into rain gear for our hike up to and through the Muir Snowfield.

Our actual hike was underway by 8 a.m. and the weather was pretty miserable. The fog/cloud cover was pretty dense, and it was raining and chilly. Most of us were wet under our rain gear, because we had been out in our under-layers before adding a waterproofed outer-layer. Also, our backpacks were thoroughly drenched and many of the packs were wet inside as well.

We hiked up from the trailhead and headed up the rocky Skyline Trail toward Pebble Creek in on-and-off rainfall. The hike to Pebble Creek went smoothly. Even though we were all in excellent shape (especially for our ages), the steepness of the trail combined with heavy packs took its toll on us all.

Pebble Creek was a broad field of smooth rocks that had a moderate-sized creek running down the middle of it. The water running down and through the stones was creating a soothing melody that threatened to put me to sleep.

By the time we reached Pebble Creek the rain had turned into sleet with an occasional snowfall burst. We rested briefly before moving onto the Muir Snowfield.

Clambering up the snow, mud, and slush we peaked over a ledge at the vast plain called the Muir Snowfield. Even in the heavy freezing rain and snow we could see the huge size and presence of the snowfield that was literally the beginning of our actual mountain climb.

My body was already screaming from the intense hike up the dirt trail and my stomach turned sour as I peered into the whiteout conditions of Rainier. On top of the heavy snow, the wind was trying to creep in under my layers and chill my bones (it was doing a pretty good job I might add). The snow was thick and produced a whiteout with only 30 feet of vision during the best times. As we went up the snowfield, our party broke up a bit as stronger hikers moved up quicker. Scott, Roy, Charles, and Scean were leading the pack with a quick pace. Paul and I were not far behind with a medium pace. And, the two Mikes were at the rear at a leisurely pace.

As I stomped up the base of the mountain, I thought about the McClure rock; which lay somewhere to my right. I knew the story about a Chemistry Professor named Edgar McClure who fell to his death in 1897. His death was the first recorded fatal accident on Rainier. The whiteout conditions were prime for just such an accident.

Death is routine on Mount Rainier. A month prior to our epic climb the mountain had killed two people. A search party on the Paradise Glacier discovered their bodies. It was evident that they had wandered off route while descending during poor visibility similar to ours.

Fortunately for us, one of the previous guided expeditions had placed *wands* (poles with little orange flags on the top) in the snow to point out the proper path to Camp Muir; which lay hours above us. For the most part, we were able to find and follow these wands.

Hours into our hike, Paul and I had found a nice pace and were pumping away in our ascent of the Muir Snowfield. Without warning, there was a cracking sound that split the quiet morning and we slowed to a stop. Looking toward Paul I wondered, *What the hell was that?* The mountain was alive and dangerous.

As Paul and I looked at each other a light rumble was growing and quickly became a viscously loud thunder. As the roar increased in volume, the ground started to shake. It was as if the mountain was shaking to frighten us away. Suddenly I realized at the same time as Paul that this was an avalanche.

My lower lip quivered and I watched wide-eyed as the color was draining from Paul's face. I am sure Paul was seeing a similar reaction in my face, but we did not have time to talk about it.

The hair on the back of my neck was standing so stiff that it could have pierced drywall. Without a moment to spare, Paul and I did the only feasible option available to our Neanderthal minds. We stood there quaking like two deer caught in headlights.

Fortunately, the rumbling earthquake sound shifted and it was apparent that the avalanche was off to our left in the Nisqually icefall. The mountain was not trying to kill us after all, it was merely warning us. I cannot relay the feelings that passed through me, but suffice it to say that it was exciting. If we had not been in a whiteout, I am sure that the avalanche would have been very cool looking. Paul and I smiled nervously at each other and then continued our trek up the snow-covered slope.

After about seven hours of hardcore steep hiking, I felt as though I could not go on any further. I was feeling the effects of the altitude mixed with the 60-pound backpack. I stopped to take a breather and questioned myself for going through this insane agony. As I caught my breath and looked up, the whiteout conditions cleared just a hair and allowed a view further up my path. Only about 100 yards up the hill were several stone structures. Camp Muir!

My heart leapt and I trudged on knowing that my pain would ease shortly. Obviously the mountain saw that I was considering turning back like a coward and therefore lifted the whiteout veil momentarily to beckon me onward into its greedy maw.

As I approached Camp Muir, I was mesmerized. There were half a dozen stone buildings up there. I could not fathom how someone found the energy to move these enormous stones around up there and build structures. It was mind boggling to say the least. We were already well above the *timberline* (the altitude where vegetation and trees can no longer grow), so all of the wood incorporated in these buildings had to have been carried up there. On top of that, the buildings looked fairly ancient and I imagined them being built in a time before plastic boots and Gore-Tex.

Walking into Camp Muir, I pulled out my GPS and read our current elevation reading. I already knew our altitude from several books I had read. However, I wanted to see it written out. Our altitude was 10,080 feet above sea level. Seeing the five-digit figure displayed before me and knowing that I had hiked to this elevation partially rejuvenated me.

The hike up there had been very rough on us all (both mentally and physically). Up until this point in my life, I had only been up to 3,000 feet above sea level (outside of a car or airplane). On my trek up Rainier's base to Camp Muir, I had gone from sea level to just above 10,000 feet in fewer than ten hours! It was taking a toll on all of us. Paul was pretty sick at Camp Muir. He was dehydrated, cold, dizzy, and probably suffering from small amounts of Acute Mountain Sickness (AMS). Mike was also suffering and not feeling well. Charles (hence his nickname: the Machine) did not appear to be worn in the least. Charles has hiked up or climbed 34 plus peaks with an altitude of 14,000 feet or more and Rainier did not seem to bother him at all. Also, he was in such good shape that he hiked up the snowfield more like a cyborg than a man. Charles also recently published the book, *60 Hikes within 60 Miles: Phoenix.*

Because of the whiteout conditions and low cloud cover, we were unable to see Gibraltar Rock until reaching Camp Muir. Gibraltar Rock is the most prominent rock feature on the mountain and can be easily seen from Tacoma on a clear day. When the blizzard calmed and allowed a peek at this massive rock I stood agape. I had seen so many pictures and expected to be amazed, but this was unreal. The rock was immense. One funny part of the mountain is if you have not been there, you think you understand the scope and size because you have seen pictures and heard stories. I am here to tell you, if you have not been on the mountain, you cannot comprehend how vast and out of proportion everything is up there. For example, many of the crevasses are more than 300 feet deep and appear bottomless and the glaciers are sheets of ice extending thousands of feet across.

I marched up to the front door of the camping hut, which was a thick wooden door that looked as though it belonged on a castle entrance. The rough-hewn stone of the building was meticulously stacked and mortared in an olden day fashion. Stepping in, I was surprised by the commodiousness. To my left there was a wall of bunks for sleeping and the right side was a long shelf where campers cooked their foods and melted snow for water.

Unfortunately, the floor was concrete and had a layer of muck and water. We had to drop our packs into this sludge since they were already wet and could not fit on the shelves.

The "hut" only accommodated a dozen people. Fortunately, only a couple of people were staying in it, and our whole party was able to setup camp inside. I had heard lots of nasty stories about staying in the hut, and the only one that I agree with is the "hard to sleep because of noise" story. The "noise" that everyone was referring to, was the snoring of other climbers. That mixed with the clinking and clanking of hikers wandering in at any hour made for a rough night's sleep to say the least. The reason I could not sleep that night was because of the torrential snoring from Mike (hence his nickname: Buzz Saw). Even with my earplugs securely inserted, I could hear Mike's erratic snoring.

When we went to bed at about 8 p.m. the weather was still bad and we could not see much of anything in the whiteout conditions. Even Gibraltar Rock, which was right next to the camp, was only visible for seconds at a time when the storm let up momentarily. We decided that if the whiteout was still a problem at midnight that we would jump back into bed and forget about climbing that evening. We all set our watch alarms to wake us at 12 a.m., but this proved pointless because I did not sleep at all and was sitting up before the beeping started.

Most climbers start their trek to the summit from Camp Muir at around 1 a.m. This ensures that your climb down will occur in the morning when the ice and snow are still frozen and hard. If you come down later than that, you chance hiking in muddy slush conditions that can prove to be very dangerous.

At midnight I sat up in bed and pulled my useless earplugs out of my ears. I had not slept one wink and yet was refreshed at the idea of climbing this mountain. Running outside to check the weather, I found the sky was perfectly clear. Without a doubt, our weather had rolled away and left behind a brilliant sky that was lit up by the full moon. Our bid for the summit would happen after all.

Going back inside the hut, I heartily informed the party about the miraculous change in the weather. Each of them grunted and groaned as they made their way outside to see for themselves. Before long, the entire hut was joyfully cooking breakfast and bustling around getting ready to roll.

Paul and his friend Mike were both in pretty poor shape after the hike up to high camp and decided that they would not attempt to summit. We agreed to break our party into two rope-groups of three men each. It took us nearly 90 minutes to cook, eat, pack, and get dressed. After that, we moved outside and started roping up. We were not ready to start our adventure until nearly 2 a.m.

For several years leading up to this crazy adventure I had planned to take the *Gibraltar Ledges* route; which made its way up the left side of the Gibraltar Rock. The neat (and scary) thing about the "Gib Ledges" route was that you get a nice 1,000-foot drop from the ledges down into the Gibraltar Chute. Unfortunately, a week prior to our trip an experienced climber slipped and fell 900 feet to his death in this same "neat" area. Apparently some years Gib Ledges is more stable than others. With this in mind, we decided at the last minute to take the *Disappointment Cleaver* route. Both routes were equally rated as easy (for Mount Rainier standards), so we were comfortable with our decision to change routes.

The rope teams consisted of Sky-high Mike, Roy, and Charles on one team and Scott, Scean, and me on the other. Clicking on our headlamps we trudged out of high camp and started on the beaten path to the top. As it turned out, the moon was full and so bright that headlamps were not necessary. Every couple of minutes I would glance at the moon and was struck by how clear and close it looked from up on the mountain.

The initial hike across the Cowlitz Glacier was uneventful and fairly easy. It consisted of a tedious one-foot-after-the-other routine that lasted about an hour. My rope team started out in the lead, as we trekked along the corridor created in the ice field by the men and women who had traveled before us. Once we arrived at the far side of the glacier, we had to make our way up a broken rock path, which consisted of ice, snow, rocks, pebbles, and a mud like paste. This dangerous mixture cut a passageway through the Cathedral Gap that brought us onto the Ingraham Glacier.

We arrived at the other side of Cathedral's Gap and faced the Ingraham Glacier around 3:30 a.m. We decided to allow the other rope team to pass us, because they were hiking at a quicker clip than we were.

After a short hike up the Ingraham Glacier, we arrived at Ingraham's

Flat, which is a common high camp area for potential summit groups. There were several tents in the "flats" as we trudged on by.

I read my GPS shortly after the Ingraham's Flat and found that we were just above 11,100 feet. I was invigorated to know that we had climbed so high in such a short amount of time.

Soon after passing the flats, we stopped to watch the sunrise; which happened around 4:20 a.m. We took a couple of pictures and pressed on with a sloth-like stride that imperceptibly moved us closer to our goal.

As we approached the *icebox* (the nickname of a dangerous section on the Ingraham Glacier), I could not believe how immense the ice blocks (called seracs) actually were. Many were bigger than houses and ominously loomed overhead in a precariously steep chute just begging to break free and crush an entire party. As a matter of fact, I remembered a horror story of an entire party of ten people and their guide that had been killed by falling seracs in this same place. As I thought about that macabre account I realized that we were going through the Icebox on the same exact month and almost the same day that it had happened back in 1981. None of the eleven climbers were recovered from that incident, which was the worst disaster in Rainier's history. Continuing toward the icebox, a chill ran up my spine as I envisioned the frozen bodies scattered all around us, under the blanket of snow. Because of the dangers in the icebox, all of the guidebooks suggest rushing through that section.

Once in the icebox, I marveled at the awesomeness. It was inexplicable and bizarre. Each ice block was a thing of beauty and they tilted threateningly toward me. With a *thousand-yard stare*, I paused and looked at the massive walls of ice. I was enamored by the sheer magnitude.

"What the hell are you doing?" Scott screamed.

Snapping to, I turned toward him grinning and looked innocently with a questioning stare.

"Dude! Move on. This area is extremely dangerous. Move!"

Waking up, I realized what he was saying and I shuffled out of the icebox. I had really been captivated by the unbelievable size and beauty of the ice blocks. This fascination had curbed my fear of being crushed. Actually being there and seeing it helped me to comprehend why people are killed standing in that section. If Scott had not yelled, I might have spent several more minutes soaking it all in.

We continued our cadence.

One foot in front of the other—

Trudge—

Breathe—

Step—

Breathe—

Step—

I was quickly starting to feel the effects of the extreme altitude and my head was pounding with pain. It was not long before I started seeing weird aura type colors and had trouble breathing. Taking a break, I spent several minutes just unclipping my backpack to try and relieve some of the crushing pressure I was feeling on my chest. To my dismay, once the pack was unfastened, I was still having trouble breathing. I rested for several minutes trying to catch my breath and finally stood to continue.

A little further up the chopped path we arrived at a crevasse that crossed our path. There was a ladder laid across the five-foot wide hole that appeared to fall endlessly below us. Under normal circumstances, a ladder would be relatively easy to cross. However, standing at 12,000+ feet wearing plastic boots that had metal crampon teeth attached to them was a far cry from normal. During my crossing of the crevasse, I stopped midway and took a photo of the bottomless crevasse that gaped at me through the rungs of the ladder. It was quite a sight looking down those sheer walls of ice. My brother Scean, being partially fearful of falling into the deep chasm, quickly crossed without peering down. Different strokes for different folks, I guess.

My rest breaks were coming much more often and I was feeling fatigued throughout my entire body. Every muscle screamed at me to stop this crazy ascent. My mind was trying to convince me that this climb was suicidal. On top of those emotions and pains, my head was literally exploding internally. I dropped to me knees from fatigue at one point and could not remember what I was doing. I sat there looking at the snow with my ears buzzing and my shallow breaths barely giving my body a livable amount of oxygen. My brother called to me and asked if I was okay. I snapped out of my dreamlike daze and looked up at him. He was wavering in my vision and the mountain was breathing.

I tried to respond to Scean, but my vision was blurry and the mountain breathed again. Squinting I noticed that Scean was hovering in the air, floating back and forth in a listless pendulum. Something was wrong.

This was preposterous! I had trained for more than four months, and there was no way that my body was not prepared for this simple task. I fought an internal battle to force myself to stand. Once up, I dizzily started my hiking cadence again.

Moments later I collapsed again. Once again I was kneeling wondering what I was doing. I picked up my head and yelled, "I need to take a rest."

Scean was baffled, because we had just taken two rests within the last ten minutes, so he decided to hike down to me and see if I was okay. He arrived and asked me how I was feeling. I explained that I was having trouble catching my breath and experiencing hallucinations. While I talked to Scean, the mountain continued to breathe, and it chuckled at me.

Scean looked concerned and was about to voice his opinion to our leader when Scott suddenly lost one of his gloves to the wind. Screaming, "That's not good!" Scott jumped up and took off sprinting out into the crevasse-laden glacier.

Scean snapped to attention as we watched the rope quickly uncoil while Scott ran onto the glacier. Just as the rope was coming to an end, Scean made a decision and leaped to his feet running after Scott.

Everything was surreal as I watched my portion of the rope uncoiling with Scean sprinting away from me. My mind finally woke and tore my consciousness awake. I suddenly realized that we were at a serious risk and it was my job as the last man to have a solid anchor prepared for an emergency. Somehow I dug deep and pooled the last bit of energy I had to focus on the problem at hand. The fastest anchor that I knew was the ice axe under my boot. I plunged my ice axe deep into the snow and quickly wrapped the rope around the shaft a couple of times before stepping onto the *adze* (the back of the axe head) and sitting back with the remainder of rope in my gloved hands.

Fortunately, Scott was able to catch his glove before we tested my hallucinogenic anchoring abilities.

Checking my GPS was a chore to say the least. My garbled mind finally figured out how to use it properly. I read that we had just passed 12,400 feet above sea level. Considering that Rainier was 14,412 feet at the summit, I deducted that we were closer than 2,000 feet from the top. At sea level I could hike a level 2,000 feet in about five minutes. I knew that these 2,000 feet would likely take me a couple of hours, but it tore me up inside to know I was this close and failing. Tears welled in my eyes as I faced the bold truth; my body would not endure the remainder of the climb.

Shortly after the "glove incident," our three-man team decided that I was not in any shape to continue up the mountain. So, we made the decision to descend from our current elevation.

At this point, Scott explained that he had brought his late Father's ashes with him to spread on the summit. He asked if we could wait while he did a little ceremony to release them at our current altitude. Scean and I both agreed to wait while he said his peace. Inside I was crushed, because I realized the sacrifice that Scott was making by turning around at this point. I fought off the tears that tried to escape as I dealt with my pride and humiliating limits.

I had already held Scott with high regard, but he now held an even higher quality in my mind. My heart bled for this extreme gesture that was being made on my account. After the fact though, I comprehend that Scott made the only rational decision possible. Yet, I still greatly appreciated the pain that he had to face when he agreed to return without finishing our summit attempt.

With our tails between our legs, we indolently rambled back down the mountain toward high camp. We found excitement in once again crossing the ladder-bridged crevasse and making our way down a muddy ice covered rock face.

Just before we got back to camp we spotted a Chinook military helicopter flying up near the summit. There must have been some sort of accident or rescue. Seeing the helicopter helped me to realize that we were in a place where people routinely got seriously injured or even killed.

We stayed in radio contact with our other rope team and found that they had made the summit. Inside I was brimming with jealousy at the gumption they had to trudge all of the way to the top. But a voice inside my head forgave me and said, *You may have died if you had tried.* This thought did not make me feel better, but I was content with the fact that my fellow climbers had made the summit.

From high camp, we slowly packed and prepared for our trip down to the parking area. The trip down the Muir Snow Field proved to be quite tedious and painful. Because it was late in the day, the snow had started to melt and become slushy. Since the snow was at least several feet deep, every step sunk our legs beyond the boot and usually to the knee. This became excruciatingly painful after only a short trek. Considering that the trip down from high camp to the parking lot took nearly four hours, by the time we were down, our knees and bodies were blown.

During our trek off the mountain, I heard something that sounded like thunder in the distance. I could not find a cloud in the sky and was wondering what that noise had been when I noticed that Mount Saint Helens was spewing a huge plume of smoke. Apparently it had just had a mild eruption right before our eyes.

I separated from the rest of our group during the last leg of the hike down. My solitude gave me time to think about my accomplishments and failings. I realized that my training needed to be more rigorous and that acclimating for a day longer at the higher altitude may have helped. I finally made it to the parking lot at Paradise and waited for the others.

Once our entire group was together, we assiduously packed the van and trailer. I peered back at the mountain for one final look and it was smiling at me. Anger built inside me—was the mountain mocking me? Without another thought I climbed into Scean's van and we headed back to his home. Before we had gotten home I was already scheming in my mind about my return to Mount Rainier. The mountain had a hold of me.

Clearly I would recommend an attempt on Rainier to anyone and everyone. It was a life-changing event that has only sharpened and clarified my requisite need for adventure.

Vaughn—zero; Mount Rainier—two!

Chapter Twenty-Three

Partly because of Mount Rainier and partly because of my early retirement from riding motorcycles at the track, I renewed my vows with climbing. A close friend and coworker Vig and his wife Quinn (who climbed at a considerably higher level than me) were gracious enough to allow me to join them on some local climbing expeditions.

In addition to Vig and Quinn, I had the old reliable twins Joe and Larry. Also, I rekindled my connection with Indy and have since become close friends with him. Along with these great climbing partners, I have also met and started climbing with Brian, Matt, Kendra, Chris, Aqua, and several others.

* * *

August 5, 2005, Larry, Indy, and I met at Larry's family ranch in Middletown at 7 p.m. While there, I was explaining the reasoning behind buying my new camera and one of the things that I love about it. While I was mid-sentence, Larry's sister, Maria, walked in and caught only part of my sentence, "I prefer small things in my hands." She shot a concerned and sympathetic look my direction—

Noooooooo! Story of my life!

We ate Paula's (Larry's mom) fantastic homemade pizza and split for West Virginia to climb at Seneca Rocks. Larry, Joe, and I had been to Seneca Rocks once before several years ago when we attended our climbing class.

Somewhere along the way in Timbuktu, West Virginia I was pulled over by the fuzz for driving through town with my high beams on. He asked for my license and registration, and when he returned he asked, "Do you know why I pulled you over, Mr. Vaughn?"

I spit back, "It's Mr. Ripley." I immediately regretted my flippant response.

Without delay, the officer asked me if I had been drinking, and I told him, "No." Then he sniffed the area a little bit and his eyes darted to the console, which was where we had our donuts stashed. I could see the avaricious gleam in his eye as he leaned in a little further and furtively asked, "Are you sure you haven't been drinking, son?"

Holding back the urge to pin his face with the power window, I again said, "No."

To which he retorted, "Your eyes look awful glassy."

It took all of my willpower to avoid saying, "Perhaps that is because I'm wearing glasses!"

He finally gave up on the 21 questions, and said, "I'm gonna let you go with a warning this time, Mr. Vaughn." I held back telling him that my *first* name was Vaughn. We rolled on.

Pulling into Seneca Rocks at 10:30 p.m., I parked and we proceeded to pitch our tents at the Shadows Campground. After listening to some girls giggling in a neighboring campsite, we fell asleep.

At 5:56 a.m. I uncovered my eyeballs and heard Indy already rustling. I popped out of my bag and sprinted for the showers. We were at breakfast by 7 a.m. and hiking to the rocks before 8 a.m. Brian, a friend of Indy's, joined us for the day of climbing. Indy and Brian ran off to investigate some climbs they wanted to do while Larry and I proceeded up the "Stair Master" (a steep, tough approach) to get to the "Luncheon Ledge" (which is the base of our proposed climb). Our plan was to climb the three-pitch "Old Lady Route," which is a 5.2 climb (read: extremely easy) that goes up 200 feet total. Because the climb started several hundred feet over the valley floor, the exposure was more like 500 or more feet.

I did not want to carry my backpack up the ascent, so I pulled out my rope bag, harness, and additional gear we would need for our climb, than left the mostly empty backpack at the base of "Old Lady." I led the first pitch, which was an easy sustained 5.2 up the West face of the Southern end. This was my first official lead, so it was a little scary (I am used to the security of being on top rope at all times).

At the top, there was a nice big ledge about 100 feet above the start. I setup a belay station and brought Larry up behind me.

The second pitch was essentially a traverse that Larry did without placing any pro (protection) on it, because there was only one dicey move.

However, the "one move" was exhilarating, because the exposure is grade A. This proved to be a bit harrowing for me, because as luck would have it, a shift of my heavy rope bag nearly popped me off of the one harrowing move. Without any pro, I would have *pendulumed* (swung on the end of the rope in a pendulum fashion) for 40 or more feet!

Not only that, but I probably would have hit about a dozen ledges, shelves, and other rock outcroppings along the way. Suffice it to say, that it would have turned into a very bad day.

From there, Larry belayed me (I was leading again), and I went up and through a neat chimney and over the crux block on top of the chimney to finish on a couple of tough moves that seemed a good bit harder than 5.2 to me. After I was up, I setup the final belay to bring Larry up.

While belaying Larry, I felt as though I was pulling him up with each tug on the rope. So, I screamed down, "Is everything okay?"

After no response, I continued my labored tug-of-war with Larry. I continued in this fashion calling down every now and then to see if he was okay. Unfortunately, the shape of the rocks would not allow my yells to get to him.

Just before Larry got to the top, I realized what all of the muscle straining weight was from. He had decided it was too tough carrying the rope bag and climbing, so he tied the rope bag ahead of himself and let me pull it up. Argh! I muttered a few choice words and helped him conclude his ascent.

As Larry finished climbing up, we started hearing serious thunder approaching from the Southwest. Because lightning strikes are so prevalent on top of rocks and rain obviously makes the rocks slippery and precarious, our situation was quickly approaching dangerous. Brian called down from another area and told us to evacuate immediately via the "Traffic Jam Rappel Station."

That was fine and dandy, except we did not know what or where the "Traffic Jam Rappel" was!

We proceeded to look for the supposed rappel. After asking a couple of scattering climbers, we were finally pointed in the right direction.

Turning the corner that was supposed to lead to our rappel, we saw what looked like a slide to hell! Both sides of the narrow path were sheer walls 20 feet tall. The trail, which was three feet wide, went down and out to an opening on top of the West face. From up top, it appeared that the trail went right out and over a cliff.

Larry agreed to hip belay me for safety and I went down to check it out.

By now, lightning was striking fairly close and in an ominous fashion.

I got out to the end of the "slide to Hell" and found a large tree there with a sheer drop of more than 180 feet. My nerves were tingling to say the least. I did not see any rappel station per se, but I figured we could *rap* (rappel) using the tree. The other problem we faced was we had one 60-meter rope and one 50-meter rope. This rappel was long. It required two 60-meter ropes tied together to reach the ground. By tying our two ropes together, we would run off the ends about 20 feet off the deck! Yikers!

As I was pondering all of this, the storm continued coming in fast and furious. I kept remembering stories that I had read and heard about folks being struck by lightning up on top of tall rocks.

Just as I felt that all hope was lost and nearly gave into doing the crazy rappel anyway, Indy poked his head around the corner. With a grin he asked, "How are you guys doing?"

My heart leapt! I thought Indy and Brian had already rappelled to safer ground. A warm and fuzzy feeling sped through my body as Indy and Brian came down and said that they would rappel with us. Looking at Larry with a smile, I noticed a huge amount of relief on his pale expression as well.

Brian quickly pointed out that there was in fact a rappel station made of chains and rings bolted into the rock face. I had completely overlooked it. Also, Indy had an extra 60-meter; which we tied to mine to create the proper length for our descent.

Indy and Brian assisted and guided us through our first "exciting" rappel in our lives. Once at the bottom I trekked over to the beginning of our climb to retrieve my backpack, and then we were heading down the trail to go back to our campsite.

Back at camp, we took a beer and pizza break. We sat with many other folks gabbing about the harrowing experience while the storm raged on. When the rain faded away, we played football and Frisbee with a nice group of ex-Greenpeace folks.

We finally got to bed at 11:30 p.m. The next morning seemed to come pretty quickly. We showered, ate breakfast, and then packed up for our trip to Cumberland for some additional climbing at "the Narrows." The ride to Cumberland was uneventful and the weather was beautiful.

All in all, it was a fantastic first lead that will always remain in my mind as a most excellent adventure with Larry, Brian, and Indiana Mark. I got my money's worth for sure!

* * *

For years I have read about and seen information related to flying in ancient aircraft at specialized air shows. In August 2005 I finally decided it was time to once again put my life on a limb and go try this adventure on for size. Kristine, Trinity, and I met my father, George, at the Bealton's Flying Circus; which is located in a farmer's field in Northern Virginia.

George had done some careful reconnaissance prior to our arrival and found a biplane that was the fastest and most maneuverable of them all. It was a 1930 open-cockpit barnstorming Fleet biplane. It only had 160HP (fewer than my Hayabusa motorcycle had at the wheel). This particular airplane was used during World War II to train pilots. I signed up for and took a 20-minute acrobatic flight as a passenger in this marvelous machine. It was awesome!

The pilot asked me if I had a weak stomach, to which I coolly replied, "Nah."

Smiling, the pilot started our bumpy ride across a cow pasture that doubled as a runway. Once in the air, I felt the freedom of this mystical open cockpit-flying contraption. We climbed at a slow rate and then suddenly did a loop. This was followed by a barrel roll and then a spin. We continued doing several more loops, barrel rolls, spins, aileron rolls, snap rolls, the Cuban 8, and a split "S" among other maneuvers.

Next, the pilot gracefully climbed up to 2,250 feet, and the plane slowed as we hit the crescendo of the climb and he allowed the plane's wings to stall. After this stall, the nose fell forward and we started to drop at an alarming rate toward the ground. During this drop, the pilot turned the biplane and we started to spin. The ground was approaching in a dizzying array of blurred images. As we drew near an eminent crash landing, the engine started sputtering, crackling, puffing, and choking. The 75-year old engine finally let out a loud bang just in time to pull our diving nose up and away from the ground. I was exhilarated and it showed with the ear-to-ear grin across my face.

The end came too soon as we landed bumpily back in the cow pasture. It was really cool sitting in that old piece of equipment straight from a time that we have forgotten (in the front seat mind you) directly under the top wing feeling the wind blow through your hair as you follow the birds and enjoy one of man's greatest creations, the flying contraption.

Try it—you'll like it.

* * *

After two months of living with my gracious aunt and uncle, Kristine, Trinity, and I moved into our new house in Brunswick, Maryland. Since Kristine and I were both from the big city, it was quite a culture shock to move out to the "sticks", but we quickly adapted. This quaint town that resides on the Potomac River is a fun place full of caring and sharing people. It is a different way of life when you move a bit away from the city. Things slow down, and Brunswick has a small town feel with lots of family activities.

Some of our decision to move to Brunswick entailed me being able to ride the train into Washington. This greatly reduced my daily stress that was derived from "rush hour" traffic. The name "rush hour" is a joke to me, since the traffic seems to last considerably more time than an "hour." Essentially, my white-knuckle escapades with the other lemmings had ended and turned into a peaceful train ride into the heart of the city each day. My train commute takes the same amount of time that I used to take driving, but now I can kick back and let someone else do the driving. On top of that, I now have time to read and keep up with e-mails. And, I get plenty of studying in. But, beyond a shadow of a doubt, the greatest attribute gained by the train is the fact that I was finally able to bang away at this autobiography and finish it.

Brunswick is a sweet town with lots of character. It has given me the gift of remembering my belief in chivalry. I am a firm and strong believer in being loving to mankind. I feel it is necessary to open and hold the door for others. And, in some ways, the inner city was slowly draining that inherent belief. This old-fashioned town that borders Harper's Ferry has given that precious idea back to me.

I truly love it, and will probably remain here for quite some time. Besides, I have lots more writing to do and I must ride the train to accomplish it.

* * *

After believing for two years that I had beaten hepatitis C, my gastroenterology doctor's office called me to explain that there had been some mistakes by the laboratory that gave me my blood test. Apparently the blood lab had mistakenly told many people that they were negative to this debilitating disease and later found out that they were wrong in many cases.

This shocked me and immediately sent my mind reeling with anguish, as I feared that I had not beaten this dreadful disease after all.

I immediately called Kristine and as usual she comforted me and explained that this did not mean that I had hepatitis again. She soothed me by telling me how healthy I was and how good things had been going. She has always been there to pick me up when I am feeling down and for that I am forever in debt and deeply in love.

Feeling comforted by her pep talk, I could not help having the feeling in the back of my mind that I actually still had hepatitis and this was some sick joke that the world was playing on me. I decided to lock out the fear and get busy (as usual) figuring this situation out.

I set an appointment to have my blood work taken and retested. After giving the blood I crossed my fingers and went on with my life.

* * *

The Washington Redskins fought their way into the playoffs during the 2005 season. My dad and I decided to fly out to Washington State to visit my brother Scean and watch them play the Seattle Seahawks. So, in the middle of January we packed our bags for a long weekend and flew out there.

Kristine and Trinity came along for the ride and Trinity got some quality time with her cousins. The game was wet and cold, which was not surprising since Seattle was working on setting a new record for days of rainfall. We pitched a tarp for cover and cooked kielbasa on Scean's grill early in the morning before the game.

As you may know, the Seahawks went on to win that game, but it was fun anyway. Since Scean is a turncoat and now roots for Seattle it worked out for him.

We spent the rest of the extended weekend with Scean, Monica, and the kids before flying back home. It was a long trip for a single weekend but worth every minute of it.

Here I was nearly 40 years old and still relishing time with my dad and brother. I suppose I always will.

* * *

Shortly after arriving home from Seattle, my doctor's office called me to explain that my hepatitis test was still negative. This was a surging relief, and Kristine and I celebrated this latest finding. It lifted a weight from my chest knowing that I had once again beaten this terrible disease.

This goes to show that I should not worry about things outside my control and I need to leave some things in the hands of the Lord and or science.

* * *

Trinity had a bad cough for several days and we decided to take her in to her pediatrician to get checked out. At the doctor's office, we found out that she had an ear infection. They prescribed Amoxicillin and we gave it to her for the next eight days.

She was supposed to take the antibiotic for ten days, but we stopped because her body was covered with a hive-like rash (from head to toe). The doctor explained that she was most likely allergic to Penicillin. He told us to stop the antibiotic and start using Benadryl to help calm the hives and allow her to rest.

So, the cough and breathing issues came back with a wrath, but the rash slowly cleared up. Kristine took her back to the pediatrician's office and they were worried about her low oxygen saturation and called an ambulance for her.

From there, Kristine and Trinity rode to Shady Grove Hospital and she was worked on in the emergency room. Her *SPO2* (saturated pulse oxygen level) was down at 84 and the doctor gave her an oral steroid that would supposedly help. They also put her on constant oxygen and periodic Racepinephrine and Albuterol Sulfate (about every two hours).

Finally we were able to take her home that evening. The next morning Kristine brought Trinity in for a follow-up appointment with her pediatrician and they again sent her via ambulance to Shady Grove, telling us that they were surprised that the hospital had sent her home.

During all of this, I was at work looking up oxygen saturation on the web and finding that prolonged lower levels can cause brain damage (later the doctor told me not to read that junk—easy for them to say!)

Trinity's treatment picked-up again and her SPO2 level was 86 (a normal level is 94 or greater). We tormented through the day before I finally went home and rested. Kristine was worn out when I arrived the next morning, because she had stayed up all night trying to keep her oxygen hose close to her. The hospital had put Trinity in an oxygen tent, because her SPO2 level dropped to 78 in the night. But, Trinity kept fighting her way out and Kristine was forced to spend the night by her side in the tent helping out.

The doctor explained that Trinity would be staying at least one more night, perhaps more depending upon some of the X-ray and trachea exam outcomes.

She ended up staying five more days, because until then, she was still having slight trouble maintaining good oxygen saturation. And, she was not eating her normal amount. Some of the lack of eating was attributed to the fact that they had her on an IV and she was not quite as hungry.

She fussed with the tape around the IV and was finally able to tear it off and remove the needle. The nurses decided to leave it out, because by now, Trinity was eating better and more regularly.

After six long days and nights, Trinity was finally allowed to come home with us. Unfortunately, she had caught a stomach virus while at the hospital and spent several of the next days throwing up. *Sheesh.*

Chapter Twenty-Four

One of my co-workers decided to make Fridays "Hawaiian shirt day." Because Ashok allows (he actually encourages this) us to dress more casually on Friday, this Hawaiian shirt day actually caught on. We all started wearing brightly colored shirts that were covered with palm trees and pineapples.

On one Friday afternoon, I was wearing my coolest Hawaiian shirt that was a delicate balance of yellow, red, and blue. It was plastered with pink flamingos and a beautiful sunset. It was a fantastic example of what Hawaiian shirts had to offer.

I was riding the train home and we were approaching my station, so I stood and filed along with the rest of the cattle to stand patiently awaiting the conductor to open the door for us. This particular day, I was waiting in a section of the train affectionately called the "party car." This car received its name because it was famous for the wild drinking and partying that happened on there. They were once filmed by a local news crew and even made the evening news!

Suddenly, one of the party animals, named Eric, called to me by saying "Hey, shirt man."

I was pretty sure he was talking to me, because I was the only one wearing a crazy shirt, but I acted as if I had no idea what or whom he was addressing.

Again, he called out, "Hey, shirt man."

I innocently turned toward him and caught eyes. He was looking right at me with a smile.

Eric said, "I am going to Vegas this weekend and I need a cool shirt. I will give you forty dollars for that shirt."

The shirt had cost me a mere $25. And I knew that Eric was mostly trying to be funny to his friends, so I shot back, "Make it sixty and you've got a deal."

Suddenly the raucous crowd went dead silent and everyone was eyeing us. Eric was being called out and put in a precarious position. Not to be outdone, he quickly pulled a wad of cash out of his pocket and started counting.

While he counted up his money, I started unbuttoning my shirt. Unfortunately I did not have a t-shirt under my Hawaiian shirt, so if he took me up on my offer, I would literally be left shirtless.

Sure enough, Eric had $60 and was willing to make the exchange. I nonchalantly removed my shirt as if this were a normal everyday exchange and handed it over to him.

As I walked topless off the train, I ran into one of the conductors that I knew and he looked me up and down with a look of surprise and then said, "I don't even wanna know."

With a smile, I walked to my car and drove home.

When I arrived home I was a little worried how Kristine would react to my being shirtless. I casually walked in and she immediately asked what happened to my shirt.

I coolly replied, "I sold it to a guy on the train."

"Oh, okay." Was her response and she went back to her routine.

This single response told me just how crazy I was. I mean, my wife of 13 years had just acted as though it was a perfectly normal occurrence for her husband to sell the shirt off his back while commuting home from work.

To this day, some of the commuters still call me "shirt man."

* * *

As I was finishing up my autobiography, I experienced a joint bleed in my ankle. I thought I would add the story, because it is entertaining (in my humble opinion). Sometimes I get bleeding in my joints (usually knees or ankles) for no apparent reason. I am sure there is an underlying explanation, however it often eludes me. But I digress as usual.

I had this medication called DDAVP that is a relatively new medication for hemophiliacs. It is taken through the sinuses using a nasal dispenser. Sometimes it will work to stop bleeding problems instead of using factor VIII. So, I decided to try it to stop my bleed. The problem is, that I lost the dosage directions over time and was not sure how much to take. I squirted two shots up each nostril and went to bed (unknowingly doubling the normal dosage). At the same time, I swallowed three ibuprofen tablets to reduce my swelling.

What I failed to realize was that DDAVP was originally created to stop children from wetting the bed. It did this by taking fluids in the body and forcing the body to absorb them. On top of the DDAVP, I did not know that ibuprofen had a similar effect. Without this knowledge, I again dosed up on DDAVP and ibuprofen the following night.

The next morning I woke with pumped forearms. I felt as though I had just finished a rigorous forearm and bicep workout with weights. My arms were so pumped that I could not make a fist. Not knowing what the problem was, I went off to work.

A couple of hours into work I started to worry because I was getting nauseous and dizzy. On top of that, my forearm pump had moved into my biceps and was starting to creep into my shoulders. I decided to avoid thinking about the issue and kept working.

Before long, my chest and back were starting to feel pumped. During this entire time I had been doing my normal hydration (I normally drink a gallon or more of water each day) without grasping the simple fact that you should cut back on water while using DDAVP.

The swelling in my arms, hands, and upper body was starting to worry me. I knew of a condition called hyponatremia from my marathon training, and I feared that I might be experiencing this. I got up from my desk with the intension of walking to the deli across the street to get something with salt in it. As I stood, I was hit with an overwhelming sense of dizziness and felt as though I might faint.

Knowing I would not make it to the deli, I went to our office kitchen and scrounged through the drawers. I found a single packet of salt, opened it and devoured it. Due in part to trepidation, I did not have any water for the remainder of the afternoon.

The time to head home came quickly, and I gathered my strength for the arduous trek to the train station. Once outside the office I felt a panic coming as I limped (remember the swollen ankle?) toward my ride home. Along the way, I stopped by a local hotdog vendor and purchased a banana hoping that some potassium might help me in this time of need.

Halfway to the station, my legs got so pumped that I could no longer keep a steady walking pace. My calves felt like stuffed hot water bottles trying to burst out of the legs of my pants. My thighs started cramping and apprehension hit as I worried about simply making it to my train. On top of that, I was starting to have trouble breathing properly and I was working myself into frenzy.

Once I was safely on the train, I nestled into my seat and reflected on the day. I realized with horror that I had not peed once during the entire day. I normally made six or more trips to the bathroom because of the amount of water that I drank.

At home, Kristine was worried about me and tried catering to my needs. She talked to my mother who had used DDAVP for her own bleeding episodes. She suggested we get me a diuretic of some sort to help me to remove the built-up water in my body. Kristine went out and bought me the pills. In the meantime, I weighed myself and was shocked to find that I had gained twelve pounds in two days!

I popped the diuretic and crawled into bed early. During the rough night's sleep, I woke on four occasions to make emergency urination trips. The next morning I weighed myself again and found that I had lost eight pounds since the previous night. My body was deflated and I was feeling better. By the following day, I had lost a total of 19 pounds in fewer than 24 hours!

Mental note to self: *if I EVER need DDAVP again, do not overdose or take ibuprofen at the same time. And, cut back on the water intake.*

Chapter Twenty-Five

Define midlife crisis. I spent much of my life mentally making fun of people for experiencing what they called, midlife crisis. You see the older guys driving around in convertible Corvettes, or walking with a twenty-something girl hanging on their arm. I always thought that I would be immune to this silliness, because I was different. I mean—midlife crisis is really just a state of mind. And, it is obviously something that is easily within our control.

Even though I thought I was immune, I failed to see the signs coming. Kristine and I weren't having sex as often as we used to. Our baby girl was frustrating us both and we were quite often tired and worn out from dealing with her. On top of that, I was starting to question my work, and how long I would continue to stay in the computer field. Inside, and physically, I felt like a million bucks. But, my age sounded old. I could clearly remember being a 19-year old kid when my dad was 40. The thing I remember most about that time was thinking that my dad was really old.

In addition to all of my signs that were building up, I had also recently given up some exciting parts of my life, including racing motorcycles on the street and track.

"What's all of this sappy goop got to do with me, and my memoir?" you ask.

I will try and gingerly explain this part without beating around the bush—*takes a deep breath*

I thought that my book was complete, and then I betrayed my wife. After spending some 80,000 words explaining my character and how I believe in chivalry and building myself into a nearly inhuman man, I cheated on my wife. I debated adding this part of my life story for quite some time and then came to the realization that it would not be fair to reveal everything else and not touch upon this story.

For my 26-day affair, I am exceptionally disappointed with myself. That disappointment did not stop me. During this foray, I never actually had sexual intercourse, but I did participate in enough tawdry behavior to call it an affair in my mind. I will never be the same because of this transgression, and I am sure that my wife and marriage have been inescapably altered as well.

I did not include this rancid tale to shock, frighten or otherwise affect you. Instead, I merely included it because it is a fact in my life story and I feel that I owe you that much. On top of that, if I can use my experience to help others, I will.

Daily I try to justify my affair with myself. I tell myself that I was having a hard time with life, that I felt as though my wife was no longer physically attracted to me, that I needed something to jumpstart me, that I was having my midlife crisis. But the truth is simple. I was weak and selfish.

Ground zero (day negative one of my breach with a chivalrous life): I went on a whitewater rafting and climbing trip during Memorial Day weekend 2006. My climbing buddy Chris put it together and had a group of twelve people willing to partake. The trip was in Fayetteville, West Virginia at the New River Gorge.

I was driving down there with Vig and his wife Quinn. We were underway Friday evening a tad after 5 p.m. A five-hour trek lay before us as we started on Route 66 heading west.

Suddenly Vig exclaimed, "Oh shit!"

Now I am not a mind reader, but that statement has always sent shivers up my spine. So, Quinn and I simultaneously asked him, "What?"

He explained that he had left their climbing harnesses back at his house. Since it is practically impossible to tie-in during climbing without a harness, we decided to go back and retrieve them. We exited the highway to turn around. Once off the highway, Quinn mentioned that her harness was nearly eight years old and she wanted a new one anyway. Following that pattern, Vig said he would not mind getting a new one, so we jumped back on 66 heading toward our destination knowing that there was a climbing store there.

Rain.

No Rain.

Rain.

No Rain.

Repeat as necessary.

As we were getting close to "the New," the weather rolled in like a hurricane and started washing away the road (only a slight exaggeration). We hydroplaned a couple of times and that made the long trip a little more bearable.

As we pulled into camp around midnight, the weather God reneged and stopped the rain enough for us to pitch our tents.

After building our shelters, Vig, Quinn, and I introduced ourselves to Ryan, Drew, Shelly, Debbie, Jason, and Zak.

Ryan had a tent that had a four-foot by four-foot floor. Somehow he managed to pull off three nights in it. Fetal I assume. On the opposite side of the spectrum, Zak and Jason both had enormous tents that could have housed the rest of our tents inside! Everyone else was normal.

Chris showed up with his girlfriend Risa and a friend, that I'll call, Renee. They arrived slightly after 1 a.m. and we hung for a bit, before falling into fitful sleep.

Saturday morning came and I uncovered my eyeballs at half past crack.

Lumbering around Vig, Quinn, and I prepared for our adventure. We boarded a bus that was going to take us a ways down the road to a point on the river where our adventure would begin.

Renee walked on the bus and for the first time I was struck by how pretty she was. The bleaching process that turned the majority of her hair blond damaged the natural auburn color and yet it managed to look good. Her blue eyes were soft and subdued.

As she walked down the bus I thought to myself, *sit with me.*

She walked past my seat and I suppose I was relieved to not have to sit next to her. Suddenly she reappeared and asked if she could sit with me. Her halfcocked smile and raised eyebrow caught me off guard as I stammered, "Come on in."

The bus ride to our white water excursion was fun thanks to the hillbilly guide that kept us laughing the whole way.

I found that Renee was frightened of whitewater rafting, so I teased her with painful drowning stories.

The river guides explained that our group of twelve would have to be broken into two groups of eight and four because twelve was too many for individual rafts. Immediately I stated, "How about Vig, Quinn, and

Renee all come along with me?" Renee was a bit frightened about the whole whitewater thing, and she knew from our ride out that I was a bit of an adrenaline junkie, but she agreed nonetheless.

When our groups separated, we picked a boat to jump on and went over to it. After we had chosen our boat and group to be with, Renee overheard the guide saying, "Okay, this is the wild group right?"

Next, another guide mentioned that our guide was the craziest of them all.

Finally, we found out that we were taking the smaller boat which would be considerably more rough than the oversized titanic that Chris and the others were traveling in.

Renee was going to ditch me for the larger and safer group. I explained to her that I would keep her safe. She looked into my eyes, and sternly said, "I am trusting you to take care of me, mister."

The New River gave us the opportunity to ride several of each class of whitewater rapids during our trip down. One of the class 3's was actually nastier than some of the 4's and 5's. We found out that a class 3 can be rougher sometimes, if it is safer.

For the most part the ride bored me until the chick next to me plopped in headfirst. We were going down a nice staircase rapid and bouncing around and such. I knew that it was my duty to make sure that Renee did not fall in or freak out, so I made sure she was okay. She was fine, so I turned forward to find the woman on my left bouncing out of the boat. My first thought was, *Man, I don't think she should be that far out of the raft.* That was when she flopped into the water. Oops.

Her husband gave a valiant effort of getting her out of the water, however, she was flailing violently and he was having measured trouble. So, I leaned in and grabbed her life vest and helped in the tug of war.

She swung like a banshee caught in a bear trap, and I calmly explained to her, "Stop freaking out, and help us get you out of the water."

Finally, we managed to get her out and she was pretty pissed at her husband. *Bad to be him, good to be me.*

We stopped for lunch on the shore and made cold cut and peanut butter and jelly sandwiches. It was nice to be out in the warm air and sunshine.

After lunch, we got back in our rafts and pushed into the water. Taking a lunch break had warmed my body up and I found that being in the raft again made me cold. Shivering, I paddled down the river.

The trip fell into the boring pattern again until I was able to actually help some more. We were going down a bouncy ride and I was filled with glee. Until—I heard Renee yelp. I barely had time to snag her life vest as she was heading into the water. She probably would have been slightly perturbed at me if I had shirked my duty and allowed her to go bobbing for apples. But, wait—there's more. Two for the price of one! As I leaned in to change my *COG* (center of gravity) I noticed that the "flailing lady" to my left was trying to take another dive in and her husband was going to let her. Sheesh! Some guys never learn. I can only do so much hero crap. What the Hell, I had nothing better to do, so I grabbed her vest too. My feet were tucked neatly under the inflated tubes on the raft floor and I performed an extreme isometric sit-up holding two women from washing their hair. This turned out to be a solid way of working the abdominal muscles. Essentially, you hold one woman with each hand outstretched while precariously bounding down a rumble and tumble and try to keep them (and you) in the rubber boat. A mere five seconds of this is all you need to feel your rectus abdominis for at least three days. Do not forget to keep your feet tucked in, or the workout will end with a wet ride and two very angry flailing women. What more could a man ask for?

The ride progressed with more rapids. Yada.

A quick bus ride back to camp brought a dip in the hot tub and a warm shower.

After cleaning up, I proceeded to drain several carbonated barley-based beverages. As the night lingered on, Renee and I managed to be sitting next to each other.

A couple of the guys ran off to the restaurant to hang and watch a live band playing. Renee and I stayed behind. She was glancing at me with longing and I realized that I needed to put this flirtation to a stop.

I happen to be a very flirtatious man, but it has always been innocent. I pride myself with a good charisma. But, my flirting has always stopped at a certain point. I never allow it to overcome me or threaten to take hold of me. Renee was different. I was in panic mode and heading in a *bad* direction.

Often I joke about the wedding band being a chick magnet. It is true. I think that girls feel a little safer around the ring. It signifies a man that is good enough for some other woman and more to the point it represents a man who can flirt but will stop it there because of his vows. Two-for-two. On top of all that, many women love a challenge (I don't write the rules).

I finally grabbed the reigns and pulled myself back. "Renee," I explained, "I am a very happily married man with a wonderful baby daughter at home."

"I know." She replied. But, she did not argue my point. This told me that my feelings were correct. Renee was attracted to me as well.

Finally, I pulled out my real firepower and hit her with, "Renee, I am HIV positive." From there, I explained hemophilia and all of the hidden horrors of my life.

At some point during our tête-à-tête I started drinking red wine instead of beer.

She was mesmerized and leaning in listening intently. I felt as though my plan to scare her away might be backfiring when she suddenly said, "I really wanna kiss you."

What the? Did you just hear me, lady?

I melted imagining her lips touching mine. I wanted to kiss her, instead I took in a deep breath, and said, "You can kiss my cheek." With that I turned my face a bit and leaned in. She pressed her lips against my cheek and purposefully held them there in a passionate kiss. The hair stood up on the back of my neck and a tingling sensation shot down my neck, through my back and ended in my loins.

Crap!

Must stop this madness.

It had been nearly twenty years since I had these kinds of feelings for any woman besides my soul mate, Kristine. I was heading for disaster. Thinking, I decided to keep talking and try and talk my way out of this. Pour more wine—yeah, that's the ticket.

We continued in a conversation and refilled our wines several times. On top of that, I could not remember how many beers I had had. These emotions mixed with alcohol to form a deadly combination.

She could sense my feelings (anyone within a mile radius must have known my feelings). She leaned in and once again asked if she could kiss me.

Again I turned my cheek and allowed a sensual kiss to happen. At that moment I realized with brash awakening that I was going to cheat on my wife.

My feelings turned dark and I cried inwardly as I allowed the coward to take over the hero in me.

Renee said that she had to go to the bathroom and I offered to walk her to the portable john on the far side of camp. *How romantic.*

When she was done I looked her in the eyes and said, "Let's go back to your tent."

She moaned slightly and took my hand and I led her on an irreversible path to adultery.

Just before sleep took me, I clambered over to my tent for some sleep.

Six a.m. came quite quickly on Sunday morning. I had planned on sleeping until 8 a.m. but the extreme religious group of bible beaters in a campsite across from ours was out screaming verses. My eyelids tried to open, but a messy mixture of sandman goop and beer God excretion plastered them down.

Pop

Finally they opened and I could see the roof of my tent. Some man was screaming about Psalms something-or-other. I am not averse to people gathering on a Sunday and going over the bible. But, yelling verses at 6 a.m. in a shared campsite is a bit overboard for my taste. Anyway, I felt as though they were purposely screaming to wake up us sinners. So, I drew in a deep breath and prepared to blast out my retort, "Don't forget Psalms 169: Shut the hell up!" However, my manners got the best of me and I muttered curses to myself instead.

I was haggard and used the excuse of noises keeping me up all night. The highway was only a minute away and police sirens seemed to come every hour on the hour. Not to mention that several of our campers were hearty snorers.

Some of our group was eyeing me differently. Or, was that just in my head? I thought, *Do they know something? How on earth am I going to make it through the day like this?*

The plan for Sunday was to hike into the gorge and get some rock climbing in. Due to the early awakening, I was ready to get down to brass tacks. However, Chris and much of the gang were not. So, the awake and ready ones (me, Vig, Quinn, and Renee) all decided to head off to the rock. The plan was that the others would catch up with us later.

We stopped for a quick breakfast before driving out to the "Bubba City" area of the New River Gorge. The parking area was a mud soaked pit from Hell. In other words, I had a blast! We clambered out after properly introducing some mud to the car and proceeded to hike to the "Tattoo Wall."

After a grueling 20-minute hike down a gully, we arrived at the "Tattoo Wall" which was located in the "Bubba City" area.

We decided to start on a 5.6 to warm-up. Renee was not a climber, so she watched as we proceeded to defy gravity. Vig led the sport climb (bolted route) so that I could do it on top rope.

As is often the case with many of my great climbing stories, I started out climbing well and then nearly flash pumped my forearm muscles on the *crux* (toughest part of the climb). Fortunately Vig came to my rescue. He managed to convince me to back down a move or two to a rest spot. My forearms squeaked out a sigh of relief as I gave them a momentary break. I then took a minute longer to view the climb carefully. Suddenly, I saw several key handholds and footholds that had eluded me. From there, I proceeded to pull through my trouble area in a much smoother fashion. Ah! No flash pump. But, I felt that this 5.6 was a hair *sandbagged* (under rated).

After my initial climb, I asked Renee if she would like to go on a quick hike. She said, "Yes" immediately. I explained to Vig and Quinn that I was a little pumped and needed to relax for a short while. Since I would just be hanging, I told them that I was going to hike around the cliffs some with Renee. Quinn gave me a look and I felt as though she was seeing right through me. *Was it that obvious?*

Renee and I walked along the rocks until we were alone and then we found a quiet spot and sat down. I poured my feelings out to her explaining that I was in love with my wife. I also explained that there was no way that this could continue. I was explaining how the forks before us were all lined with pain. In some ways I was actually trying to convince myself that this was wrong and would not work.

She was sad but understanding. She had a good head on her shoulders and knew as well as me that what we were doing was wrong and it could only end with hurt.

We both agreed that it was best to end our affair before it went further and became more passionate. We finally stood and returned.

Along the way back, I explained that there would be no communication between us, because that would only make a tough situation tougher. She understood and agreed.

We walked back to the climbing area with our heads hung low. Along the way I thought how I could have avoided all of this heartache and pain by simply doing the right thing last night. *I am such an idiot!*

Back at the rocks, I continued doing some more 5.6's and 5.7's, and got two hours of climbing in, before Chris and his ragtag band of straggling zombies rolled into town. It turned out that they zigged when they should have zagged during their hike in and it took them considerably longer to get to our climbing area.

Shortly after they arrived, Ryan and Jason climbed another 5.6 that we setup. And then, Jason followed up with a splendid climb of the 5.7. Zak and Drew battled with the 5.6 only to be overcome with tired, blown arms and dented egos.

At one point, I was belaying Chris on a 5.7 while his girlfriend Risa lay sleeping near my feet. During his arduous task of floating toward the ground (as I lowered him), he managed to kick a four-inch diameter flat rock free without realizing it. I was lucky enough to be looking up and saw the weird object descending at a rapid rate (not terminal velocity mind you, but fast). I thought, *Hey, look at that whistling thingy flying right at me. Neat.* Suddenly, I was gripped with fear as I realized that it was a rock. Snapping to attention, I locked both hands on the rope jerked Chris into a stop and flung my body at the rock wall (which proceeded to bounce and bruise me).

During my leap, I screamed, "Rock!" And the others fled the scene.

Risa was lying under a blanket oblivious to the goings on. Thank God the rock missed her (and me). I was glad that I did not drop Chris to his death a mere three inches from his girlfriend (that would have been bad).

Climbing ended sooner than necessary, because my shoulder was blown. Then, during our hike out of the gully I somehow managed to injure my ankle.

After getting back to camp, we cleaned up and then headed to Dirty Ernie's Rib Pit for some dinner.

I sat at a table with Renee as I asked myself, *What am I doing?*

Earlier in the day I had made a clean break from this torrid affair and here I was building it back up. I validated it by thinking that it would end after this weekend. No reason to control my feelings right now when I could enjoy myself for one more night.

Back at camp I clambered over to my tent and feigned going to sleep. After about fifteen minutes I snuck out and crept over to Renee's tent. Zipper noises abound. I imagine that everyone at our campsite knew something was going on.

Afterward I tiptoed back to my tent slightly before daybreak.

Finally I was able to get a small amount of sleep. Oh well, I will get plenty of sleep when I die.

Once again, Renee and I had agreed that sans communication was our best course of action.

We crawled out of tents early and packed up. After saying "Goodbye." Vig, Quinn, and I trudged back up the highway to the city and society.

* * *

My strategy was to cut off all ties to Renee after that weekend fling. My plan was working fine until one day later when I got the itch. During our time together she had asked if she could get a copy of my autobiography rough draft, and I had told her I would send her one. Realizing I had not gotten her home address or a way to send it to her, I convinced myself that I merely needed to contact her and get this info.

I called her and before I knew it, we were talking and e-mailing.

I used getting my book to her as a ploy to see her. Each evening I would leave work and go to her work. From there we would spend some time together and then she would drive me to the train station to allow me to return to my *other* life.

I called my buddy, Ben and explained the situation to him. He was livid. He could not believe what I was doing and told me so. Most of his anger was pointed at the blatant fact that I was a hypocrite talking about chivalry and such and then turning around and doing this.

I completely agreed with him. I was ashamed for the way I was treating my wonderful wife. I felt pathetic and weak to say the least.

I arranged to visit Ben under the premise of going down to help him through some tough times and Kristine easily agreed that I should go see him.

My plan was to drive down with Renee early Saturday morning and introduce the two of them. From there, I was hoping that Ben could talk some sense into us and then I would make the return trip home that afternoon.

To make matters worse, Kristine and I were more fervent then ever. It was as if this affair had given our relationship a renewed energy. We had a wonderful passionate night. Then the next morning I drove into Washington, DC to pick Renee up. I hated myself, as we piled into my car and started our long trek to Charlottesville, Virginia.

On the one hand I had the perfect life at home. Sure Kristine and I had our problems, but for the most part, I was extremely happy with our marriage. And, we had little Trinity between us creating a family worth dying for. Kristine was a loving woman who had always been there for me. She has essentially thrown any chance at a normal life away by committing to me. She knew when we were married that the odds were pretty slim for us to have children. She also accepted the responsibility of possibly becoming HIV+ and the risks associated with this. On top of these noble things, she took me under her wing knowing that one day she would have to stand beside my bed (perhaps for months) watching me wither away and die a young man. Kristine has poured her heart and soul into our relationship and this was how I repaid her.

My mind fought a fierce battle trying to untangle this mess that I had created. *Suicide?* Out of the question for Trinity's sake at the very least (thanks kiddo for saving me yet again). *Leave my family?* Out of the question. *Leave Renee?* Turn my back on these powerful emotions? *Keep both lives and go on happily ever after?* Not fair to anyone including me.

Before I knew it, we had arrived at Ben's house and it was time for introductions.

As I said, I planned to stay for part of the day and then head home—my plan went by the wayside after I drank a bottle of ten-year old Laphroaig scotch upon my arrival.

Ben commenced yelling at me in a gentlemanly fashion. Renee sat and soaked it all in. Ben's biggest point was that it was unfair to Kristine to not let her know this was happening. Of course I knew he was right. But, I did not begin to know how to explain this to her. I was terrified of what that might mean. As I drained the bottle of scotch I blurred and began blathering about me. My selfish wants and needs. How I had spent a lifetime being selfless and sacrificial, and it was time for Vaughn to do something for himself. Cliché.

Kristine called, and I explained to her that Ben and I had been drinking pretty heartily and I would not be returning that afternoon. I told her I would spend the night and drive home the following morning. She was pissed, and rightfully so. Now I was creating a rift and dragging Ben into it.

Inwardly I wish to be a role model. I truly want to set a good example for others. I feel that I have had some tough decisions and tribulations in my life and I have usually managed to find a way to turn them golden. In this case, I had created my own ugly turmoil.

Ben, Renee, and I went out to dinner and we drowned our sorrows in more alcohol. I drank two gin martinis and proceeded to step into a realm of drunkenness that I had not seen in years. *My poor liver.*

After managing to find our way home, Ben and I quibbled a bit more about this rancid situation that I was putting Renee and me in. You see, not only was I damaging my life with this entire event, but Renee's as well.

Her friends and family were all worried about her. Many of her friends already hated me with passion comparably to our passion toward each other. On top of that, I was hurting Kristine, Trinity, my family, and friends to boot.

The next morning I dropped Renee off at her home and sped to my place where I reconciled Kristine's anger at me for being gone so long. *A shell of a man is what I had become.*

* * *

A couple of days after the "Ben trip" I decided to tell Kristine about my mendacious second life. Renee and I continued e-mailing, talking and seeing each other for short rides to the train station. On June 6, 2006 (that's right folks, 666) I went with Renee for a drink and dinner at a nearby Thai restaurant. I could barely eat a thing as I thought through what I would say, and why.

Kristine saved me the ulcer that was sure to come on the ride home when she called me at the restaurant. I started in on another lie about how I was late and grabbing something to eat before catching the last train. Suddenly my mind screamed, *Enough.*

At that very instant Kristine insightfully asked me, "Is someone there with you?"

Ahhhh. The question was put before me. It was my turn to walk the talk. *Mouse or man?* I lifted my head and eyed Renee as I responded, "Yes." After a deep breath I continued, "I am at dinner with another woman."

Kristine could not or would not believe me. She insisted on talking to Renee. I queried Renee who fearfully shook her head, "No." I believe I had shocked Renee as well by bluntly and honestly telling my wife in an instantaneous moment.

I talked to Kristine a little longer before she again insisted on talking to Renee. Finally Renee sighed and agreed to talk to her. They only spoke for a moment and I do not know how it went, but Renee was polite and brief.

I explained to Kristine that I would be home a little later and we would talk about all of this in great detail. With that I hung up.

My heart leapt at the undo pressure that had been released. Relief moved through my body as I felt the truth setting me free. Had I known that this would be merely the beginning of an onerous trip, I might have been exacerbated instead.

Finding that I had missed the last train, Renee offered to drive me the 60 minutes up the road to my place. Fortunately she would only have to drop me off two minutes from my house at my car. The storm had begun.

* * *

Now that Kristine knew, I thought the rest would be easy. She would ask for a divorce and we would part our ways. I felt that I deserved for her to leave me after what I had done.

Instead of kicking me out, I found that Kristine still loved me (perhaps now more than ever). Thank God.

We stayed up long hours talking through all of this, and I finally called Renee to tell her that Kristine and I were going to try and reconcile our marriage. She was pissed to say the least. She accused me of using her to fix my marital problems. All of the yelling that she did hurt me, but I knew that she was merely lashing out due to her own pain. So, I took it like a man and humbly apologized. Finally she hung up on me, and Kristine and I continued our talking into the night.

* * *

The problem with ending a relationship on such a harsh note is that both parties eventually feel guilty and want the other to know they are sorry. I felt miserable about the way I had treated Renee, but could not e-mail or call her because I feared we would start seeing each other again.

Renee solved this dilemma for me by e-mailing me an angry note asking why I had not apologized to her yet. This opened a floodgate of my emotions and we started e-mailing back-and-forth again deciding that e-mail would be a safe vent for our feelings.

Finally Renee and I both agreed that it was best to stop all forms of communication and get on with our lives.

* * *

This side story starts in Romney, West Virginia at 1:30 p.m. on Friday June 9, 2006 when I was casually riding through town with my top down, sunglasses on, and sly grin smeared across my weathered face. For you see, I was on my way to Seneca Rocks for a weekend of climbing with my friends. Suddenly drizzling water forced me to pull over and put my top up. Top latched, and five seconds later a category four storm rolled through and around me. This latest development assured me that Indiana Mark was sure to be there tonight—the weather God was sending his standard warning about climbing with Mark!

Driving on the switchbacks at maximum wet traction velocity was a blast.

I arrived at Seneca Rocks West Virginia at 3:02 p.m. and the place was empty except for Roger and Anne I quickly took up an entire tent pad with my enormous tent. Afterward, I setup my lounge chair and started pounding Guinness. Ah, climbing vacations are sweet. Just what the doctor ordered.

Folks started moseying in and my friend Kendra was one of the first, so she pitched her tent. We hung. More folks rolled in. And so on, and so forth—we ended up with a crowded 70 people at this event.

No dinner and twelve Guinness later, Larry showed up with a bottle of 17-year-old scotch from Liam for my birthday. God Bless Sweet Liam. The scotch was exceptionally smooth and woody tasting. Later in the night, I pulled out the double pie iron and started cooking up grilled cheese sandwiches over our capacious fire. Life was good and we had not even climbed yet!

Met lots of COo.oOL folks from all over the world. Indy really is the king of bringing nice peeps together. Fact.

Five fifty-four a.m. and my eyeballs were uncovered manually (serious tugging and pulling was involved). Was it really four hours ago when we went to bed? It felt like I had only received 45 minutes of partial sleep. ARGH! I needed to drink more tonight. No worries, I was sure I would. Kendra was already awake and wondering what to climb. I offered my lead services on "Old Lady Route" (a three-pitch 5.2) with a chance to finish on "Windy Corner" (5.4) if she felt up to it. She was game! Indy planned to take the majority of our group out for caving all day, so I found another victim—I mean, wanton climber, named Amanda. Amanda had not climbed in several years and was excited about getting up on something fairly easy.

We headed out and hiked up the lactic acid inducing stone stairway known as "the Stair Master."

Using doubles (two 8.5 mm ropes, instead of one thicker rope) we darted up the first pitch of "Old Lady." At the top of pitch one you find some of the most extreme exposure available on a 5.2 (at least that my limited experience has found). You go up the West face of the South peak and this gives you about 300 feet of exposure, because the valley continues down below where the pitch actually started. But, the real exposure happens when you crawl through the little crook and start the second pitch on the East face. This belay station is a solid 550 feet above the valley floor.

When Amanda crawled through and saw the breathtaking view, she turned white and appeared ready to puke. I soothed her by explaining that the climb was truly a 5.2. Of course I failed to mention that the very next move was fairly dicey.

Amanda expressed her fears and together we decided it would be better for her to downclimb and wait for Kendra and me. She was relieved to see that I was willing to make this change. But, I did not see how I could have done otherwise (it was the right thing to do for all of us). The climb was only going to get more invigorating and she was already having a troublesome time. So, she downclimbed with her chin held high and sat for the next three hours to await our return. Exposure can be a very fearsome nemesis.

After leading the first pitch, I led the next pitch too and zippered up the traverse with protective gear. Mostly I did this because Larry failed to place even one piece last time and I nearly pendulumed for 40+ feet into jagged edges. Anyway, the one move on the traverse was exactly how I remembered it—NOT A 5.2! Damned east coast sandbaggers.

Kendra did a good job following and cleaning gear. She was a hearty sport and willing to take a chance on what I thought was "Windy Corner" a 5.4 third pitch variation on "Old Lady." I led once again (Kendra had not placed traditional protection before, so we thought it would be best if I did it, since I had done it two times before—YIKERS!). Pulling through the fun little chimney I started dreading the overhanging funky finish of the pitch (I clearly remembered wetting my pants the last time I did it). Yanking up my harness and taking a deep breath, I moved in for the kill. *HOLY CRAP!* This was a sick couple of moves for 5.4, even by Seneca standards. Mentally, I screamed at myself, *Suck it up wuss!* Breathe. Look down at the 600-foot drop to help remove your fears. I finally leaped onto the final bulge and dangled momentarily on the overhanging pumpy section thinking about the manky piece that I had placed about six feet below my feet. Scrambling for a hold, I managed a forehead to forearm mantle that took me over the tough part and I breathed deeply with relief as I pulled over the final part of the climb. Five-four! What the?? I wondered, *Who rates this crap?*

Kendra followed up in smooth fashion and climbed like a champ. She also mentioned that the climb felt a tad tough for a 5.4, but she was used to the gym and just accepted the fact that it was tougher here at Seneca Rocks.

After a quick rappel down "Traffic Jam" (about 185 feet of pure fun), we hooked-up with Amanda and headed back to camp.

Back at camp, I picked up Tony Barnes' new version of the *Seneca Climbing Guide*. The new guide was considerably nicer than the old one. All of the impossible to see red dotted lines had been replaced with yellow lines and were much easier to see. Also, he had added some routes—including "Expletive Deleted" (5.7); which it turns out was the variation that I had led during our third pitch. So, for the second time, I had successfully led a 5.7 pitch thinking it was only a 5.4 (which happened to be the toughest traditional lead of my short trad life). I am glad I read the rating *after* doing the climb, because I would have never even attempted it otherwise.

Kristine showed up with baby Trinity and brightened the camp. They were the reason for the circus-sized tent.

Drinking did not start until 4 p.m. this time, but I drank faster to make up for it. We headed over to the restaurant for some pizza and camaraderie with Kristine, Trinity, Kendra, Amanda, Eric, Becca, Aqua, and his wife.

Back to the camp, the fire, the rest of the bottle of scotch, and beer. This fellow Martin bought some bottles of wine and we took turns chugging that also. All we needed was some Banana Schnapps and everything would have been complete (hurl city).

The next morning at 4 a.m., Trinity (16 months old) decided to wake up camp early. Heh heh.

Eight a.m. woke me and I found my ankle to be a bit of a problem. I was having another bleed in that confounded joint. So, climbing would be improbable. It turned out to be a problem, and I did not get to climb—but, Kristine, Trinity, and I did do some breakfast at the "4U" restaurant with Melanie and her two boys Benny and Lukey before heading home.

Fun times. I wish the rest of my life could be this easy.

* * *

Where were we? Oh yeah, talking about my breach with an honest life. I was able to go six days without a peep before I finally broke down and e-mailed Renee. She responded and we e-mailed for a couple of days. I was growing my feelings again and decided that I had to see her. This time I decided to see her with Kristine aware. I justified this by telling myself (and Kristine) that I was still trying to figure out our marriage and I needed some time to do that. Together, Kristine and I thought that a short partial separation would help me to figure that out. I explained that I was planning on spending the night in DC to figure things out. I told Kristine that *if* Renee was willing to see me, I planned on seeing her.

Kristine was broken, but only wanted our relationship to work if my heart was in the right place. So she let me go after explaining that it would not be fair to figure this out in Renee's arms.

I called Renee and ended up staying at her place for the night. As we parted in the morning, Renee reiterated what Kristine had said about it not being fair to try figuring out my marriage with her in the picture. We both agreed that this had to stop, and as mature adults we ended our relationship by telling each other how much we cared about one another. We sat and cried for a bit and then walked out of each other's lives.

* * *

Alas, I must conclude this chapter—

Where does the affair part of my story come to closure and end? Right here. Right now.

On June 21, 2006 I was still confused early in the day about what to do. I bartered with my inner self and begged to have both women. Simple—cake plus hungry equals eat.

Early in the day, Kristine called me at work and told me that she did not want me having any contact with Renee from now on. I agreed.

After Kristine and I hung up, Renee gave me a call at the office. It was apparent that we both still had feelings for each other. When we ended our conversation, Renee asked me to stop contacting her until I had this figured out. And, in so many words, she begged me to figure it out in a way that would work for us.

I sat at my desk transfixed upon the options that lay before me. Fading into a daydream I envisioned Renee and me moving far away from all of this and living happily ever after. But I could not keep that vision lucid because Kristine and Trinity always crept in and asked me what they had done to deserve this. On top of that, I could not imagine life without Kristine in it. She always makes me so happy.

I soul searched and found that I still loved my wife ecstatically. While soul searching, I thought of our wedding song, "Glory of Love" and felt the words etched into my mind. "I am a man who would fight for your honor." I cried.

What has happened to me?
Where has my belief in chivalry gone?
Is this inescapably impossible to fix?

In the past, I wrecked two important close friendships in my life because friends of mine cheated on their significant others. I destroyed these friendships because I could not forgive close friends for doing this terrible thing to their women. And yet here I was, the king of the hypocrites, doing that very same thing. I wondered when I changed the rules in my favor. And, what gave me the right to throw people's lives around carelessly and with such reckless abandon.

Then and there I realized what I must do. I would not contact Renee again. I had to go home and be the man that Kristine had always believed I was. Slamming my fists into my eyes I felt the weight lift from my shoulders as I faced the easy truth. I had a wife and child at home who adored me. They were waiting there for me to figure this out and come home.

In that instant I knew what must be done and how to do it. I completed my day's work and headed home to tell Kristine that I had made my choice.

The stars must have been in alignment. For when I arrived home, Kristine had a hot bath drawn for me. Surrounding the tub were sweet smelling candles. She helped me off with my clothes and got me in the tub before leaving me to sit and relax. In the background Jim Brickman was playing all of my favorite piano songs.

I chose to fight for my family.

"What about Renee?" You ask.

As I said early on, Renee and I had never actually had sexual intercourse. I feel like President Clinton mentioning this, but I believe that it is an important point. I am not justifying what we did. I feel that our transgression was just as bad as if we'd actually had sex. But the simple fact is that we did not.

I am confident that Renee will move on and find love. She will grow from this experience, as I have, and use it to empower her instead of consume her. She will miss me, and I her. But I have no illusions—she will be fine.

"Men who cheat always cheat again." you cry out.

I am a consummate flirt and naturally charismatic. However, I am also a very strong willed man. I cannot presume to promise the future. But, I can promise that I will try my hardest to ensure that nothing like this happens again.

"If I had it all to do over again, what would I do?" you ask in desperation.

I would tell Kristine about my needs and wants. I would not let sexual tension build over time. I would write love letters and send flowers all of the time. I would come home, cook dinner, and give massages. I would work at making our love life better. I will do those things now more than ever!

Finally, "Have I learned anything from this experience?"

Hell yes. Kristine and I had been together for more than 23 years. And, happily married for more than 16. Nothing in life can take that away from us if we do not let it. I love my family with all of my heart, and contrary to my brief belief, there is not enough to share with a mistress.

On top of all of this, I now realize that I took my wife's love and care for granted. She has always been there for me and never did anything to deserve such a terrible thing. I will never be able to understand how she must feel about this betrayal, but her fight and effort to stay with me through this shows me how much of an idiot I was.

* * *

After this situation was closed, Kristine and I both saw individual counselors and a marriage counselor. We have renewed our vows and become more committed than ever before. This horrible mistake that I made has also opened communication channels between us. Fortunately for me, I have a loving and understanding wife who stood by me during and beyond my time of deceit.

My eyes are open and I am trying to build a less judgmental man of myself. Chivalry is back and a force to be reckoned with. But, forgiveness and understanding are also here with more power than ever before.

Learning from one's mistakes is a virtue. In this case I did learn a painful lesson. Living for the moment lasts just that long—a moment. It's ephemeral. However, living with the guilt from a moment lasts a lifetime. Not a day goes by that I do not kick myself for the pain that I caused around me for my transgression. I can't take back my crime, but I can learn and grow from it. Each day I reflect and use my disappointment in my choice as a tool. Instead of being negative and tearing myself apart, I try to focus on the fact that I am human and I will stumble and fall. The key to life, in my opinion, is picking yourself back up after your falls and not making the same mistake twice. Unfortunately this mistake did more than give me a bleed in my ankle. It hurt my wife, family, and friends. There is no simple Factor VIII solution to this blunder. For that I cannot forgive myself. But, I work each and every day to mollify the damage.

My soul mate believed I was worth the effort. That is enough for me to never do this again.

Chapter Twenty-Six

On another of our climbing adventures, Vig and I traveled with our lovely wives and Trinity up to New York to climb at the Shawangums (the Gunks) in the Mohonk preserve just outside of New Paltz, New York.

Most of the time we were there it rained, but we were able to get a little climbing in on our last day. The rock was moist and slick at best and filled with puddles, mud, and slime in other areas. Suffice it to say that the conditions were not perfect for climbing.

We made the best of it and climbed several climbs as the sun slowly dried up the water and sludge. On one climb, Quinn led the first pitch and I followed her. When I got up to her belay ledge I had a sudden uncontrollable feeling of vertigo. I literally felt the world expand and then the treetops below spread open as if calling me. I nearly fell with dizziness and nausea before getting a grip and looking at the wall. Quinn asked me if I was okay and I casually responded telling her I was fine.

Quinn didn't think any more of it, but it was all that I could focus on. I tried a couple of times to look back down at the fall below me and found that dizzy sensation slamming back into my gut. *What is happening to me?* I thought as I tried to reason this out. I had eaten breakfast and was properly hydrated. My mind fought for a physical answer that it could not find.

Finally I fought with my inner self and insisted that I get control of this fear. I controlled my breathing and forced another look at the exposure before me. I was calmer this time, but still had the tingling and fear. Pinpricks stabbed at my nape and threatened to make me vomit. I was able, with time, to overcome my unexpected phobia, but it lingered in my mind as we continued climbing.

During my next climb I felt calmer than ever before and I was climbing beyond my normal abilities. I created a oneness with the rock. It was weird to think that only minutes earlier I was ready to hurl at the thought of being so high up and now here I was climbing without a care in the world.

After rappelling down off the last climb of the day I was coiling up the rope and preparing to leave when I got an abrupt and sheer pain in the back of my neck. I winced at the feeling and suddenly had another in my thumb. Seconds later I was feeling sharp excruciating pains in half a dozen places on my body. My mind raced to figure out why this was happening to me. I feared that perhaps I was having a stroke or something. I had no idea what it must feel like to experience a stroke, but I imagined that this was possibly it.

Suddenly it became clear where my pain was coming from. Looking around I noticed hundreds of angry hornets dive-bombing my body. They were taking no prisoners as they swung in for repeated attacks. I started slapping them one-by-one and realized that they would down me well before I could put a dent in their ranks.

Running into the woods slapping at my pained body parts I passed Vig and Quinn in a screaming tantrum. Vig laughed thinking that I was making some kind of obscene joke before realizing that I was being attacked. After I had gotten about 40 feet from their nest, the hornets started leaving me alone.

It turned out that chaos and random luck had dropped my rope on a ground nest of these festering demons. While I was coiling up the rope I must have disturbed them and they came-a-callin'. I learned the hard way that I am not allergic to hornets. Later that evening Kristine and I counted no fewer than 24 stings. Ouch!

The stinging fest and such put my vertigo experience on the back burner. But it did not take me long to start thinking about that again. I also associated the hornets as a sign that it was time for me to hang up my ropes for good. I realized that up until now I had been extremely lucky to not have sustained a serious accident and decided to stop rock climbing in pursuit of calmer pastures.

At the same time of putting down my cams and carabiners I picked up my dusty guitar and started playing again. Shortly after this decision, I purchased a new electric guitar and was falling in love with music yet again. Fortunately my cousin Greg had a similar love of music and we have strengthened our relationship through it.

* * *

Only days after my decision to hang up my climbing ropes, a climbing acquaintance named Carlos had a serious accident at the Gunks. He fell pulling two pieces of protective gear with him and slammed his helmet-covered head in to the rock. He received a multi-part fracture on the right side of his skull, broke his left cheekbone, left scapula, and fractured his T5, T6, and T7 vertebrae. On top of those fractures and breaks, he damaged the structure in his ear and a nerve in his face. He also bruised his lung and got pneumonia to boot!

Suffice it to say that Carlos has a long road to recovery and will probably have lingering effects for the remainder of his life.

If that accident had happened to me, as a hemophiliac, I would be dead from internal bleeding before I even arrived at the hospital. Looking at this incident helped to affirm the fact that I needed to mature and move forward with my life in a direction away from climbing. In a painful sort-of way, Carlos helped me to make a clean break from climbing.

Chapter Twenty-Seven

Deciding to get back into off-roading after a hiatus, I started investigating the latest vehicles. One thing that I have found is that technology has really changed. This is not always for the better either. I still haven't found a vehicle that is better suited for trail running than my CJ-5 Jeep was. However, I did find a very nice off-road vehicle in the Toyota FJ Cruiser. I did some serious research before deciding to go with this truck.

Traveling to the dealership, Kristine and I were not sure which color we preferred. My heart was set on the Black Cherry and she really liked the Voodoo Blue or Sun Fusion (Yellow).

These days, we never buy a vehicle the first day we test-drive them. We normally spend a pretty good amount of time with our noses buried in the *Consumer Guide* and in magazine articles. We also surf the net and checkout Edmunds.com. This purchase was no different. I was certain that I wanted an FJ Cruiser, but I let the salesman stew for three days while I "thought about it."

During my thinking about it time, I noticed a single sentence hidden in the depths of one of my four-wheeling magazines. It mentioned that Toyota was planning on releasing a *TRD* (Toyota Racing Development) version of the FJ Cruiser. It would have a different exhaust, wheels, shock absorbers, and best of all, a roof that was matched with the body color (standard FJ Cruisers come with a white painted roof, regardless of body color). I was elated and hurried down to the dealer to put myself on the waiting list.

When Kristine and I arrived at Darcars Toyota in Frederick, Maryland, the salesman had no idea that Toyota was making a TRD version of the FJ. I asked to speak with a manager. The manager was helpful, but he explained that Toyota would not be making a TRD version of the truck. He told me that if they were, he would have heard about it before it showed up in some magazine.

I was perplexed and yet sure that I wanted the TRD version if it was coming. So, I asked if there was a waiting list yet and the manager sighed as he reiterated, "There can't be a waiting list for a truck that does not exist."

Determined to get my way, I wrote out a check for $500.00 and handed it over to the manager. As he took my check with an odd look on his face, I said, "If you are right, we will simply tear this check up in a month and I will purchase a regular FJ Cruiser. But—if I'm right, you will keep this check as my deposit and put my name first on the waiting list. Fair?"

Shaking his head and smiling, the manager said, "Fair enough."

Needless to say, one week later I received a phone call from the manager. He simply stated, "Mr. Ripley, I apologize for not believing you. There is in-fact a TRD version of the FJ Cruiser coming and I have put your name first on the waiting list."

By the time I picked up my truck, the waiting list had grown pretty large and I heard that many people on the list called for weeks after I picked up my TRD to ask if it was still available. I was officially a happy camper.

* * *

One week after owning the truck, another driver wrecked into it. Fortunately the only damage was to my front bumper. After some thought, I decided to upgrade my bumper to an aftermarket one that would allow me to add a winch. Along with the winch, I added some mud tires and ended up with a formidable off-road machine.

Before long, I had found and met with many local FJ Cruiser owners for four-wheeling adventures. We decided to start an off-road club called the FJ Bruisers and we now have more than 122 members. If you like to off-road your SUV and live within four hours of Washington, D.C. (at this time, the Bruisers serve Maryland, Virginia, DC, Pennsylvania, West Virginia, Delaware, New Jersey, and New York) checkout our website at: www.fjbruisers.org or simply join us for some mud talk at www.fjbruisers.org/forum.

* * *

For my fortieth birthday, Kristine decided to have a huge surprise party for me. She started polling my friends and before long she had more than 100 guests planned. I discovered the party by opening a letter that was addressed to me about a D.J. playing at my party. This turned out to be a boon for Kristine, because she was overwhelmed with the handling of such an affair.

Together we decided to hold the party at a local hotel reception hall and even had one of my favorite local bands, "the Reagan Years," play for us. We had catered dinners and an open bar as well. All-in-all 101 people showed up for this shindig and it was a great success.

During one point my cousin Greg (he was the M.C.) asked folks to come up and share stories. I was amazed by the stories, which brought back a flood of memories and happy times.

Near the end of the party, Greg called me up front with my wife and they presented me with my birthday gift. All of my friends had chipped in and bought me a Gretsch Chet Atkins semi-hollow body electric guitar. It has 24-carat, gold-plated hardware and a brilliant orange body. It is perfect! Shouts to hear me play had me plugging into the band's equipment and throwing out a couple of drunken songs. My eyes welled with tears as I looked out to the reception hall of standing friends who were cheering me on.

I couldn't ask for a better group of friends and most of all, such a wonderful wife. The party was just what the doctor ordered.

* * *

Kristine and I decided to have another baby. Well—at least we decided to attempt to have one. We started all of the in vitro shenanigans again (this was our fifth in vitro attempt). We had two fertilized eggs (embryos) implanted and they took. On July 23, 2007, we found out that Kristine was officially pregnant and would be having the baby sometime around March 28, 2008.

w00t!

Kristine's hCG (human chorionic gonadotropin) levels indicated that the embryo was growing at a healthy rate. On August 1, 2008 Kristine was able to see the little heartbeat through a sonogram.

In October, we found out that the baby was a boy. This was great news, because even though I have twelve nieces and nephews, none of them carries on the Ripley name. On top of that, I consider one girl and one boy to be the golden ratio.

* * *

On Saturday, February 25, 2008 I drove up to Deep Creek Lake to my buddy Rick's cabin on the lake. My purpose was to take a dive in the frozen lake to raise money for the Special Olympics. I hadn't done any special training for this event, and my nerves were tingling. I was ten minutes away from Rick's house when my mobile phone rang. Kristine's water had broken! *How was this possible?* Our baby boy was not due for 5 more weeks and yet here he was ready to enter the world. Butterflies took turns dive-bombing my stomach.

After talking about it for a while, Kristine and I decided that I could go ahead and do my frigid dive and then drive straight home. The only two major fund raising events that I have done have happened right as my children were being born … Weird?

I met my friends at Rick's place and we all drove over to the lake, where the temperature was ten degrees with wind-chill. Speaking of wind, it was blowing pretty firmly and was promising to make our swim miserable.

Before we could go out into the water for our polar bear swim, the local fire department had to cut through more than twelve inches of ice. The firemen were wearing their winter water rescue gear and they waded out to chest deep water, before letting us run in.

They grouped us into small groups of about 50 people and the groups took turns running into the water for no longer than five minutes. Basically, it was mayhem. When they said we could get wet, our group just started running and screaming. I hopped into the freezing water and my body immediately screamed with agony. I was pleasantly surprised to find that all feeling quickly went away. After a couple of steps in, I was one of the few who dove head first into the water and started swimming.

I swam under water all of the way out to where the rescue workers were and high-fived one guy before returning to the shore. Stepping out of the water was considerably worse than being in the water. The cold air instantly shocked my body. On top of that, the wind was threatening to freeze me on the spot. Somehow I managed to fight my way back to a heated tent and changed into dry clothes amid fellow shivering bodies.

I went back out and hugged my goodbyes before jumping in my truck and zooming home to greet my sweetheart.

* * *

Kristine's water broke on Saturday, February 25, 2008 and she was admitted to Frederick Memorial Hospital. The doctor informed us that we would be having a baby within the next couple of days. Long story short, we finally started to induce labor via a pitocin injection (pitocin is a synthetic version of oxytocin; which is a hormone produced by a woman's body that causes contractions) on Monday evening.

Kristine elected to have the epidural anesthesia to eliminate most of the pain associated with a vaginal birth. She was very brave during the entire process and I am always amazed at how she handles tough situations. I know that she is terrified of things like this, and yet she puts on her *game face* and moves forward. I have always been in awe of her control and willpower. Kristine is a powerful person with a special attitude toward life and she makes me extremely proud.

The pitocin started working pretty quickly and before we knew it, Kristine had her first contraction at about 4 a.m. The fact that it felt like a long night to me makes me wonder just how women do this! It is very taxing and my part was easy for the most part. I basically just had to stand there and give her supportive words and massage her feet, yada. I cannot conceive (no pun intended) how you manage the pain and turmoil of giving birth, but it is a beautiful thing that everyone should experience.

Kristine's contractions starting coming closer together and they were lasting a little bit longer. We knew that a baby was coming. Finally the birthing assistant had her start actually pushing with the contractions. I caught my first glimpses of our baby's head as he crowned.

I can understand why they say people pass out and/or vomit sometimes during this process. I was queasy from a lack of food and lack of sleep. I had been standing on my feet for countless hours. On top of all that, I was staring at a stretched and bloody vagina with a head coming out of it. Um … Yes, it is amazing, but damn! Keep in mind that I had the easy job. I merely had to watch this and give occasional massages. Kristine was doing some pushing things with her body that hurt me just thinking about it.

Because Kristine was having trouble feeling her lower body, the nurse turned off the epidural drip. She announced that Kristine would start feeling things in a very short amount of time. I wasn't sure how she would react to that. But, taking it in stride, Kristine battened down the hatches and kept pushing when asked. She was going through agonizing pain and there was nothing I could do to assist or relieve her anguish. I was talking, soothing, and basically frustrating her. I felt like a third wheel at times, but I know that my presence was helping.

The doctor appeared and took a look. She explained that we were ready to have a baby. She inserted several fingers into the opening and started forcefully stretching the entire area. My God! It was working. The baby's head came further out than ever before and each push was getting us closer.

Finally, with one extra big push and the scariest scream I have ever heard, our little boy literally just popped out and landed in the caring physician's hands. Tuesday, February 28, 2008 at 6:31 a.m.—Xander Maverick came into this place we affectionately call Earth. He was premature by almost five weeks. Weighing in at 5 pounds and 13.5 ounces, he was 19.5 inches tall. Even though he was a tiny little fella, the hospital informed us that he was properly formed and would be going home without a stay in the NICU. Double w00t!

I cut the umbilical cord and we ran home! Well, there was a couple of forms to sign and some sleeping, but essentially we (Kristine) were done with the hard work.

* * *

When Xander was only a couple of weeks old, Kristine noticed a lump that was appearing on his lower abdomen. I thought it looked like a hernia and we decided to get a medical opinion. Sure enough, he had a bilateral reducible inguinal hernia on both sides. We brought him in for surgery and sat in agony as our baby went under the knife.

The operation only lasted about 45 minutes and everything went smoothly. The doctor explained that one side was pretty bad off, but that it was fixable and he patched up our baby boy. Due to his young age, Xander needed to stay in the hospital for 24 hours, so Kristine elected to stay with him and I went home to take care of Trinity.

Chapter Twenty-Eight

I had planned a bicycle ride along the Chesapeake and Ohio Canal Towpath for quite some time. I've always wanted to do it. Once we moved to Brunswick, I realized that we lived two miles from the canal. It itched at me. After some thinking and planning, I finally decided to do it. I talked to my friends and forum members. Many people said they would do it with me. I knew that list would dwindle as the date approached. However I started my training assuming we were doing it in the early Fall of 2009.

Because I am hard headed, I decided to ride the trail uphill. People will argue that the grade is very slight and there isn't any difference between up and down. I'm here to tell you that there is a difference. Slight for short distances, yes. But after 190 miles, it is extremely discernible.

My training was a cross training of sorts. I continued doing my weight lifting using the High Intensity Training model. I was building a solid muscle base that would endure the 184.5 mile bicycle ride. At the same time, I rode a recumbent bicycle twice a week, doing HIIT (High Intensity Interval Training) for 35 minutes per session. HIIT is a mixture of two minutes of slow easy riding followed by one minute of extreme intensity as fast and hard as you can muster. Then you repeat it again. I was doing this for ten repetitions each workout. Also, I got out on the C&O canal once per week for a moderate ride of between 18 and 40 miles.

As the ride closed in on me, I found that Pete and Andrew were going to be my riding partners. There were still a few stragglers saying they would go, but they weren't training consistently. My experience has been that they wouldn't make it. So, Pete, Andrew, and I did some of our rides together to workout paces and so on.

I had ridden 40 miles on two occasions during my training. Both times were tough and this distance was considerably shorter than the 60 plus miles we would be riding each of the three days. I knew I could muster some endurance and push through these long rides, but I wanted to be as prepared as possible.

Friday, September 19, 2009 at 6:31 a.m. Andrew and I started loading our bicycles on my truck. We packed tons of Gu, Power Bars, and bottles of water. We piled into my FJ Cruiser and headed to Pete's house. Our plan was simple (they always start that way). We would drive down to DC and park my truck there. My buddy, Jerry, would pick it up that evening and drive it home for me. From there, we would ride 184.5 miles from Washington, DC to Cumberland, MD on our bicycles. Months of training had culminated to this event. *Easy Peasy!*

We picked up Pete and drove downtown. Once there we searched for parking near the Thompson Boat Center, which is where mile marker zero on the canal is located. Downtown parking is hard for my FJ, because I need 6'9" of clearance. Most garages down there are under 6'6". We finally found the perfect garage at the Kennedy Center. It was 7' tall! It is the tallest one I have ever seen in DC. In the blink of an eye, our parking situation was solved.

We each had bike racks located behind our bicycle seats and medium sized bags attached to them. Pete and I also carried camelbacks with water and paraphernalia. We rode out of the Kennedy Center parking garage and into the gorgeous morning with grins on our faces!

We located the canal trailhead around 9:52 a.m. and then took some photographs.

Just then a man and woman rode up on a tandem bicycle. They told us that they had ridden all the way down from Pittsburgh, PA. Hearing this made us feel weak. Then I thought, *Meh—It's downhill the whole way from Pittsburgh!* This is how I justify and console myself.

I digress.

We took off quickly and were in Great Falls before I knew it. The ride was easy. However, I had already developed a cramp in my left calf. We weren't riding faster than our training and we hadn't gone that far, so I chalked it up to nerves. I took a couple of photos of the falls, ate a snack and moved on.

The rest of the day was uneventful (for the most part) and relatively easy. Just before home, Pete realized that he had been riding on a broken spoke. It had warped his rim and the rear brakes had been on for a good part of his ride.

Passing the Monacacy Aquaduct, I remembered all of our training days that had brought us through that section of the canal.

We had ridden a total of 57 miles that first day. Pete had ridden 15 of those miles with his rear brakes on. He is a machine!

At home, we tracked down a local bicycle shop, *the Bike Doctor*. It's located on Buckeystown Pike in Frederick. Awesome shop! The owner and his mechanic stayed past closing time, fixing and truing Pete's rim. Then they gave him new brakes and tightened up his bike. They are a fantastic group there and very concerned about our safe trip. I absolutely recommend them to anyone in the Frederick area who needs repairs or bicycle parts and so on.

Arriving back home, Kristine had put together a delectable meal that consisted of salad, pasta, and steak. It was FANTASTIC! And, much needed. We talked about the day and encouraged each other.

Andrew stayed next door at his house and Pete stayed as a guest at my place. During the night I had to wake up and do some updates on databases for work. It was a challenge and wore me out mentally. I only got a few hours of sleep and worried how I would perform on our longest day. We were scheduled to ride about 72 miles on day two. Yikers!

Day two started well. My right knee was a touch sore on the outside, but nothing I couldn't ride through. I packed three Advil and promised not to use them. We got underway around 9:14 a.m. and rode strong for most of the day.

Just past Harper's Ferry, we found a large cave that women, children and ex-slaves used to hide in during the Civil War. I could feel the spirits of fearful people lingering in the shallow cave. It was eerie and amazing wrapped into one dark package.

Along the way, we ran into a section of the canal that was closed due to flood damage. We had to ride on the road for a bit. This was tough for me, because it was a bunch of moderate hills. My knee was bothering me again. Pete and Andrew made it look easy. As we passed a pasture full of cows, I thought to myself, *I sure am hungry.*

About 20 miles before our stop in Hancock, my knee sang out with excruciating pain. Suddenly, with only 12 miles left, I didn't think I would make it to our hotel in Hancock. I stopped and writhed in pain. I popped the three Advil and inwardly wished for it to start working immediately. I tried walking beside my bike for a minute to stretch it out and I couldn't even do that. I was considering calling Kristine and throwing in the towel.

I literally could not walk without severe pain shooting through my knee and up to the base of my spine.

Andrew and Pete offered to cut our pace in half for a while and see how I did. We had been riding about 14 MPH. I decided to bite the bullet and literally gritted my teeth for 15 or more minutes at about 7 MPH. It slowly warmed up and the pain subsided. I assume the three Advil were kicking in. We made it to Hancock and proceeded to the Triangle Bar and Grill on Main Street. Dinner was awesome and I was starving! We burned more than 5,000 calories during that day's ride (We burned 14,000 calories total over the 3-day ride).

Once we got to our Hotel, we ordered a pizza, wings, and cinnamon bread. We ate another dinner. *Yum!*

The final day started out cold. We went outside to a chilly 47 degrees. *Burrrr!* Climbing into the saddle, I realized just how sore my gluteus maximus was. It was swollen, sore, and ready to be done with this ride. I had popped some Advil before leaving my hotel room, so the knee was under control. The day promised to be good.

We headed down to Weavers Restaurant, and had the best breakfast that I have had in quite some time. I got cream chipped beef on biscuits with two poached eggs on top. The whole town had a very nice appeal and seemed friendly. Afterward, we mounted up and got under way. It was our final day. A 60-mile ride lay before us. Prior to this three-day weekend, I had never ridden further than 40 miles and now I was doing one and half times that (or more) each day!

The last day went quickly. My pain came and went furiously, only to return again. My hands had lost all feeling in them, except an incessant tingling that threatened to drive me mad. My neck was tired and worn from supporting my head and helmet. Shoulders and trapezius muscles were tight. I don't even wanna talk about my triceps and forearms. *Sheesh!*

The Paw Paw tunnel is a magnificent and amazing creation. It is 3,118 feet long and took about 14 years to make. It is wicked cool!

If you are claustrophobic, you will need to skip this one. It was pitch black in there and I kept feeling like I would simply ride off the trail and into the slimy canal waters. It was a bit freaky in there without headlamps. I had a headlamp with me, but refused to use it, because Andrew and Pete didn't have one. In the immortal words of the Three Musketeers, "All for one and one for all!"

When we got to Lock number 69 I wanted a photograph. But a guy and girl were there making out. I felt weird about taking a photo with them in it. I considered asking them to "pose" under the Lock 69 sign. Then realized that it would be pointless and invasive. Instead I pedaled on thinking how funny it was that he had invited her to Lock 69 to neck. *What a romantic.* Actually, I was jealous that I hadn't thought of it.

The last ten miles were furious. I had just finished my audio book, *The Road* by Jack Kerouac, at mile marker eleven. What a fantastic autobiography straight out of the *Beat* generation written by the king of Beat. I dug it immensely and pondered upon the fragility of mankind in a preponderance of heaven and hell that surely came together to single-mindedly stare into my mind's eye. Stepping back and looking at myself through my brother's prismatic periscope, I wondered, *is life merely a dream?* Yeah man, right-on, ahem, and all that stuff! You dig?

After Jack's lovely book was done, I turned on some John 5 and cranked it. It was my turn to set the pace and I went too fast a couple of times. I was so hyper about the finish. I counted each of the last ten miles out loud. I chanted them and signaled Pete and Andrew with my fingers. Excitement coursed through my body. I was electric and my inner self was on fire.

We rode the last mile three abreast. Three friends, nearly broken by the dirt and gravel trail, finally at our journey's end. Triumphantly riding into Cumberland with our heads held high, we created broad smiles on our faces.

Standing before us was a group of nine people. Our waiting wives, families and friends. It was a magical moment. They had created a finish line banner for us. We burst through the banner to cheers. It was awesome!

It is 184.5 miles from D.C. to Cumberland via the canal path. Our jaunts off the canal added up to a total trip distance of 190 miles.

After the celebration, we went to the Manhattan Grill, two blocks away and drank champagne and ate another wonderful meal.

As usual, I must recommend this trip to everyone! Go up hill from DC to Cumberland, if you dig—I had to.

* * *

Where were we? Oh yeah … Life!

Mount Rainier continues to call me and I decided to answer. I will be returning to Washington State to finish what I started so many years ago. The plan was to make another attempt in the summer of 2009. However, my brother Scean has been having some medical issues and his doctor warned him against climbing the mountain at this stage. So, it has been postponed. I will climb that mountain—oh yes—I will climb that mountain.

Kristine worries about my safety on this treacherous journey. I soothe her, and explain that I will be prepared and safe. She looks at me understanding and knowing. *Love.*

Man against nature. I think about the mountain and how it peered at me with glee when I retreated the last time. This time around I will train harder. I know in my heart that Rainier knows I am coming. I fantasize that it knows and cowers at the thought. The truth is however, that the mountain looks forward to meeting me again. It delights in the idea that it can send me home with my tail between my legs for a third time.

No. Not this time.

Chapter Twenty-Nine

After five fun-filled and exciting years at the Department of Justice, I decided it was time to move on. I had been talking with executives from a small technology firm aptly named, Emergent. The group was small and cohesive. It was exactly what I was looking for, so I started investigating and discussing possibilities with them.

As you can imagine, I built some pretty strong relationships with coworkers at the Department of Justice. During my five years, I worked closely with many divisions, departments, and small units such as, the Federal Bureau of Investigation, Bureau of Alcohol, Tobacco, Firearms, and Explosives, US Attorneys, Office of Federal Detention Trustees, United States Marshall Service, Drug Enforcement Agency, and Bureau of Prisons among others. I met and worked alongside of some of the brightest and nicest people that I will ever meet. I was privileged enough to work on some of the most important programs in the world. I would not trade my experience at Justice for anything, but clearly it was time to move on ... So —

I met with the owners of Emergent, Greg and Paul, and tried to figure out how and where I would fit into their business plan. Paul, the vice president, was excited to have me come on board, and immediately visualized some key areas I could help with. He made me feel like I would make a great addition to their company, and he comforted me by showing me how I could be best utilized. Before I knew it, I was accepting an offer letter and I handed in my resignation to the DOJ. I was brought on as the director of technology and architecture and immediately fit into that role.

I started with Emergent in March of 2010 and have never looked back.

In my opinion, the work in the commercial world is considerably tougher, but comes with less stress. Tough I can handle, and stress I prefer not to. Squeezing me into the small team was fairly easy because the entire group was very welcoming and happy to have me come on board. I instantly made friends with Jason, Paul, Michelle, Sarah, Colette, Roxanne, Jessie, Kacie, and Bryan. I also met and became friends with folks from our satellite office. All-in-all, the group is not only tight, but extremely friendly and fun to work with. We enjoy each other's company and we all work well together. I can see that this will be a strong bond that maintains for a long time.

* * *

I didn't drop my book this time. And, my elbow was not sore … But there it was Mount Rainier—peering at me through the airline window. I unbuckled my seat belt and crossed the slim aisle. Leaning over Kristine and Trinity, I put my head right up next to Xander's and we stared together with our mouths agape. The mountain was out there and it was calling me by name.

My non-stop flight to Washington was uneventful. At 14,412 feet, Mount Rainier is among the tallest peaks in the 48 contiguous states. It also has one of the largest glacier systems in North America. Rainier is famous for creating its own weather systems and having extremely hazardous conditions. For this reason, many people travel from around the world to train on it before attempting Everest.

However, I am getting ahead of myself—let's back up a few months and talk about my training and preparation for this arduous task.

My training was pretty straight forward. I weight lifted a full-body routine twice per week. And, three days per week I did cardio on my VersaClimber machine. My cardio routine involved doing HIIT (High Intensity Interval Training). Essentially, I did one minute of maximum output cardio, getting my heart rate close to my maximum. Then I followed that minute with a minute of slow paced cardio. I repeated this for a total of 10 sets of each.

Along with the weights and cardio, I also did some yoga about two or three times per week. I was doing two different styles of Vinyasa—slow and flow. Yoga helped me to have limber joints and a healthy, strong structure. Most of all, yoga has helped me to center and find a calm mindset.

In a perfect world, I would have added some extremely heavy backpack training on some tall stairs. Also, my cardio training was only for about two months. I would have changed that to four or more months worth of mountain specific exercise.

Once it was loaded with all of my gear and the two liters of water I carried up the mountain, my pack was about 69 pounds.

Scean, Mike, Sarah, and I drove to the Cougar Rock Campground on the evening of Monday, June 28, 2010. We setup camp and crashed. Early the next morning, we packed up and drove the last 15 minutes to the Paradise parking area. Once in Paradise, we checked in at the ranger station and found out that a storm was due to arrive mid-day on Thursday. Luckily, our plan was to complete the summit in the early morning on Thursday and be well on our way down before the storm even arrived.

From the ranger station, we walked over to the Paradise Inn and ate a very filling breakfast. I ordered French toast, sausage, and some over easy eggs. Everyone else got the buffet breakfast bar. I think the waitress simply pulled my order off of the buffet. *Hehe.*

We left the restaurant, donned our heavy backpacks, and got underway at approximately 9:39 a.m. Pacific Standard Time.

Prior to hitting the trailhead, we all lathered up with Titanium Dioxide sun protection. Titanium Dioxide is basically 50+ SPF sunscreen on steroids. Up on the mountain the clouds tend to be skimpier, the sun is more aggressive due to altitude, and it reflects off the snow doing nasty things to parts that normally don't see the sun.

Once on the Paradise Trail, we got up to Panoramic View and did a nice switchback with some pretty exciting exposure (risk of severe injury and/or death). Looking down off the icy switchbacks, I realized that if one of us fell here, we'd most likely live, but chances are the person would end up with a broken leg, broken arm, and some serious lacerations.

Getting past the momentary excitement, we pushed on to Pebble Creek and arrived there at 1:46 p.m. Moving right past the snow covered creek, we eventually the Muir Snowfield. The snowfield is about halfway to Camp Muir, so we celebrated our arduous task by whooping and hollering.

We kept a sensible pace and managed to get up to basecamp without extreme exertion. However, that didn't stop me from asking for a five minute break every 30 minutes or so.

After a long and hard push up the snowfield, we finally got to Camp Muir at about 7:09 p.m. So, our trek up from the parking area took a solid nine hours. That's ridiculously slow, but we were utilizing a sensible pace that kept us all with reserve energy.

We found that the archaic shelter had plenty of space, so we wouldn't need to setup our tents Tuesday night. Sleeping in the shelter is nice and relatively easy. You are completely out of the wind and weather. The most obvious advantage is that you skip pitching and taking down your tent.

We spoke to a ranger at Camp Muir and he said that the weather had been updated. The approaching storm was going to hit earlier. According to the latest reports, we were now looking at a pretty serious storm system that would hit at midnight on Wednesday night. This was when we were planning on waking for our summit bid. Our stomachs turned sour at this news, but we decided to push on to the Ingraham Flats.

From Camp Muir, we headed out onto the Cowlitz Glacier and went through the Cathedral Gap. While heading up the gap, a rock fell off the overhead cliff and I had to sprint away from the line of fire. It is amazing how many seemingly innocent dangers exist on the mountain. At any moment, one of hundreds of tragedies awaits you while climbing on Mount Rainier.

While roped up, Mike was leading, with his daughter, Sarah behind him. Scean followed Sarah, and I was tail gunner. I should also mention that Mike's pace was perfect and the reason why we were all so strong. A faster pace would have worn us out, and we wouldn't have been able to keep pressing forward.

After we got through the Cathedral Gap, we marched on to the Ingraham Glacier and headed into the Ingraham Flats camp area.

The views are unbelievable from up on the Ingraham. Directly below you is the Little Tahoma peak, which is a rocky spire and amazing to view from the Ingraham. Also, the crevasses are some of the biggest and most deadly on the whole mountain. Looking up the Ingraham, you can see right up to the summit of the mountain. Everything up on this glacier is breathtaking and utterly unbelievable.

Standing on the Ingraham, I stared pluckily around at all of the beauty and danger surrounding us. As we trekked down from Cathedral Gap, the Ingraham Flats camp area revealed itself ahead of us. The tents stand so stark against the backdrop of ice, rock, and snow. It is hard to explain how foreign tents and mountaineers look up on the side of the mountain at this height. The last thing you expect to see up here is any sign of civilization … Yet, there it is before our eyes.

The hike from the gap to the campground is relatively flat and safe, so we picked up our pace and gladly marched into the pitched tents and fellow climbers.

At approximately 2:17 p.m. we arrived at the Ingraham Flats and pitched our tents. Since we were expecting a very windy storm, we decided to dig a tent pad that would leave a nice, solid, and tall wall around our tent.

Scean dug out our campsite as I tried to catch my breath. He made a wonderful three-wall shelter around our tent. Unfortunately, the winds that showed up later that night came from the exposed side ... *Figures!*

Once the tent was pitched, and we had moved our gear in for safe keeping, we dug a little kitchen area for cooking snow and creating our water supply.

While waiting for the water to boil, I decided to send a message to my wife, Kristine. Earlier in the week I had set up the "help" button on my SPOT GPS to send a smoochie-koochie love letter to my adorable wife. The thing that I overlooked was that even though no one else would see my message, they would see that I had pressed the "help" button. Little did I know the consequences of doing this.

Apparently, many of my friends were following our trek and they each saw my supposed cry for help. Before you know it, every hospital, fire department, and the ranger station had been called and alerted of my last known coordinates. *HA!*

A Rainier Mountaineering, Incorporated (RMI) expedition guide came to our campsite and asked if we were the Ripley party. We said yes, and he asked if everyone was okay in our party. Again we said yes. Then he explained that we had accidentally pressed the "help" button on our SPOT. *Oops!* Lesson learned—*now can we move on?*

Shortly after making meals and filling water bottles, we settled in for sleep. As I nestled in, I caught a glimpse of Little Tahoma out our tent flap. Without a doubt, it was the most spectacular tent view I've ever had in my life. So exhilarating and astonishing that I cannot convey in words what it felt like. I twisted up some earplugs and inserted them into my ears. Falling backward, I allowed my tired body to overcome my excitement, as I slipped into a deep slumber.

Scean's watch alarm went off at midnight, but I was already awake for a few minutes prior. Sitting up, I pulled out my earplugs and smiled at my brother who was already sitting up. Opening up the ten flap, I peered out at the night sky, which was pleasantly clear ... The calm before the storm. We decided to rope up and head up the Ingraham glacier to make an attempt at summiting. *Perhaps the weatherman was wrong...*

Everything is slower at higher altitudes and 11,000 feet counts as a higher altitude. Getting on our layers of clothing, climbing boots, and crampons took quite a while. We left our campsite for the summit at 1:18 a.m.

Our hike started in fairly clear skies, but it quickly changed into heavy clouds and then snow and wind. We were only about an hour out of our campsite when the dangerous weather started rolling in. Further up the Ingraham glacier, the weather worsened rapidly and the trek became lugubrious.

As we trudged up the mountain, the weather continued to darken. The winds picked up over time, and a small flurry of snow turned into an all out snow storm. The wind was blowing at a steady 30-40 MPH. To add insult to injury, an occasional surge would come through and give us gusts of over 70 MPH.

We continued our cadence.

One foot in front of the other—

Trudge—

Breathe—

Step—

Breathe—

Step—

Déjà vu all over again?

We leaned into the wind. We struggled. We pursued our goal of reaching the 14,412 foot summit. Up around 13,308 (about 1,100 feet below the summit) all of the other climbing teams (there were about five or six going up to the summit at the same time as us) started turning back to head down the mountain. Everyone who passed us on their way down said that they were turning around due to the increasing nasty weather. We were literally the last team on the mountain.

At 5:54 a.m. we were stopped for a break and the wind was fiercer than ever before. I crept up to Scean and asked him what he thought. He said that he was willing to go on. I knew that I was strong enough to make it another 1,100 feet in altitude … However; the melancholy weather was beating us up in many ways. I asked Scean to hike up to Sarah and Mike with me. They were already together talking about the situation as well. When Scean and I arrived, I could see the worry in everyone's eyes.

I asked Mike what he wanted to do. He was stoic. I knew that everyone was capable of making it. I knew that everyone really wanted the summit. I also knew that we were risking a lot, because the weather was progressively getting worse and we were only going higher into more dangerous territory.

After a moment, I spoke up. "I think it would be best to head back down." I continued by adding, "The weather is getting worse, and our downclimb is already going to be treacherous."

Everyone seemed momentarily sad to hear me say this, but they each realized that I was correct. Within moments they all agreed. We started to head back down the mountain.

Going back down the Ingraham was challenging to say the least. The wind stepped up another notch, and the blizzard was torrential. Every step felt dangerous, and I found myself trying to counterbalance against the wind. Occasional breaks in the whiteout would show us the huge crevasses that were only yards away from our path. Some of them were downright evil looking and lay beside particularly nasty sections of the glacier. Inwardly I was glad to be going down with some of my energy remaining. Not to mention that the weather worsened by the minute. A wayward blast of wind would come along immediately following a lull in wind. A few of those squalls had to be pushing more than 90 MPH!

Along our route, we got to jump over four crevasse openings and we used a ladder twice to cross a very wide crevasse that lay right in our path. Exhilaration barely describes the flood of adrenaline as you leap over a seemingly bottomless hole in the ground. Crossing the ladder is another level of insanity! With crampons on, the ladder becomes an indescribable hazard and falling at this point would prove extremely dangerous. Suffice it to say that we got our monies worth right there and then.

After a nasty struggle in some of the most atrocious weather that I have ever encountered, we finally got back to high camp at the Ingraham Flats. The estimated time of arrival was 8:03 a.m.

Scean and I told Mike and Sarah that we were going to lie down for ten minutes and catch our wind before taking down the tent and preparing to head down to Camp Muir. We both collapsed and fell immediately asleep. We slept for a couple of hours. When we woke, both of us were surprised we had fallen asleep. Fortunately, Mike and Sarah weren't waiting for us, because they had slept too. *Talk about worn out!*

We packed up our gear, roped up, and headed down the mountain slightly after noon. By the time we got to the Cathedral Gap, the storm had picked up so much that I thought we might blow off the trail. I was extremely glad that we weren't stuck up near the summit with this latest bout of wind and snow.

When we got down to Muir, a ranger approached us and asked if we had seen a solo climber. Two guys also walked up with fear in their eyes and asked if we'd seen their climbing buddy. We hadn't seen him and we couldn't help. The mountain claimed another victim on this day; fortunately it was not anyone from our party.

After a brief stint at Muir, we trekked down the snowfield. The lower we got, the slushier the snow was—Slushy snow is dangerous and slippery. Crampons do not work well in slush. Plus you posthole (post holing is when your boot punches through the top of the snow and you sink in, sometimes up to your knees). It is painful and tedious.

Feeling like a lifetime later, we strolled into the Paradise parking area at about 7:15 p.m.

I am done with this confounded mountain. I feel that I have gotten a lifetime of adventure out of it. It is time to tackle another goal. Also, Scean and I feel that we have obtained our goal even if we have never finished on top. Besides, who's counting?

Vaughn—zero; Mount Rainier—three!

* * *

One final note to address is my latest purchase. After five years without a motorcycle, Kristine and I decided that I could get back in the saddle as long as it was a cruiser style, as opposed to a crotch rocket. So, I went out and bought a Harley-Davidson Dyna Fat Bob. It is a naked (no fairing or windshield) cruiser that has a lot of style and class. I love my new motorcycle and I ride it everywhere. It has become my daily driver.

If the Hayabusa was a beast, this is beauty. Don't get me wrong, it has an edge to it, but it is sleek, stylish, and gorgeous. I added some aftermarket pipes to get that deep and throaty classic Harley sound out of it.

If you pay close attention, you might just hear me approach and then blast past in a streak of deep red and chrome.

Afterword

There are many people and things in life that have swayed me into the successful businessperson that I have become. My business success has stemmed primarily from a select group of managers and coworkers who have supported me throughout the years to make me a better employee and manager.

Without the faith and support of my boss George from Lewis of London, I would have never gone out and tried to make a better living.

Then there was my boss Bob from ADP who not only believed in me, but also carefully helped me to plan future goals and assisted me in strengthening my belief in myself.

Along the path, my supervisor Dick at Dyncorp taught me about the power of a mentor and the influence that I have on others.

After Dick came Jeff who helped me make leaps as a manager at Acecomm and eventually led me in the direction of starting my own business.

At Bay Technologies I had two mentors with completely different ways of looking at business. Cathy stimulated my mind in ways I had never thought of. She showed me the importance of clear rational thinking and expression. With her help I found that there is a tenuous balance between being the wild-and-crazy guy and being the strong mature person that everyone turns to.

Along with Cathy, George helped me to understand that there is more to life than work. He ameliorated and sculpted my rigid beliefs into creative passions. He introduced me to the lucid path of ambition intermingled with fun.

At the Department of Justice, my director Ashok reiterated that you must have fun. By then this philosophy was well engrained in my thought process and yet he managed to give me more oomph in this area. Ashok took me under his proverbial wing and showed me how to control and focus my creativity into something awe inspiring. He carried me over many hardships and helped me to believe in the businessman that I have become.

My manager Beverly constantly affirmed my strengths and helped me get leverage on my weakness. She focused on the positive things in life and this has rubbed off on me too.

Charlie showed me that you must never show fear. Regardless of how arduous a task or project is, you dive in head first without looking back.

Mildred simply believed in me. In some ways, this was more powerful than any of my previous managers. She also spent time sharing a philosophy on life that will remain with me forever. Of all of my bosses, managers, and leaders, Mildred and I connected the most. She is a kindred spirit on this path to enlightenment and I am sure that we will remain friends for the rest of our lives.

Most recently I started working with Emergent. Obviously Greg and Paul have rubbed off on me. Their differing management styles and outlooks have helped to amalgamate a level of business acumen in me that I have needed. I am putting another notch in my belt with Emergent, but I am also adding value to this small company. I look forward to a long working relationship with this class-A group of people.

In addition to all of the work related inspirations, I owe most of my work ethic foundation to my dad, Kim. Throughout my life he has been there to teach me how to handle situations that inevitably arise. His unique way of handling what life deals out was passed on to me and has assisted me in facing challenges every day. He was my first (of many) heuristic coach, who showed me the world of computers. He also introduced me to the business world by giving me an opportunity to work at his land-surveying firm at an early age.

* * *

Interestingly, my most influential "life coach" came to me in a strange fashion. I was watching the movie *Shallow Hal* when Anthony Robbins popped in and made an indelible impression on me. I was immediately in awe of his presence and confidence. Soon I was searching the web only to discover that he was the biggest life coach out there. Before long, I had purchased all of his books, CD's, and videos. Tony Robbins has empowered me through his insight to do the things that I always wanted.

Alongside Tony, I have found a surprising path to success by reading and listening to a fellow climber, Eric Hörst. Eric has written and published several books on physically improving yourself for climbing and more recently, he started motivational inspiration in his *Mental Wings* program. He is also the creator of the *H.I.T. Strips* that I used to train my finger strength on my indoor climbing wall.

Besides Tony Robbins and Eric Hörst, I also owe much of my inspiration and healthy outlook to Stephen Covey and Deepak Chopra. Both of these men have stimulated and educated me in countless ways.

Lately I have been reading and listening to Robert Kiyosaki's *Rich Dad, Poor Dad* series and Timothy Ferriss' *The 4-Hour Workweek*. I have been using these inspirational authors to obtain the next level of my life; which is business owner and investor.

In addition to the many authors I have read (I read about four books per month), there are family members and friends all around me who influence me in fantastic ways. I am a firm believer in surrounding yourself with friends who want to achieve more in life. I quickly found that I followed in the tracks of my close friends. Together we create a harmonious amalgamation of go-getters.

God also plays a big role in my success and happiness. I have a hard time with manmade organized religion, but I have a powerful belief in a creator. It is this belief that has carried me through tough times over-and-over again.

Without a doubt, the greatest contributor to my success has been from my wife, Kristine. If it were not for Kristine, I would still be at ground zero. Kristine has given me the strength to step past my paradigms and do things I would have never imagined before she was here. She is my soul mate and has been with me through the toughest of times. Every time I face diversity or trials, Kristine is there to help guide and support me.

On top of all of those powerful stimuli, I also have my brother Scean who grew up faster than me and introduced me to that pattern of maturity. Scean was there to bonk me on the head when I stepped off the righteous path. He has always supported me in ways that only a brother can. If it were not for my loving brother, I would not be the man that I am today.

Last but nowhere near least, Mom raised me and stuck by me through thick and thin. She was always beside my hospital bed and she nursed me through countless injuries and bleeds.

* * *

All in all I am an exceptionally happy person. How I got there is a complex puzzle created by character making decisions and changes. I walk around life with a big smile planted on my face. This happiness has gone through its ups and downs, but it has always remained with me. I suppose the key to all of this bliss is the many blessings that I have.

If I could sum all of my traits and successes into one word, it would be chivalry. I firmly believe in the *Golden Rule* (do unto others, as you would have them do unto you). By following a chivalrous life and always looking for ways that I can help others, I have enriched my life beyond anything I could ever imagine. Chivalry is not just a fancy word with a neat meaning; it's a way of life.

I do not believe in luck, and yet I feel like the luckiest man in the world. I do not believe that God interferes with this journey, and yet I feel like omnipotent blessings surround me. I do not believe in wishes, and yet all of my wishes have come true.

I am not opposed to positive thinking, but I do not believe that you should foolishly say, "I am positive, therefore it is so." I think there must be a method to your madness. My positive thinking stems from the very fact that I have done things to make myself more successful and happy.

* * *

As far as what I do goal-wise to achieve my high level of success (that I demand of myself), it is a fairly simple process. I have a scale / chart (that was derived from my own ideas mixed with those of countless self-improvement coaches, family, and friends) that I follow with the most important aspects of my life. Essentially, I choose the eight most significant parts of my life: spirituality, family (spouse and children), relatives (parents, siblings, cousins, etcetera), health, work, friends, hobbies / extracurricular stuff, and community (the world). I rate each of these eight parts individually with a number from one to ten, where one is horrible, and ten is the absolute best.

For instance, I rate my current work level at seven, and would like to push myself harder to achieve an eight or even nine. A level ten is practically impossible (but a great goal area to keep you improving toward).

Once you have all of your parts rated, add the ratings together and then divide by the total number of parts (in my case I use eight parts). This average rating that you compute gives you a total overall life value. I consider an average of eight an exceptional life and where my goal is. So, I need to work on each thing (except maybe hobbies; which I seem to be an expert at) to get them at an average of eight. It is my belief that each of these pieces should be at least equal to six (above average) in order to achieve true success. And, my overall score should be eight in order to lead an exceptional life.

I use Dr. W. Edwards Deming's cycle of improvement to work on each of these areas. Simply put, his cycle is: Plan, Do, Check, and Act (also labeled "Action"). In this way, you can continually improve any part of your life by simply repeating this cycle in a never-ending pattern.

I am working on it, but it is a tough thing to improve one's quality of life.

* * *

I will finish this chapter on life success by tackling an often-overlooked piece of the life pie: Health. Because of the virus that my body fights everyday, I do not have the luxury of overlooking my health. Perhaps this is a boon.

In any case, I am a firm believer in keeping your body fit and in shape. Remember, your body is your temple.

That said, I must first warn you that working out and exercise can be dangerous. You can be seriously injured, crippled, or killed from physical exercise. My ideas and opinions presented here do not constitute a recommendation of or endorsement for any particular or general use. People are individuals and react differently to exercise. If you choose to workout (or follow any advice from this book), you do so at your own risk. I strongly recommend getting a complete physical and doctor's approval before starting any type of strenuous activity (especially if you are over the age of 40, or have high blood pressure, genetic heart problems or conditions, or elevated cholesterol levels).

With that painful disclaimer out of the way, let's talk about fitness. First I do not believe that you should jump in willy-nilly and start working out without a plan or idea of where you want to go. You would not add an addition to your house without first deciding your exact requirements and then drawing up plans to follow through with the addition. On top of that, throughout the process, you would continually go back to your plans to assure that you are staying on track. This is the same way that I tackle health and exercise.

I start by figuring out what my final outcome is. In my case, my final out come is this:

I want to spend the rest of my life living in a body that is vigorous and healthy. Along with this outcome, I want to maintain a pain free structure that is strong and allows me to do things like mountain biking, hiking, and moving friend's furniture without worrying about pain and damage. I believe in functional muscular strength, as opposed to "show" muscle. Finally, I want to be free of nagging neck aches, backaches, and other bodily aches that come along in life.

My outcome is actually broken into segments of long-term outcome, annual outcome, and quarterly (every three months) outcomes.

Once I determined my outcome, I set goals to reach that result. My goals are:

1. Follow a nutritious diet that precludes all trans fats and avoids saturated fats;
2. Eat five to eight smaller meals throughout the day;
3. Drink a gallon or more of water every day;
4. Weight lift for strength;
5. Use cardio-related activities to increase my respiratory and circulatory systems;
6. Stay abreast of fitness and nutrition information and always improve;
7. Stick with this plan through thick-and-thin!

Utilizing these simple goals, I have been able to get myself into a healthy 190 pound body that has only nine percent body fat.

Once I established what my goals were, I then drew up an exercise routine that works all of the major muscle groups in my body. I meticulously workout two days a week using the *H.I.T.* (high intensity training) that was invented by Arthur Jones and improved upon by Dr. Ellington Darden and John Philben. Regular rest days between workouts help my body to repair from the rigorous training. And, on top of that, twice per year I take an entire week off to allow my body to strengthen and heal.

If and when I do my cardiovascular workouts, I make sure that I do them for at least 45 minutes per session. And, I work to keep my heart rate at about 80 percent of my maximum predicted heart rate. You can find your maximum predicted heart rate by subtracting your age from 220. Remember that this number is simply an approximation and is not written in stone. As a matter of fact, I have had my heart rate more than 15 beats per minute higher than my predicted max!

I do a full body workout each day that I weight train. Because I use H.I.T., these workouts only take me 27 minutes to complete. I have tried many versions of high volume training (multiple sets and exercises), throughout the years, but I find that H.I.T. gives my body the single-best and most efficient workout available. On top of that, I do not have the tons of hours that are required to do a "standard" weight lifting workout. H.I.T. is not for everyone, because it is truly intense and extremely hard to accomplish. There are times, after just 27 minutes of training, that I feel like vomiting and collapsing.

If you are interested in learning more about H.I.T. visit my forum www.vaughnripley.com/forum and chime in on the fitness conversation.

Programmed exercise has been proven to lower cholesterol, decrease your chances for heart problems and prolong your life. On top of these essential benefits, I find that it also improves my spirit, energy levels, and sex drive. It straightens my posture and keeps my entire body fit and pain free. And, perhaps the best benefit of all, you look better on the beach!

If you want to get started with working out and staying healthy, you may find that an online forum (like: www.fitnesslifeforum.com) is the perfect place to start. A forum is a great place to meet people with similar goals. And, it usually has some qualified professionals who can help you design your plan and meet your goals.

On top of my daily fitness routines, I also set at least one major goal per year. These goals are extreme fitness tasks like running a marathon, bicycling the C&O canal, climbing Mount Rainier, swimming across the Chesapeake Bay, and so on. The idea here is to make the task tough enough that it requires months of training to accomplish. With that in mind, you will always have something out there that you are working toward. I find that this helps me to stay focused on my training.

* * *

In conclusion if I can pass on one piece of knowledge it would simply be this: live life to the absolute fullest, for the simple reason that it is precious and not boundless.

I face many obstacles on a daily basis and fight them off to continue this arduous journey through life. After combating shingles, my face was left permanently scarred. The year's worth of hepatitis C medication removed a large portion of my natural fat in my cheeks and face to leave a skeletal facade behind. And, the numerous HIV medicines I ingest have altered parts of my physical structure including giving me a bloated belly and hunched back that will not go away with a low body fat and physically fit anatomy. However, I work ardently at forgetting about these things and improving myself in every way possible. I focus on the things I can change.

For more than 23 years I have dealt with daily diarrhea, peripheral neuropathy in my feet and hands, periodic vomiting, occasional joint bleeds, hives, random pains, depression, sleep problems, nightmares, night sweats, trouble waking in the morning, dry eyes, sensitivity to sunlight, allergies, loss of fat in my butt and face, added belly fat and bloating, gas, sore throat, phlegm, skin problems, and nausea. All of these problems have brought me down at times, but I pick myself back up and think of ways to better myself. Worrying about these silly effects is a waste of my time. I choose to grin and bear it. I try to avoid focusing on the things that I have *no* control over.

Perhaps I should remove the hazardous adrenaline-filled aspects of my life and lead a safer path. To this I answer with a resounding, "Nay." After all, I have yet to bungee jump!

"What will this self-proclaimed jack-of-all-trades do next?" you ask. I was thinking I would try out writing fiction.

I believe that my *raison d'être* is to share my shortcomings and successes with you. In this way, I hope that I can touch you and show you a different view. Perhaps one day you can open my eyes to something as well.

I often wonder, *What will life throw at me next?* And, *How will I combat it?*

The cool thing about life is that you never know what's comin'. But I can tell you one thing:

I relish the fight!

To contact me, e-mail: survivor@vaughnripley.com

Or, go to: www.vaughnripley.com/forum and join in the fun discussions!